THE IRISH MYSTIQUE

Also by Max Caulfield

NON-FICTION

Tomorrow Never Came

The Easter Rebellion

FICTION

The Black City

The Irish Mystique

by

Max Caulfield

PRENTICE-HALL, Inc., Englewood Cliffs, New Jersey

Extract from "In Memory of Eva Gore-Booth and Con Markiewicz" reprinted with permission Macmillan Publishing Co., Inc., from *Collected Poems of William Butler Yeats* copyright 1933 by The Macmillan Company, renewed 1961 by Bertha Georgie Yeats.

Extract from "The Ballad of the White Horse" from *Collected Poems of G.K. Chesterton* reprinted by permission of Dodd, Mead, and Company.

Translations from the Gaelic by Dr. Douglas Hyde on page 120 and elsewhere reprinted by permission of his literary executors.

Extract from *The Metrical Dindshenchas* reprinted by permission of the Royal Irish Academy.

Extracts from *Translations of Ancient Irish Poetry,* by Kuno Meyer, reprinted courtesy Constable and Company Limited.

The author is deeply indebted to Professor James Carney of the Dublin Institute of Advanced Studies for permission to use his translations on page 128 and elsewhere.

Poem translation page 140 taken from *Early Irish Poetry* edited by James Carney, Mercier Press, Cork and Dublin, 1965. Reprinted by kind permission of Anne O'Sullivan.

I am indebted to Messrs. Gill and MacMillan for permission to use the translations of poems by the late Dr. Daniel Corkery from *The Hidden Ireland.*

Extracts from "The Midnight Court" translated by Frank O'Connor reprinted by permission.

I am deeply indebted to Dr. Liam de Paor, College Lecturer in History, University College, Dublin, for permission to use his translation of the poem by Donatus, Bishop of Fiesole.

Printed in the United States of America
Prentice-Hall International, Inc., London
Prentice-Hall of Australia, Pty. Ltd., North Sydney
Prentice-Hall of Canada, Ltd., Toronto
Prentice-Hall of India Private Ltd., New Delhi
Prentice-Hall of Japan, Inc., Tokyo

10 9 8 7 6 5 4 3 2 1

Library of Congress Cataloging in Publication Data

Caulfield, Malachy Francis, date-
The Irish mystique.

1. National characteristics, Irish. 2. Ireland–History. I. Title.
DA925.C33 309.1'415'09 73-6748
ISBN 0-13-506162-8

CONTENTS

ACKNOWLEDGMENTS

I can only feel appalled at this inadequate method of thanking all the charming and hospitable people who put themselves to such trouble to aid me with the preparation of this book. What follows is by no means an exhaustive list, for many indicated that they would prefer to remain anonymous. Nor, human memory being so fallible, is it possible to feel other than uneasy in the knowledge that names are bound to be omitted inadvertently. During my refresher trip through my native country, much information, too, was often gleaned through the bottom of a glass darkly. It still is an almost impossible country to work in. One is simply *battered* with talk, food, drink, activity, parties, and shenanigans until, through sheer weariness, the mental processes shut down. It is all magnificent—and the trouble is I have never learned to live magnificently. But then, who outside Ireland has?

In London I was greatly helped by Dominic Behan, the late René MacColl, Vincent Mulchrone, Patrick O'Donovan, Dr. Brian Inglis, Andrew O'Rourke, then first secretary of the Irish embassy, Barbara Kelly, and officials of the Irish Tourist Board.

In Cork I was vastly indebted to Captain Sean Feehan and James Healy, who took me everywhere and introduced me to everybody and told me everything.

In the Mizen peninsula there was Patrick Murphy himself, fount of all knowledge and kindness.

In Limerick there were Tom Tobin and Brendan Halligan, good companions and good journalists.

In Lahinch, Michael Vaughan, restaurateur supreme.

In Milltown Mallbay, Martin Telty, one of Ireland's greatest musicians.

Somewhere in Clare, Luis LeBrocquy.

In Belfast, Denis McGrath, James Kelly, James Boyd, and the late incomparable Ralph Bossence.

In Dublin, Mr. and Mrs. Cathal Oge O'Shannon, Mr. and Mrs. Eamonn Andrews, Mr. and Mrs. Michael Viney, Mr. and Mrs. Douglas Gageby, Garech Browne, General M. J. Costello, Mr. and Mrs. Desmond Guinness, Jack White, Patrick Lynch, James Fitzpatrick, Ulick O'Connor, Mrs. Nuala MacLoughlin, Nicholas Leonard, Anthony Lennon, Terence de Vere White, Edward Delaney, Liam Robinson, Rhonda Kelly, Sean MacReamoinn, John Horgan, Father Fergal O'Connor, Father Tom Stack, Father Michael Cleary (and at Maynooth, Drs. J. G. McGarry and Brendan Devlin), John Huston, George Campbell, Paul Durcan, Michael MacLiammoir, Mary Maher, Felix O'Neill, and Stanislaus Lynch. It was a particular pleasure and privilege to talk to Sean O'Faolain. Lastly, but certainly not least, I am indebted, not only for help and information, but also for light and laughter, to that man who has created his own mystique, Benedict Kiely.

Max Caulfield
London

We are a nation of brilliant failures; but
we are the greatest talkers since
the Greeks.

OSCAR WILDE

I

A SMALL BEAUTY

She is a rich and rare land;
O! she's a fresh and fair land,
She is a dear and rare land
This native land of my mine.

No men than hers are braver–
Her women's hearts ne'er waver;
I'd freely die to save her,
And think my lot divine.

She's not a dull or cold land;
No! she's a warm and bold land;
O! she's a true and old land–
This native land of my mine.

Could beauty ever guard her,
And virtue still reward her,
No foe would cross her border–
No friend within it pine!

O! she's a fresh and fair land,
O! she's a true and rare land–
Yes, she's a rare and fair land–
This native land of mine.

THOMAS DAVIS

Nineteenth century

The Irish live on a moderately agreeable, largely unspoiled island which has an impressive quota of legends and a romantic history long antedating the birth of Christ. On the whole, they are a people of attractive gifts. A charismatic race of genial humor and frequently ready wit, they are, in the main, kindly, gentle, hospitable, and magnanimous, with well-developed spiritual qualities nicely balanced by their notable toughness, hardiness, and tenacity.

None of these qualities in itself is either remarkable or uniquely Irish. Yet together they appear to be mixed in such a pleasing proportion that the Irish stand out as a strongly favored people. They have won a respectable renown for themselves as missionaries and teachers, poets and prize fighters, doctors and lawyers, military leaders and cannon fodder, navvies and tavern keepers, actors and politicians, dramatists and philosophers, artists and thinkers, wits and buffoons. Their epic fight for national liberty and religious freedom, described by the nineteenth-century French historian Augustin Thierry as "one of the noblest and most touching episodes in all history," has lasted for over seven centuries and served as an inspiration for subjugated peoples throughout the world. "The Irish," Lord Macaulay once observed, "were distinguished by qualities which tend to make men interesting rather than prosperous," and in many ways they are more accurately characterized by their struggles than by their victories. Their greatest achievement is unquestionably themselves.

Nevertheless, one sometimes suspects that more is heard of Ireland than such a small country really warrants or the virtues of the land or its people justify. Much of this is due to the dispersal of Irish people throughout the world, which has some analogy to that of the Jewish Diaspora. Ten times as many Irish live outside the ancient motherland as in it, and they have carried the fame of their island with them. Part of the total Irish tragedy—for the Irish are, above all, a tragic people—is that only a tiny fraction of the expatriate Irishmen left their country willingly. The majority have been the victims of political or religious persecution or of famine or economic disabilities of the most extreme kind. They have left with a sense of ineradicable bitterness toward those responsible for their exile, mainly the English, which has served to heighten their already intense love of Ireland—a love that in very nearly a mystical way has always characterized the Irish people. Even the great eighteenth-century statesman, Edmund Burke, who could scarcely be accused of normally allowing his emotions to rule his head, once declared that he loved Ireland "with a dearness of instinct that cannot be justified by reason."

An intense love of country, a feeling that they have been thrust unwillingly from their homes, a bitterness toward those who treated them savagely and with contempt—have led many Irish of the dispersion to exaggerate the glories and achievements of their race. To the Irish at home, who cannot fully understand the motives and conditions of the exiles, some actions of Irishmen abroad prove embarrassing. The extreme chauvinism of the Saint Patrick's Day parades in America, for example, makes Irishmen in Ireland uncomfortable, largely because they are unaware that such demonstrations are a reaffirmation of the exiles' right to human dignity—part of a declaration of rights by those who, when they first left Ireland for America, encountered the same anti-Irish, anti-Catholic prejudices from which they had just escaped.

Not that an exaggeration of Irish glories can be blamed entirely on the exiles. Extolling things Irish became an important and integral part of the campaign in the second part of the nineteenth century to restore the self-respect of the defeated and abject Irish people—at least the Catholic part of it. Only by arousing them from apathy and torpor, it was thought, could they be helped to regain that sense of national dignity necessary to carry through the political program upon which their leaders had decided. To some extent, therefore, exaggeration became a political weapon in the struggle to eliminate direct English rule of Ireland and to allow Irishmen again some say in their own destinies.

It is natural, too, that a people reduced to degradation should reflect on the past achievements of their race; should see them, perhaps, in more glowing colors than they actually deserve; should pounce on each new achievement, however modest, and elevate it beyond its merits. When a man is ignored, he tends to shout louder in order to get a hearing.

In addition to this Irish penchant for exaggeration, there were and are other important factors obscuring or distorting what, for want of a better term, one has to call *the real Irishman*. In the first place, there was the *Stage Irishman*, and associated with him, the cult of *sham-Irishry*. Furthermore, the literature of modern Ireland has tended, inadvertently but inevitably, to add to the tangle of myth, cliché, and self-perpetuated romanticization that might be called the *Irish mystique*.

"Ireland was surely made by nature to be a comfortable land," once stated the London *Times*. "Doubtless also its beauty, its warmth of colour and romantic wilderness have reacted on the temperament of the people."

Bernard Shaw, in fact, had an idea that the Irish character was largely due to the climate. "Your wits can't thicken in that warm, moist air." Irishmen, certainly, are forced to live with one of the most varied and unpredictable climates in the world. As they say in Ireland, "We haven't got climate, we've got weather." Even when the sun is shining, one must be more or less *en garde*, prepared for a squall. I remember starting off across the Upper Lake of Killarney under a relatively cloudless sky and being caught in a small cloudburst before we were halfway across—even as the boatman, doing his traditional bit for Ireland as we all dived for shelter under a much-used tarpaulin, tried to pass it off with the remark "Ah, isn't it only a heavy dew." One spends half one's life in Ireland dodging in or out of doorways or seeking shelter under trees or thick hedges, trying to avoid abrupt downpours.

The Irishman's sense of humor makes the most of it, of course; wherever you go in Ireland there will always be a wiseacre who will point to a nearby mountain or island and announce, "Now, when you can't see that, it means it's raining, and when you can, it means it's going to rain." Yet, in fact, the persistent Irish drizzle (or as it is sometimes called to distinguish it from everybody's else drizzle, "mizzle") has an important dispiriting and hampering effect. It is the continual clumping in and out of houses in wet boots; the dampness invading and at certain times of the year chilling the very marrow of the bones; the sudden imprint of a dog's wet paws on a kitchen floor that are as much my own recollections of Ireland as is a memory of drawn-out, sun-filled days that often make Ireland as beautiful and dramatic as Corsica. When the brilliant dark green for which the island is famous fades away to a color that hasn't even got a name, when one sees an Irish farmer struggle with his few acres of bog, mountain, or lakeland and subjected to pitiless rain, one senses that this is a source of that pervasive melancholy that alternates in Irish society with irrepressible gaiety.

It does not seem, however, that the Irish weather can be blamed for the fact that the modern Irishman notoriously lacks a well-developed visual sense—except where it touches his compact landscape. Although Irishmen respond to scenic beauty, the people as a whole are remarkably apathetic with regard to architecture or civic beauties. The explanation, like most others in Ireland, is rooted in history. Put briefly, native Irish culture was rural as opposed to urban, and even today the gregarious Irishman's one desire is usually to live in the center of forty acres of land with no house but his own in sight, secure in the knowledge that he can always cycle to the nearest pub and the warmth of human comfort within half an hour. The village, the town, the city appear to retain for him dark reminders that it was invaders who built these places, that almost every brick was laid at the price of Irish blood or liberty. Yet, as I say, the Irishman retains a constant visual awareness in relation to landscape, perhaps heightened because his country has produced no great painting, no great architecture.

The look of Ireland in many ways is less interesting than the feel of it. One gets a slightly isolated, backwaterish, peripheral feeling there. When I lived in Ireland, I had this constant impression that the country was largely ignored or not even known. Until the recent troubles in the North again focused world attention on their affairs, Irishmen almost boasted of their country's smallness and isolation. In a way, smallness and isolation had taken the place of the English as excuses for Irish frailties and lack of achievement. All of which was in strange contrast to Ireland at the end of the eighteenth century, when Irishmen felt themselves at the center of great affairs, secure in the knowledge that one in every three people in the British Isles was Irish and the interest of the greatest of empires focused upon them in the most gratifying way.

Yet, small and undistinguished though she now finds herself, Ireland is neither poor, underdeveloped, nor small by United Nations standards. There are more than one hundred members of that organization smaller than she—for example, Holland, Denmark, Sweden, and Greece. She is in the top quarter of the world's wealthy nations—which shows, perhaps, how wary one has to be of statistics. What she is, however, is smaller in population, more isolated, and by and large less industrially advanced than any of the so-called developed nations, although within the past decade she has been buying her way into technology and world markets with conspicuous success. Paradoxically, many Irishmen see isolation as a blessing in disguise. For Ireland's lack of population, although obviously debilitating in terms of economic survival, means that one can move easily about the country, in a way indeed that almost savors of the eighteenth century. Ireland, for all her disasters, allows the human personality to breathe.

Delight in the pastoral thinness of Ireland's population is blunted, however, by an awareness of the tragic conditions that produced this situation. Today the Irish population, including the six northeastern counties which politically are part of the United Kingdom, is a mere 4,243,803. This is less than half of what it was before the Great Famine and the epidemic of evictions that punctuated mid-nineteenth-century Irish history. The Famine of 1845-47 resulted from a blight on the potato, the staple food of the rural population. It was followed within the next forty years by a series of bitter evictions, or land clearances, which resulted when the large landlords discovered that it was more profitable to graze cattle and sheep than to allow people to cultivate small farms, some as little as one acre. Although this policy helped increase the ordinary Irishman's hatred of the English, Caltholic landlords of the old Gaelic stock often behaved as badly or indeed worse than their English and Protestant counterparts. Even so, the Famine and the evictions—the latter a parallel to similar clearances in the Scottish Highlands—are critical points in the Irish destiny and are the main causes of the shift of the common people to the United States and Australasia, as well as to Britain herself.

Ireland's commercial and industrial backwardness are due to almost as many causes as Irishmen have grievances, yet to a considerable extent the blame rests on the exploitative policies of successive English governments from the time of Elizabeth I onward. English governments naturally considered their first duty to be to their own subjects, and their policy toward Ireland was to extract as much wealth as possible from the island. Although they were willing to nurture some commerce in Ireland, they refused to tolerate any enterprises that clashed directly with English interests.

Consider wool, for example. For some time the basis of England's wealth was her wool trade with the Low Countries. When Ireland tried to develop a wool trade in her turn, the English government of the time quickly sat on it. Ireland had long been a nation of great seamen, but when she tried to develop a mercantile marine arm, British Navigation Acts stultified such enterprise at its birth. Finally, when technological advances made an Industrial Revolution possible, Irishmen found that "the Ould Sod," lovely though she was, had neither the coal nor iron upon which they could erect such a structure. They were left to contemplate the eternal beauties and get on with the "dreaming! the dreaming! the torturing, heart-scalding, never-satisfying dreaming!" that George Bernard Shaw, that most romantic of Irishmen, once talked about. In short, Ireland had few options left to her. The beautiful romantic wilderness that evokes admiration from tourists today and makes a sentimental Irishman's heart melt is in fact incapable of supporting Ireland's population at anywhere near the standard of living obtained in the rest of western Europe except, possibly, in the Iberian Peninsula. The land was destined to remain fair, lovely, unspoiled—a country ideally suited to pastoral agriculture, that most backward of all agricultural forms. Out of her twenty-one million acres, only twelve million are fertile, or profitable, land. Today, fortunately, the stony, barren acres have begun providing an income in the shape of tourism.

Compared with England, which has dominated her for so many centuries, Ireland's natural resources are meager. The very terrain of Ireland would make an agricultural student weep. Of the twelve million acres of profitable or productive land, a large proportion is mixed with bad land, so that a small farmer is often dealing with a kind of patchwork quilt. The Irishman's basic plight—the factor which introduces a spirit of stoicism, frustration, apathy, and even fatalism into his character— is that one-eighth of the entire Irish land surface is pure mountain, supporting nothing but coarse grasses and heather, which have no value except to graze sheep. In addition, thousands upon thousands of acres are merely peat bog—called *turf* in Ireland—which has the merit of supplying fuel but nothing else.

Analyzed even thus briefly, it seems incredible that such an unpromising mixture should produce an environment that affects every Irishman's emotions to so great an extent. There is little logical reason why Ireland, considered as landscape only, should have this almost mystical effect. The mountains are so old and so eroded—some of them are the oldest in the world, and all are much older than the Himalayas—that they are now scarcely foothills by Alpine standards. All over Europe, indeed, there are landscapes much grander and more dramatic. Yet part of the Irish "secret" is that everything is more or less according to scale, so that eminences which are merely hills tend to look almost as magnificent as mountains elsewhere seven or eight times higher.

The great blessing so far as the individual is concerned is that the mountains lie mainly in a spectacular fringe around the 2,250-mile coastline. Almost none of this is spoiled in any way. On a good day, I suppose, western Ireland is as near as most of us will ever get to Paradise. Yet, wild and cut off as parts of Ireland look and are, one is never quite overcome by a sense of desolation, of nonhabitation, particularly of nonhistory, such as one experiences, say, in Canada. Always, round this bend or on the other side of that hill will be a solitary cottage. There will be someone walking the roads, however distant the interval. Every bay, mountain, field, and rock yields a story, either from genuine Irish history or from the mythological pre-Christian past. One stumbles into something sticking out of the sand of the seashore and it may turn out to be a bleached bone from the wreck of an Armada galleon—for it was Ireland's west coast that destroyed the Spanish Armada, and not the gunfire of English sailors.

Ireland can be considered divided rather handily into two parts. The dividing line is the river Shannon, 230 miles long, running north to south. To the east of the Shannon lie the richer lands of Ireland: the thickly meadowed good earth round Dublin, reaching into Royal Meath where, on the Hill of Tara, stand the remains of the *rath*, or palace-cathedral-fortress, of the ancient High Kings of Ireland. The best Irish land runs down through the great plains of horsy Kildare into the mellow counties of Kilkenny, Tipperary, Wexford, and Waterford. Yet, such is the nature of the Irish countryside that almost within sight of O'Connell Street, the main thoroughfare of Dublin, lies one of those lyrical wildernesses that stirs an Irishman's fondest instincts. This is the region known as the Wicklow Mountains—an area of superb scenic variety, where wooded glens alternate with moorland eminences, all topped by the graceful little nipple of Lugnaquilla (or the Sugar Loaf), the third highest mountain in the country. Here, in a valley carved out of the folding hills by Ice Age glaciers, lie the somber waters of Glendalough, guarded by that unique Irish symbol, a Round Tower.

What tears at an Irishman's emotions perhaps as much as the physical beauty which usually surrounds him is that wherever he goes, he is certain to stumble across the artifacts of his ancestors, reaching back into history and prehistory. The generations tread hard upon each other everywhere. In Glendalough, for example, once lay one of the greatest monastery schools in Western Christendom. Today there is little left; a few ancient and interesting buildings, pre-dating the Viking descent on western Europe, and a Round Tower built to thwart those savages are all that now remain of the old City (for all monastic settlements, however small, were called Cities). Glendalough is also famous for its memories of Saint Kevin, the Irish Francis of Assisi. Kevin, indeed, seems to have had an extraordinary rapport with wild creatures; for instance, he was supplied daily with a fresh salmon, brought to him by an otter, as he stood waist-deep in icy water reading his breviary. On one occasion a blackbird alighted on his outstretched hand and began building her nest on it. Kevin—so the legend goes—as a penance, allowed the nest to remain there until the bird had hatched her eggs.

West to the Shannon and then right across it stretch the flat, rather dull Irish midlands until, suddenly, one is in Roscommon, the heartland of ancient Ireland. Perhaps today the quietest and doziest of all Irish regions—remarkably similar to some out-of-the-way spot in the Loire valley of France—this country holds the almost indiscernible remains of Ireland's proudest and most ancient capital, Cruachan. Although for most Irishmen Tara stands as the great symbol of their Gaelic past, Cruachan in fact was the ancient seat of Celtic majesty; indeed, the authority of the High Kings of Tara derived from the monarchy first established at Cruachan sometime before 100 B.C. Today, however, except for the imprint of old fortresses, little remains on the green hillocks where sheep now graze. Yet the society that once existed here still lives on in the Irish *Iliad*—the *Tain Bo Cuailgne* [tawn bo quel-gne], or *The Cattle Raid of Cooley*, the greatest expression of the Celtic literary genius. A central figure in the epic is Queen Maeve, the first and perhaps still the most striking of all the "wild Irish girls" who have threaded Eireann history. Her palace—an affair of stone and timber—stood here.

Neglected now, ignored almost, is a red granite memorial stone marking the grave of Dathi, High King of Ireland and the Scottic race. The last but one of the pagan kings of Ireland, his authority is now claimed by Queen Elizabeth II of England. A remarkable man, Dathi extended Scottic conquests to almost the whole eastern half of Britain. After leading an army through France as far as Piedmont, he languished seven months at the Castle of Sales studying classical manuscripts and observing the disintegration of the Western Empire. On his way back to Ireland, he was killed by a flash of lightning at the foot of the Alps, and his Scottic army carried his body on their shields through France, Britain, and Caledonia to its last resting place in this forgotten spot.

Roscommon itself is a necklace of somnolent lakes opening off the river Shannon. Many of them are extraordinarily beautiful with hundreds of islands; some still cradling stone carvings and monuments connected with the Druidic religion and its memories of sacrificially burning human flesh. Once through this sleepy region, the traveler finds himself amid the splendor of the west, where Ireland still retains some aspects of a misty Gaelic world of ancient talk, poetry, and music. From wild Donegal, which geologically is part of the Caledonian Fault of the Scottish Highlands; through the fabled land of Sligo, with its myriad cromlechs and cairns dating from a culture older than that of the Celts in Ireland; from the enchanted mountain of Knocknarea, where an enormous mound of stones marks the grave of Queen Maeve; by way of barren, stony, and windswept Connemara; and finally to majestic Kerry in the southwest, with its exotic palms and saxifrages and its overpraised, tourist-inundated holiday resort, Killarney—a traveler will find Irishmen living a life that has hardly changed in centuries, a life that millions of Irish overseas keep fresh in their imaginations and remember with a sense of longing.

It was in western Ireland, on the Aran Islands, that the dramatist John Millington Synge discovered those entrancing speech rhythms that make *The Playboy of the Western World* such a classic; it is in Sligo that Ireland's greatest poet, W. B. Yeats, lies buried under Benbulben, no longer dreaming of

> The light of evening, Lissadell,
> Great windows, open to the south,
> Two girls in silk kimonos, both
> Beautiful, one a gazelle.
>
> . . . .
>
> The innocent and the beautiful
> Have no enemy but time.

The scenes here are picturesque—donkeys pulling creels of turf or ambling along with panniers of it; perhaps a black-shawled woman of the older generation sporting a fine red petticoat as though she were a character in a Synge play; thatched, whitewashed cottages (although these are disappearing fast); fishermen in their *bawneens* (white undyed woolen jerseys) and tam o'shanters out in their *coraghs* searching for basking sharks; caravans of red-haired tinkers and their families straggling along the white, winding roads as though journeying to some Irish Samarkand.

An Irishman loves this part of the world with a feeling not dissimilar to that of a Tokyo businessman who goes home in the evening and changes into a kimono in an attempt to recapture the ancient life of his ancestors. This is the Ireland of enormous Atlantic rollers crushing a gallant coast; of fantastically shaped pinnacles of rock, with their splintered fragments disappearing into the Atlantic like the ruins of an ancient causeway to the Americas. Here lies traditional Ireland.

This, then, is the Irish land poised on the old edge of the world, not all that much changed since the last Ice Age. When one goes in search of the sources of Irish charm, the gentle moods, vivid coloring, and pervasive tranquility of the West cannot be ignored. The surroundings themselves have helped to create the human beings–have raised, supported, fortified, influenced a people vastly different from the bawdy, rumbustious, if generally good-humored, *bowsie* of the Dublin pubs. Even a stranger while here senses that he is reaching back into something special–the kind of community, perhaps that American hippies and all the other tortured, twisted, lost-children of the Western world, without knowing it, really seek. "The only sounds are the occasional cry of gulls and, less frequently, the lowing of a cow wanting to be milked. The smells of the air are all of hay and the sea. One's total feeling is of being in a far place, untouched by what the twentieth century calls 'progress,' " writes an American journalist. The idyllic grandeur of the west is often breathtaking, but what is particular about Ireland–what is an integral part of the Irish mystique–is that this place is for humans. Men are at their ease here.

Good fortune or ill fortune, depending on one's personal reactions to urbanization, has determined that Republican Ireland should have only four cities, only one of which really qualifies as other than a large town. Dublin, the capital and once the rich center of the great Viking empire, is a city of color and vitality which in the immediate post-Second World War period earned for itself the title "the largest open-air lunatic asylum in the world." It now holds almost one-quarter of the total population of the Republic, which is just under 3 million. Estimates are that soon Dublin will have changed to an unrecognizable extent, with a population rising to at least 1 million–thus probably destroying its unique village-like society and totally obliterating all traces of those graceful Georgian buildings which give it so much of its distinctive character today. Cork has a population of 129,000; Limerick, until a decade or so ago a sleepy old town with fine Georgian terraces, but now a bustling center for the nearby Shannon Industrial Estate, has 74,000 people; and Galway, once the great port for Irish trade with Spain and, so legend has it, Columbus' last stop before starting across the Atlantic, has 28,000.

Once one leaves these relatively small towns, which are the closest things to cities Ireland has, the country's architectural impoverishment–in particular, its domestic architectural impoverishment–becomes dispiritingly apparent. There is a relatively decorative area stretching roughly from Dublin to Cork where, as the writer Sean O'Faolain has said, "One can still feel the Norman influence." Clonmel, for example, has a stone gateway rather similar to those one associates with such Norman towns as Rouen; Kilkenny, "a fine town" in Irish terms, boasts the great turreted castle of the Butlers, one of the two most important medieval Norman-Irish families; Youghal has a picturesque Clock Gate and a whiff of the genuine Elizabethan in the house called Myrtle Grove, the old home of Sir Walter Raleigh; and Kinsale, built on steep hills around the old harbor, looks like a transplant from England's glorious West Country. But none of this is really Irish.

The rest of Ireland is not without its odd, delightful surprises–delightful and surprising because they appear like oases in an architectural Sahara. Adare, in county Limerick and only a few miles from the original Hollywood, has a manor, medieval castle, abbey and churches, and some English-style thatched cottages; Westport, in county Mayo, with a canal running along its main street, looks faintly like a miniature Amsterdam; Listowel has a noble square–and a typically Irish signpost that shows two arms pointing in opposite directions to the same place!

To be fair to the Irish spirit, each little town or village turns out to be a warm and friendly place where it quickly becomes apparent that there are more important things in life than viewing neat little cottages with roses round the door or even impressive chateaux. Nevertheless, to a visitor who envisages Notre Dame or Saint Peter's when he thinks of great European glories, any idea of an Irish mystique in the sense that there is a French or Italian mystique may appear unfathomable. No Parthenon, Versailles, Colosseum, Sistine Chapel; no soaring spires of Chartres, Renaissance opulence, or baroque splendor; none of the rococo extravagances of Würzburg or even the charming cottages of Shakespearean England. One has to try to remember that as recently as the seventeenth century the Irish were still burning towns, still fiercely resistant to urban culture.

Yet no Irishman would like you to leave the country with the impression that it is entirely devoid of architectural–or at least, archeological–interest. Certainly few countries possess such a rich litter of ancient stonework within such a small area. There are no fewer than forty thousand prehistoric earthen or stone forts in the country. There are horned cairns, round cairns, dolmens, cromlechs, long and V-shaped passage graves, ring-barrows, lake dwellings called *crannogs,* raths, tumuli, souterrains, and beehive stone dwellings called *clochans*, which are rounded and corbelled like the interior of well-known megalithic chambers elsewhere (not dissimilar, indeed, to Agamemnon's tomb at Mycenae).

Some of the most impressive megalithic tombs in Europe can be found at Brugh-na-Boinne, not far from Slane Hill, where Saint Patrick lit his Paschal fire in the year 433. There is no denying the fascination of such miniature Christian oratories as the one that clings five hundred feet above the sea on the island of Skelling Michael, off the Dingle peninsula in Kerry. This island of sharp, impossible pinnacles, was one of the last and most westerly retreats of Christianity when barbarian invaders swept over Europe and was a place from which the reconquest of western Europe for civilization began. The Gallarus Oratory in Kerry dates from the eighth century and looks like an upturned rowboat; built of unmortared stones, it is fitted together with such precision that despite twelve centuries of Atlantic storms it still stands solid, its interior bone dry. In addition, there are more than eighty Round Towers, the tallest of them reaching 108 feet. These slender, rocket-shaped titans, perfect in their symmetry, balance, and conception, were Gaeldom's ingenious and unique defense against the Vikings, for they offered no cornerstones a determined attacker could prise out. When the alarm sounded, monks and students clambered inside these towers and drew up the ladder behind them.

Ireland also has several small, native-built cathedrals dating from before the Norman invasion. In one way they show how backward and isolated Irishmen were, yet in another they indicate how the Irish might have had some interesting individual contribution to make to architecture if they had not been overwhelmed. Notable are "Saint Kevin's Kitchen" at Glendalough, which has a steeply pitched roof out of which rises a tiny round tower, and Saint Brendan's at Clonfert, which was built in a style called Hiberno-Romanesque and which has a decorative doorway consisting of a round arch of five orders with ornate round and octagonal columns, the whole ornamented with carved heads, animals, and abstract patterns. Perhaps the gem of these native—and, if you like, naïve—cathedrals is Cormac's Chapel on the Rock of Cashel, which was cunningly oriented by its builders a few degrees north of east so that the rising sun shines through its altar windows in May, the month of the Virgin to whom it is dedicated. One also should pause to look at the interesting Transitional abbeys, with their mixture of native elements and the new continental influences, as well as at some of the numerous Norman abbeys and friaries now lying buried amid clustering ivy and lichen and tall grasses—mementoes of Henry VIII's decision to dissolve the monasteries.

Despite its many excellences, the whole collection is enormously inferior to England's, which may or may not be a tribute to the ferocious nature of war between Gael (the native races) and Gall (foreigners). Reminders of this fierce struggle also can be seen in Norman castles, with their broken spurs and cracked battlements showing on the skyline, or in odd fragments from Tudor or Jacobean times, which remind us that until the eighteenth century such was the turbulent state of Ireland that nearly all Irish country houses were simply haphazard, jumbled oddments made from medieval keeps and serving as little more than dark, windowless towers intended as fortresses in a hostile countryside.

Most of what decent post-medieval architecture exists in Ireland remains a gift from the English. The brilliant Anglo-Irish society which became master of Ireland following the "settlements" of the "Irish Question" in the days of Cromwell and then William of Orange not only gave an extraordinary luster to Ireland in all the arts and sciences, but also supplied such glittering specimens as Carton House (former home of the Dukes of Leinster) and Castletown, Bantry, and Westport—all fine edifices which give Ireland a veneer of high culture. And there is, of course, the rather tattered, pawnbroker-fondled diadem that is Georgian Dublin itself.

The very existence of these places—which if carefully restored and preserved would clearly add to the country's tourist attractions—is often too much for the stomachs of intransigent "patriots," who tend to feel that it would not matter if many of these things were literally knocked down—because they are symbols of the past oppression of Irishmen. Nor can one say that their feelings are not altogether understandable.

II

IRISH STYLE—OR THE COME-AND-HAVE-A-DRINK SYNDROME

I found in Munster unfettered of any,
Kings, and Queens, and poets a many–
Poets well skilled in music and measure,
Prosperous doings, mirth and pleasure.

I found in Connaught the just, redundance
Of riches, milk in lavish abundance;
Hospitality, vigour, fame,
In Cruachan's land of heroic name.

I found in Ulster, from glen to glen,
Hardy warriors, resolute men;
Beauty that bloomed when youth was gone,
And strength transmitted from sire to son.

I found in Leinster the smooth and sleek,
From Dublin to Slewmargy's peak;
Flourishing pastures, valour, health,
Long-living worthies, commerce, wealth.

PRINCE ALFRID OF NORTHUMBRIA'S
ITINERARY THROUGH IRELAND

Translated by James Clarence Mangan
from the twelfth-century Irish

"My God!" said Sean O'Faolain. "*Is* there an Irish mystique?"

"Yes."

"You know, the very idea scares me." He pulled thoughtfully at his pipe. Through his window I could see Killiney Bay, which we Irish, full of our inferiority complexes, call the Irish Bay of Naples. Needless to say, it has no volcano, extinct or otherwise.

"It's something new, is it?" he inquired.

"No. It means the Irish *thing*."

"That's a tall order then," he said, refilling his pipe. "I suppose why people are interested in us today is that they have this idea that Ireland's a lovely old place, with quaint, lazy ways, and that we're indestructible; that we'll never change. I'd say it was all nostalgia, wouldn't you?"

"Couldn't it be simply that it's because we're such a lovely people?"

"What about Joe MacCarthy?"

"Every race produces its head cases."

"No, I'd rather go for the idea that it's nostalgia. The Americans have destroyed their own country, the English are busy ruining theirs, and the Germans and other continentals are going mad, locked up in bursting cities with motor cars everywhere and the threat of The Bomb or something awful like that constantly hanging over them. I often see them out there on the west coast, standing on a bit of rock and getting salt-sprayed from the rollers, and you can almost hear them say, 'Isn't this really lovely?' It's the tranquility of it all."

"The way we take life nice and easy?"

"Yes, but that's our trouble, you know. The things that have kept Ireland as she is—the old folk values, in other words—will no longer work in the modern world. And that puts us in a dilemma. Today we're absolutely torn between wanting to produce fellows with cold, clear, rational-type minds and a people who value the old, easygoing, delightful society—a people who believe leisure and companionship are more important than 'success'—whatever that is—or money. What we're really talking about, I suppose, is not *what* the Irish mystique adds up to—but is it going to last?"

It was nearly sunset when the minibus driver spotted a pitchfork lying in the middle of the road. He tried to swerve but was too late. First came a resounding clank, then a little farther on, an ominous note from the wheel.

He had been caught miles from nowhere, naturally—somewhere, in fact, along Ireland's Atlantic edge. Resignedly, he got out, surveyed the battered minibus he had hired in Dublin, unearthed the wheeljack, then fumbled about for a while trying to fit it before suddenly realizing that it was the wrong size.

He ought to have known, of course, This, after all, was Ireland!

And Ireland, of course, is a country where people tend to leave pitchforks in the middle of the road—when it isn't cows, sheep, horses, fairy bushes, prehistoric raths, Ogham stones, or early Christian monasteries.

The correct procedure in Ireland under such circumstances is to get out, draw yourself in a deep breath of air, savor the glorious evening, and wait to see what will happen. In this instance, the minibus driver did just that and had but a short wait. Suddenly, from nowhere in particular, there materialized an elderly man carrying a mammoth jack that clearly could as easily be used to change the wheel of a Jumbo jet as to shoe an ass. He soon had the wheel off and its replacement fitted. The traveler proffered effusive thanks.

"Ah, 'twas the half of nothing," replied the Samaritan.

Although still conditioned to the monosyllabic conversational patterns of southern England, the driver abruptly felt an urge to talk. The presence of Irishmen tends to loosen the tongue, if not addle the brain, I'm told. He confided that he was on his way to stay at the castle of the Queen of England's uncle.

"Oh, you'll be comfortable there, so."

Here was a man who had his perspectives absolutely in order. Then, with no sign that he thought it unusual that a man driving a conveyance of which any self-respecting tinker would be ashamed was on his way to stay at the castle of the Queen of England's uncle, the Irishman took his leave, and with the enormous wheeljack slung carelessly over his shoulder, disappeared into the dusk.

My novelist friend, Lionel Davidson, once booked a holiday at a country hotel just beyond the Dublin suburbs. Despite my assurances that Irishmen on the whole were a maligned lot who ordinarily were neither more nor less efficient than anyone else, he took the precaution of confirming the booking by letter and then by telephone. Then, having paid his deposit and got back a receipt for it, he wired ahead his estimated time of arrival before taking off from Heathrow. He had every reason to feel that even in Ireland nothing could go wrong after such preparation.

And, indeed, everything went fine—at least to begin with. Irish airlines deposited him in Dublin on time. The Irish Customs waved him and his family through with all the affability of a bank manager confronted by a customer clutching gold nuggets in his fist. The could-do-with-a-wash taxi got them to the other side of Dublin without actually running into anything, although in Davidson's words, "Cyclists, donkey-carts, and pedestrians were flying at us from all directions." Safely deposited outside the country hotel, he and his family approached the front door, which was shut. Tight. He pulled at the Edwardian doorbell, waited for a while, and then, when the last clangings of the bell had faded away, he decided to investigate. He walked round to the side of the hotel and entered through the conveniently open French windows. He found himself in a dining room with rich, dark woods, white linen tablecloths, and heavy hallmarked silvery cutlery. He went on into the hall, where he found a grandfather clock kicking up a fuss. As he hesitated, a large Saint Bernard ambled out from somewhere at the back. Davidson patted its head and then looked up as footsteps sounded on the stairs.

"Oh, are you the manager?"

"Good God, no!—who are you?"

"Just arrived. Looking for the manager."

"You needn't bother, old man. He's not here. There's nobody here. Hardly ever is."

"What?"

"Nobody. There's nobody here. You might see someone once a week or so. Otherwise, there's nobody but guests. Apart from the odd skivvy, that is—and they're never the same two days running."

"What does one do?"

"Like everybody else, my dear fellow. Just help yourself."

Helping yourself involved moving into the only bedroom not already full of other guests' belongings. It was a large room, with feather-mattressed beds. Davidson had specified a bath *en suite*, but the only w.c. lay a good half-mile along high-ceilinged corridors, and the only washing facilities were a pitcher of water, a bowl, and a marble-topped washstand. If not exactly *fin de siècle,* the ambience was no later than 1910.

His wife's first reaction was to urge an immediate return to Dublin, where one could try to get into the Shelbourne or Royal Hibernian. Still, it was late, and at least they had a roof over their heads. They could always sue the President, Mr. Eamonn de Valera, in the morning.

They didn't get a chance. According to Davidson, they were awakened by the din of larks and bright sunshine warming their faces. They decided there was a nice, delicate nip to the air—quite different from what they were used to in Kensington. They had slept well, and it was with a sense of buoyancy and, indeed, a feeling that they might be embarking on an adventure that Davidson moved to the window. Below, he saw a wide, pebbly, horse-carriage drive and beyond it a garden, which in contrast to its English counterparts, seemed to reflect an extremely permissive attitude toward the raising of plants: no more than a haphazard collection of roses, brambles, and hedges. It obviously had never seen a pair of shears during the lifetime of anybody living. The lawns were easily recognizable because this was where the grass stood only a foot high; beyond this was a field proper, distinguishable from the lawns because the grass rose to the haunches of the horse grazing there. Davidson drew in a deep breath of the fresh, sparkling morning—it had rained overnight. Beyond the field proper he could see a lake, the water now still as glass. As he and Fay stood admiring, a mallard squawked a trail across the lake and rose into the air. Off to the right, one of the gentle Irish mountains provided a blue backdrop. The previous night's irritation disappeared with the mallard. Baths *en suite,* a formalized system of management—these and the other impedimenta of urbanized man no longer seemed congruous or needful. Ireland had worked its magic on them, and de Valera would be safe from the lawsuits of peevish tourists for another day.

One difficulty about introducing such anecdotes is that they present a distorted view of the environment in which the Irishman lives. The Ireland-the-Quaint syndrome can rightly raise the hackles of natives in a way even criticism of the IRA can scarcely do. The problem is that the ordinary Irishman, leading a relatively staid—or, as is often said, "genteel"—existence, sees nothing very special about Irish life. The character that others affect to perceive in Irish society or in Irish individuals seems to him to mirror the exceptional rather than the normal.

Irishmen hate the idea that strangers should find Ireland "quaint," "romantic," "funny," because they are aware that such concepts originally were invented as defensive mechanisms by the English upper- and middle-class moral conscience. Although they delight in comedy and flamboyance, Irishmen are sensitive: full of psychological bruises and hurts. Thus, as the country increasingly attracts visitors who often assume superior airs, Irishmen have to some extent established a reputation for not having a good word to say about anybody—which comes on top of a reputation for not having a good word to say for themselves. In fact, however, the Irish are a truly charitable and generous-natured people, although this is a secret they try hard to keep.

There is another true story about an American journalist who, cynical enough to believe that there were no people left in the world who would help a stranger without first demanding a reward, drove into Connemara and deflated his tires in a fairly remote and inaccessible spot to see what would happen. Were the Irish really as kind and helpful as they were said to be? Like gazelles from the undergrowth the country people gathered, and after a dozen or so different ways of rescuing him had been discussed and rediscussed, a final cooperative moment produced a foot-pump from somewhere, and he was reinflated. When he arrived back in Dublin, he told friends there that he had never felt more ashamed of himself. It ought to be noted, of course, that at no stage of the events described did coin change hands. Country Irishmen (formerly called peasants) have great natural dignity and pride (all the louts live in the cities); help is given the stranger as part of the natural order of society. Corruption is spreading slowly, of course; but normally it is only in towns or at places frequented by tourists, such as Killarney or Blarney Castle, that one comes across "the guide" or other unsanctioned and unofficial person who expects a handout for a minor service.

Part of the Irishman's secret, in fact, is that he is a bamboozler *extraordinaire.* Thus, while there are elements of truth about the anecdotes I have quoted, another truth is that neither Ireland nor the Irish ever seem quaint or romantic once you have become familiar with them. The Irish, in fact, consider themselves a deadly serious people and usually have a number of things on their collective mind that are the antithesis of escapism. At the time of writing, for example, these include the problems of the North and the Common Market, the intellectual (*sic*) conflicts within the Catholic Church, the educational deprivation of the poorer classes, the growing industrialization of the country, the probable extinction of the small farmer (backbone of the country), the desirability of further Economic Programs, the new role of the Bishops, Women's Liberation, and even the disappearance of the properly baked and unwrapped brown wholemeal loaf. The agenda is flexible, the issues usually the same as those which occupy newspaper headlines throughout the western world, with fairly hearty obtrusions of items of parochial interest only. In short, if it's leprechauns (or more properly, *liópracháin*) a visitor is after, most of them appear to be running motels or working in the civil service.

Nonetheless, although the greater part of modern Irish literature portrays an Irish society much less romantic or quaint than that of Staten Island (which is sheer exotica for most Irishmen) and, indeed, less enticing than the back streets of Wolverhampton or Stoke-on-Trent on a wet Saturday night, both contrasting conceptions can be true and false—at one and the same time. As a whole, Irishmen really are minefields of ambiguity, ambivalence, and *chassis* (as a character in one of Sean O'Casey's plays calls anarchy). One of a dozen different explanations is that the country lacks discipline, cohesion, and homogeneity; so that given half a chance, every vagary of the human character is likely to obtrude itself upon Irish society.

Like it or not, the Irishman cannot help seeming romantic, quirky, and quaint—at least to others, if not to himself. Consider this, for example. While traveling through county Cork once, I came across an item in a local newspaper referring to a case which had been brought before the local magistrate at Causeway, county Kerry. It seems a farmer was summoned for "allowing his donkey and cart to wander unattended on the public road at Ballinascreena." Garda Michael O'Brien of Ballyheigue testified to Justice John B. O'Farrell that he had found the donkey and cart wandering along the road from the creamery "with no sign of an owner." The defending solicitor, Mr. Robert Pierse, interrupted to explain that the donkey involved "was a stepbrother of a donkey which became famous on television but which died recently." It seemed that the television donkey had been trained by its owner to respond to the commands of a dog; its stepbrother, however, was still only in process of being trained.

On the morning the crime occurred, according to Mr. Pierse, the owner took the donkey to the creamery, but "the dog and the donkey had a row on the road" on the way back. "This sounds very comical," the solicitor went on, "but the old donkey used to react to the dog's bark; but this trainee-donkey does not react properly. On this day, the dog and the donkey had some kind of a row, and the donkey went off."

Justice O'Farrell: How is it your client was not around?
Mr. Pierse: He was out the back of the house.
Garda O'Brien: He was not out the back.
Justice: If he was around, he would have seen the donkey going off.
Mr. Pierse: It was the dog that caused that.

In the upshot, the defendant, Thomas Diggins of Drumnacurra, was given the benefit of the Probation Act (suspended sentence), but the Justice emphasized that he was "against any kind of animals wandering along the public road and possibly causing accidents."

So that if it is not pitchforks, Ogham stones, early Christian monasteris, or indeed, fairy bushes that are to be found cluttering Irish roads, then it might be donkeys who are stepbrothers to television stars but who will not obey the commands of dogs who are put in charge of donkey-carts.

What is attractive to many people who are tired of the pulsing crowds and the pulsing lifestyle of the modern urban scene is the conspicuous absence of these things in modern Irish life. It is this absence that, when one begins to get accustomed to the slapdashness, haphazardness, over-optimism, and sheer natural bone-laziness of the Irishman, helps to make the country seem as comfortable as slipping on an old shoe or suddenly discovering how pleasant it is to stop banging your head on a brick wall. However, the Irish tendency to take one's time about doing things ought not to be confushed with the Mexican *mañana.* The Irish can be an energetic people, even if they do not regard work as sacred. Everybody is always *at* something in Ireland, always busy—even if it is only at doing nothing. The corollary is that everybody is also elusive. One morning in Dublin, for example, I discovered that:

A newspaper editor was not available because he had gone to Killarney on a report that "the fish are biting."

A Dublin businessman connected with the rag trade was not available either, because "he's gone off to the races at Punchestown."

A well-known film man could not keep an appointment he had made the previous evening because he had been called away urgently "to go hunting in Galway."

In one of Dublin's more old-fashioned public houses, where fresh-faced, befreckled "curates" (barmen) draw foaming pints of stout and talk in shy, soft, country brogues, a man mentions that he has been trying to get "the hoult of" a well-known Dublin personality whom we shall pseudonymously call Seamus MacKeown. I could not help but overhear the following conversation:

"So you're wanting Seamus, is it?"

"I am."

"Have you tried his office?"

"I have."

"Ah, well, then you might as well give up. Didn't I get hold of his secretary the other day and wasn't the poor girl distracted by him herself? 'Sure it's not that he isn't where he should be. He isn't even where he shouldn't be!' she yelled."

I had always believed that most allegations of fecklessness, elusiveness, unreliability, and so on, were tales invented by Englishmen to run down Irishmen. Yet having run into a man who was probably the finest of modern Irish composers, I am no longer quite so certain. I met him at a party outside Dublin one evening, and after I told him I'd like to talk to him about Gaelic music, he invited me to stay the weekend at his home in county Cork. "Now, I'll meet you at the Hotel Metropole, in Cork city, next Saturday evening at six o'clock. Then we'll go on to my place. You'll stay the weekend, of course?"

"Do you want me to phone to confirm?"

"Ah, not at all—what's there to confirm? Besides, I'm not on the phone."

"Six o'clock, then?"

"On the dot."

On the following Saturday, therefore, I drove from Dublin to Cork along some of those wide, traffic-free roads that the Irish Tourist Board spends millions of pounds annually publicizing. At first I found myself caught up in an unusual stream of heavy traffic flowing south—as bad, indeed, as anything to be met with outside London, Paris, or Rome. Then as I passed the Curragh racecourse I discovered the explanation: They were on their way to the races. After that, driving became sheer pleasure. There were odd encounters with stray sheep and cattle, and once I had to slow down for a line of tinkers' caravans. In one town I had to slow down again for what I took to be a First Communion procession of children. All the way, breaks of brilliant sunshine alternated with gusts of belting rain. Sharp at six o'clock, however, I presented myself at the reception desk at the Metropole Hotel, Cork.

The girl receptionist noted my name and then said in a soft Cork brogue, "Mr. Blank presents his apologies, but he can't meet you, unfortunately, as he's had to go up to Dublin. But he'll see you at the offices of Telefis Eireann next Tuesday at one o'clock."

On yet another occasion I took part in what seems in retrospect an epic search for the late Brendan Behan. An English magazine had asked me if I'd look up Behan while I was in Dublin and see if I could persuade him to write an article for them. It seemed that all their earlier efforts to contact him had failed, but they felt that as I was on the spot, I might be able to assist. Accompanied by a local reporter whom I had asked to contact Behan on my behalf, I drove to the late dramatist's house at Ballsbridge. As we drove out from the center of Dublin I inquired:

"Have you talked to Behan yet?"

"Have I talked to the bloody Pope?" replied the reporter. "And haven't I been up to the house at least five times? Now is there any particular pub he'd be in? Good God and His Gracious Mother, Beatrice hasn't a glimmer. What about his friends?—Oh, he has nothing but friends so long as a penny lasts."

In the Behan kitchen, Beatrice Behan was sitting at the table, smoking, her sleeves rolled up. "You're terribly unlucky," she said. "Didn't himself just go outside that door five minutes ago!"

In The Bailey, a pub opposite the famous Davy Moran's made immortal in the pages of James Joyce's *Ulysses*, we ran to earth one of Behan's pals. Oblivous, apparently, of the fact that it was now 7:30 P.M., he explained, with every sign of reasonableness, "I was to meet him here at four o'clock." Then he added, "But you'll find him in Neary's or MacDaid's for sure." And then he further added, as if he were giving me some form of cast-iron guarantee, "He's got the mother with him."

Armed with such seemingly recondite information, we made for Neary's. They hadn't seen him for four days, and at MacDaid's they hadn't seen him since before the previous Christmas. At Flood's they suggested we should try Peter's, but of course at Peter's they hadn't got him either.

However, what Peter's did promise was that later that evening they would have "the father and the mother."

So in due course we returned to Peter's, to find that the promised developments had, at least, half-developed. For there, sitting in a semi-doze, by himself, a battered old hat on his head, was Stephan Behan, "the father."

"Can you tell me where Brendan is?"

Stephan waved a pudgy hand in the general direction of the Liffey. "Oh, somewhere there. . . ," he muttered, and lapsed into a full doze.

There seemed little point in pursuing the search any more that evening, partly because we had no further clues but even more importantly because Peter's appeared to be rapidly filling with Behans and their kin, the semi-Behans. At one stage there seemed to be so many of the clan present that I had a feeling Brendan Behan must be the epicenter of a local kind of Malthusian manifestation. Peter's indeed became so full of Behans that I began to get the uncomfortable feeling that Dublin was inhabited by no one else. In the middle of it all, the Ould Wan suddenly made a dramatic appearance. She turned out to be a straight lift from a character in one of Sean O'Casey's plays.

"What will you drink?" I asked her, as we all shuffled and scraped our chairs around.

"Oh, only a small Jameson," she said, as though she had just taken the pledge.

"I was looking for Brendan," I explained hopefully

"Oh, God bless you!—haven't I just left him this minnit."

"Where?" I asked wildly.

"Outside there. Didn't he drop me off in the car."

I got to my feet so rapidly that I actually knocked the chair back onto the floor. The Behan matriarch laughed as though I were a professional comic. "Ah!" says she, "sure you needn't stir yourself. He's gone by now!"

Sometime later, Jack White, a fine Dublin novelist, invited me to lunch. He turned up two minutes *before* he was due, drove me to a charming hotel magnificently positioned between the Wicklow Mountains and the sea, a place where tables were busy and there was a lot of laughter yet all of it carefully controlled, the chatter being kept to a quiet, well-behaved pitch. The Dublin Bay prawns here seemed to me the size of Spanish lobsters, while the Cork lobsters looked the size of baby dinosaurs. White himself had a Wexford steak smothered in Hennessy brandy (the original Hennessy being a member of the Irish Wild Geese who fled to France following the Jacobite defeats in Ireland). Our talk centered mainly on the advantages of living in Dublin vis-à-vis a megalopolis such as

London, where Jack had worked for a while for the *Irish Times*. "Here the environment is more natural, somehow," he said. "You can bring up the children in a happier and more innocent way. And you don't have to worry about them being raped or assaulted the way you do in London."

Benedict Kiely, novelist, critic, short-story writer, incomparable raconteur, and the finest boon companion to be met with in all Ireland (not excluding the late famous Ralph Bossence of Belfast, the fastest draw with a witticism I've ever met), said he would meet me in The Bailey at 12:30 P.M. to "talk about Ireland." As we had been talking for three days nonstop about nothing else, this offer may have seemed a bit superfluous; but it was agreed that we had not yet gotten, as they say in America, down to the nitty-gritty. Ben promised he would pour out facts, statistics, tables of comparison and analysis, relative values, and some theories of his own that would, he confidently assured me, "explain everything." God bless Ben Kiely!

At 12:30 P.M., however, Ben was not there. Neither was he there at 12:45 nor one o'clock. The "curate" smiled reassuringly. "Ah, he'll be in all right, if he said he'd be in." It was a few minutes past two when Mr. Kiely finally appeared. "Didn't I tell you he'd be in!" declared the curate triumphantly. Kiely couldn't understand why I was attaching such importance to such a small matter as an hour and a half. "What's all the hurry about, anyway?" he asked in genuine incomprehension.

Indeed, what was all the hurry about?

Later there was a telephone call for me suggesting that "we all meet up in The Bailey this evening and then go on someplace." One never has any clear impression of who "we all" are or, indeed, where "someplace" is. The Almighty, it is clear, is supposed to get off His big chair and get down to working out fate in such a way that it turns out to be a grand evening for all of us. I suspect, in fact, that prayers are sometimes said to The Little Flower in this respect, so that she can go and prod The Big Fellow, sometimes known as Yer Man Himself. Anyway, I met "this sairtain crowd" (as Ben Kiely keeps describing gatherings of two or more people) at The Bailey, where the party included the following Dubliners: a short, squat man who said he had been born in and normally lived in Rome, but was in Dublin on "an extended weekend" (which already had lasted four months); a Japanese businessman or journalist (it was never made quite clear which) from Tokyo or Hokkaido (again it was never made quite clear which); an Irish-American from San Francisco; and a blonde girl from Munich who had taken out Irish citizenship. There was also a tall, heavy Englishman with a cockney accent who was studying at Trinity College. There were three assorted Irishmen, one of whom was so handsome—with dark, black, curly hair and cherubic countenance—that we waited rather anxiously for some of the women hovering about on the fringes to assault him. There was a great deal of talking and a considerable drinking of the local brew before the Dublin writer Ulick O'Connor joined the party, when even more talk was generated. Finally, after an indeterminate space of time spent convivially in this way, the party, now swollen to about eighteen members, poured out into Duke Street and entered an odd-looking collection of cars, one of which was a two-stroke French job very popular on continental roads in 1952 and which had apparently just "come in" in Dublin. This belonged to the handsome Irishman, and although it was clear that he was fairly "short of the readies" (lacked sufficient funds), this in no way diminished his stature, particularly among the ladies. I was sharply reminded of Ulick O'Connor's remark: "Ours is a classless society. We don't care whether a man has money or a title. The only thing that matters is his personality. We have an aristocracy of personality." And also of Sloan Wilson's comment that "the Irish have a social democracy only our [American] grandfathers can remember. No one in Ireland yet imagines that a man's wealth is a true measure of his worth."

The two-stroke had a top speed of thrity miles an hour, but the handsome Irishman could not have been more enthusiastic about her if she had been a Rolls-Royce. "I've got sixty-five miles to the gallon out of her—mind you, that's allowing for freewheeling going down the hills," he proudly informed us.

In short order the little two-stroke had deposited us somewhere in Howth, a well-to-do Dublin suburb, where we were to listen to a jazz concert given by an American artist named Maynard Sinclair. The hall was packed, there was wild enthusiasm for Sinclair, and an attractive young lady who had something to do with organizing the concert flirted outrageously with the handsome Irishman, then with O'Connor, then with the cockney, then with me, and finally with the man from Rome. When the Irish-American nipped in and asked if he could escort her home, she suddenly yelled out with laughter, "G'way with you—amn't I married?"

"So what?" demanded the Irish-American doggedly.

"But, my God!—haven't I got seven children?"

She also had a figure Elizabeth Taylor would have envied.

Eventually I found myself ensconced again in the two-stroke and driving to Dalkey—another well-to-do suburb, but this time on the other side of Dublin. Here the event involved some kind of a social "do" whose origins were lost in the mists of time. The leader of our party, which had now swollen to two dozen people, approached the man on the door, whispered something in his ear, and we all trooped through without, so far as I could see, paying any admission. The handsome Irishman immediately went over to the jazz band, borrowed a clarinet, and proceeded to blow himself nearly inside out as he joined in the din. Some of us went off to see about drinks, and I noticed that the tables were full of seated but unescorted ladies. At first I imagined that this might be like one of those Berlin places were strangers go to pick up women by telephoning them at their tables; but it turned out that the ladies were not unescorted but were alone only because their men were busy drinking at the bar. At approximately 2:00 A.M. the band leader announced the last dance. Immediately, someone sitting next to my right ear demanded to know "Well, where are we going next, then?"

"Next" turned out to be a large Victorian house with truly enormous rooms, overlooking Dublin Bay. The walls of one of the reception rooms were covered from floor to ceiling with paintings created by our host. A long discussion then began, during which the host made the point that Irish painters–presumably he had himself in mind–were very badly treated by the international critics and that it was a shame they had never received the same international recognition that Irish writers did. "If I were an artist in Outer Mongolia and painting in camel-dung or something, the big international magazines would take me up all right and make a real fuss. But there it is; nobody ever pays any attention to Irish painting. We have to settle for the fact that Ireland always gets ignored. As George Moore once said, 'We'll never be great until we get a big army!' "

The host's opinions drew the comment from someone that "It isn't as if Irish artists aren't dedicated, either. George Campbell spent a whole year working on a canvas and then put his foot right through it because he didn't like it!"

Upstairs, the party seemed to be proceeding in a relatively orderly manner. Nobody did anything out of the ordinary, except talk. There were no signs of any hell-raising, and everything took place in the quiet spirit of true gentility. Then, at 3:30 a new wave arrived, out of which walked a tall, statuesque brunette who sat down beside me. She disclosed that she had been born in Yorkshire, was married to a Swedish architect, and that they had lived in Mexico, San Francisco, and Rome before settling down in Dublin. "That's my husband there," she nodded, indicating a willowy figure stretched out on the floor, a drink in his hand, talking earnestly to a small group of four. She said she "didn't think we'd ever leave Dublin now" and listed the reasons for this decision: easy accessibility to country and sea; good theater, cinema, restaurants; marvelous pubs; hectic social life; cheerful, easy pace of society; and the best place she had ever discovered for bringing up children. "You can let them wander off on their own anywhere, knowing that nobody's going to assault them or murder them." She admitted that Dublin had its drawbacks. "You sometimes get the feeling that we're mentally very isolated in Dublin, that we're too far away from the main centers of European culture or from where everything is happening. So we traipse off to London every now and then, hoping for mental refreshment. But the trouble is that everything over there is so superficial–so that instead of getting anything, we constantly find ourselves giving."

It is 4:30 and voices are heard complaining that "it's only the shank of the evening" when we finally take leave of this party and I find myself once again in the two-stroke. "Now where?" askes someone. "Bed!" I shout, but am immediately voted down. "Ma Mulligan's!" suggests Ulick O'Connor. "Ma Mulligan's" turned out to be a ham-eggs-chips restaurant which never closes. Here we ate ham-eggs-chips while O'Connor and I discussed Leonard MacNally, one of the most extraordinary rogues in Irish history: a spy and informer for the British Government at the time of the Irish Rebellion of 1798; a brilliant barrister who defended the great patriot Robert Emmet after his abortive Rising in 1803; a talented writer and composer who wrote operettas and that lovely song of Olde England, "Sweet Lass of Richmond Hill." I remember thinking, "Ireland, is there no end to your absurdities and contradictions?" Finally, came the dawn and finally, blessedly, bed.

Dublin being no more typically Ireland than London is England or New York the United States, I decided to see how Irishmen conducted themselves in a moderately prosperous town such as Limerick. Apart from a new industrial significance, Limerick is also famous for the Siege of Limerick, one of the great events of Irish history and the last stand of Catholic Ireland–in this case, in support of that Catholic convert James II against the invading British and Dutch hordes of William of Orange. Limerick ham is also among the genuine delights of the Irish table. It had been suggested to me that I should call on the Protestant Bishop of Limerick, Dr. Wyse-Jackson, to get a view of how the minority in the Republic felt about the changes in the state since the British left, fifty years ago. Dr. Wyse-Jackson expressed the opinion that the Protestant minority in the Republic (only five percent of the population) could not have hoped for better treatment. Everybody had "leaned over backward" to make them feel they were "Irish and at home." While we were talking, the Mayor of Limerick called to pay his respects to the Bishop. Eventually, I asked the Mayor how he would define *Irish style.*

"You mean, I take it, in the sense that Americans talked about the Kennedy style while John Kennedy was in the White House?"

"Yes."

"Well, I don't think we have a *style*, do you? Or maybe we've too many styles. Anyway, I can tell you one thing–any style I might have as Mayor of Limerick would be nothing like the Mayor of New York's. The Irish, as you probably know, have some queer ideas of what city functionaries are for. Do you know there's hardly a day that some fellow doesn't come rushing into my office—somebody I went to school with, of course—and without as much as a by-your-leave, demands, 'Here, lend me five pounds will you—and I'm in a hurry.' "

I drove on from Limerick to Listowel, one of the most pleasant and cultured towns in the whole Republic. Here I called on Bryan MacMahon, playwright, novelist, and director of the Abbey Theatre, Dublin. Bryan left his classroom—he is also a teacher—to buy me a coffee at a newly opened coffee bar in the main street. I found him bursting with local pride and eager to let me know that even though Listowel looked a small town, it was still a place to be reckoned with. As he spoke I became conscious of how important education and academic qualifications were in Ireland. Here as in Dublin, a university degree seemed to be considered almost an end in itself, rather than as a means to an end.

MacMahon was proud of the fact that all four of his sons were university graduates. They had been taught everything through the medium of the Irish language rather than the English, he said. I asked him if the use of Irish had not hindered their education and preparation for the bigger world outside Ireland. "Well, people will tell you that their children are badly educated because they are taught everything through the medium of Irish," said MacMahon. "But all my children were taught in this way—and they all got their degrees. In fact, one of them won a scholarship to Harvard and is now doing law there." He was almost as proud that "almost every second person in this town has a university degree. The house next to where you're sitting has two—and there are two more in that house across the way, for example. Do you know that we have Listowel people at this very moment teaching at the Mayo Clinic, at Harvard, and at Rome University? We've only got a population of three thousand, but we've got six schools in this town, including a technical school and St. Michael's, a classical college. Now, would you tell me of any other town anywhere else you've ever heard of that could best that?"

Not only was Listowel and its hinterland well catered for educationally, but the area had produced more well-known authors than any comparable area in Ireland—or anywhere else for that matter. There was Maurice Walsh, who wrote *The Quiet Man,* and earlier authors such as James O'Connor, Seamus Wilmot, Tom McGreevy, and George Fitzmaurice, whose plays had recently been revived with great success in Dublin. "And to that little lot, you can add John B. Keane, a fellow playwright, and myself today." Listowel, it seemed, could boast of being the best-read town in the country, thanks mainly to a man named Dan Flavin, who once owned "that shop you see across the way." It seems Flavin insisted that "every mother's son of my generation were made to spend our pocket money on books. And if we didn't have enough, he'd slip you a book he thought you ought to read anyway." MacMahon remembers Flavin giving him a copy of James Joyce's *Ulysses* "when I was only a nipper. It was a copy straight from Sylvia Beach's famous shop in Paris. 'Now read that—but don't let your mother see you,' he told me."

From Listowel I headed south to the Mizen peninsula in county Cork, where I called on an old London friend who had retired to this tip of Ireland. He had found himself a delightful cottage at Crookhaven, a small harbor near the end of the peninsula, where a firm called Celtic Fisheries has its headquarters. This is a largely French-owned concern which has a concession to fish the mineral-rich waters in the vicinity for lobsters, crabs, and other shellfish, which they ship daily to the Paris market. One evening, as I stood watching the sun sink behind the slight rise of hills I got talking to an eighteen-year-old Irish beauty who struck me as having the same fair hair and cool, classical beauty that was so much admired in Grace Kelly, the film actress, now Princess of Monaco. The girl was called Jane O'Neill, and at the time of our conversation was a chemistry student at University College, Cork. I have met many of the world's famous beauties—Ingrid Bergman, Elizabeth Taylor, Sophia Loren, Audrey Hepburn, Cyd Charisse, and others—but Jane was as beautiful and, I felt, probably a lot better educated than most of them.

She and her girl friend had just returned from Lough Derg, where she had been with her father on an annual pilgrimage. Lough Derg is and has been for fifteen hundred years famous for Saint Patrick's Purgatory, the name given to a small island where the saint himself once wrestled with demons and devils. In the Middle Ages its fame was as great as that of Saint James' of Compostela in northern Spain. At Lough Derg Jane had fasted for forty-eight hours, breaking her fast once only with a piece of light toast. She had managed to stay awake for twenty-four hours, doing "The Vigil" and praying continually, one of the penances involved. She had gone round the Stations of the Cross in her bare feet, across stony ground, three times every twelve hours she was there. Comparing her experiences and background with those of members of the drug-addicted generation one runs across in London, New York, and other big centers, I asked her if she didn't think she was being a bit "old-fashioned and slightly unrealistic."

"No," she replied, "why should you think that? It's true that even in Ireland many of the youngsters are turning away from the Church and becoming agnostic. But on the whole, they are few and far between. Anyway, a year ago I decided that each year I'd devote part of my holidays to a retreat [a period of contemplation, accompanied by fast and penance]. So last year I went to Lough Derg, and now again this year. I went mainly to mortify myself. You see, I believe that by mortifying myself, I'll actually help myself to lead a happier life. The idea of getting to heaven is only secondary. The main purpose is to experience acts of self-denial, for I believe self-denial is something that's becoming increasingly important in this world, and increasingly necessary. People don't seem to realize that they'll never get everything they want in this life and that sooner or later they'll have to face up to disappointment. I believe that by conditioning myself, by mortifying myself, I'm preparing myself to face up to anything that may happen to me. Mind you, I went to Lough Derg with two other intentions. I wanted to make a small sacrifice as a recompense to God for helping me to get through my examinations, and I also wanted to say a special prayer for peace among all peoples."

"Are you a religious girl, then? Do you consider yourself particularly religious?"

"No—at least I don't think so," she smiled. "I mean, I wouldn't call myself a bluestocking, would you?" I assured her that I emphatically would not. "No," she went on, "I go to Mass every morning during Lent, but otherwise only on Sundays. I join in the family Rosary every night before going to bed—but then I think most Irish people still do that, don't they? Not that I pay too much attention to ritual—actions are obviously much more important. But ritual does help you not to forget that you are a Catholic and that you have duties and responsibilities.

"I go out quite a good deal—to parties and dances and that sort of thing. But I don't accept all the invitations I get. I find most parties are too superficial to be much bothered with them. I still expect Daddy and Mammy to lay down the rules for me, even though I am eighteen, but I find that they're very sensible, so I don't feel that I should be up in arms and in rebellion. For instance, they'd never stop me going to a dance or a party just because it didn't end until 3:00 A.M. But if they did give me permission to stay out until that time, they'd expect to see me home not later than four.

"I have no intention of marrying before I'm twenty-three, simply because I don't believe in early marriages. You see, I believe that when women do marry, they ought to take care of their families. So they should try to make their contribution in other spheres before they get married, not afterwards. For instance, as soon as I get my degree, I intend to spend the first year working in Africa as a lay missionary."

After meeting Miss O'Neill, I worked my way round from the Mizen peninsula to Kenmare and then I took one of the finest scenic motor drives in Europe—the 110-mile drive round the Ring of Kerry. On the way I visited such places as Parknasilla, where De Gaulle spent some time after he retired as President of France, and Waterville, where Charlie Chaplin and his wife Oona are frequent visitors. In Killorglin, where they stage the famous Puck Fair, the first pub I called at had a young university student serving behind the bar. His family owned the pub, and his name was Philip O'Sullivan Beare. One of his ancestors had gained fame during the Elizabethan period—as a rebel chieftain. Philip was able to tell me a good deal about the social life in a town like Killorglin. "I suppose the statistics I'll quote you must seem a bit odd to foreigners," he said. "I mean here in this small town, with a population of less than a thousand people, we have no fewer than thirty pubs. Seems a lot, doesn't it?"

"Kerry men must be a thirsty lot," I agreed.

"Well, now, while we're still at the statistics, we have one hundred university students in this town, including myself—so we're not all in the pubs drinking all the time. But, in fact, we've got that number of pubs because the licences date back to the days when Ireland had twice its population and a town like Killorglin had a good population. But the real reason, of course, is that on Fair Day you have people coming in here from miles around, and if we'd twice as many pubs they'd still all be packed after the main business of buying and selling is done. Actually, if you came back here in the evening, you'd be surprised at all the activity in this town. Most of the farmers around here are very prosperous, and some of them seem to be able to afford to come in and drink all night, seven nights a week. And they still put their sons on to be doctors."

"How about the generation gap?"

"I don't think there is much of a one—certainly not in this part of Ireland. If there's a gap like that, you might find it up in Dublin, particularly among the Trinity crowd, half of whom aren't Irish anyway. But so far as I can see, we still have this mixing of the generations, as we've always had in Ireland—and always will, I believe. All of my generation have their own ideas, of course. In a country where every young fellow knows that one out of two has to emigrate, we've all got to keep up with the times. But that doesn't mean we're going to reject our elders. We talk to them naturally, and they talk back to us naturally. We recognize that we've got so much to learn from them—say, even in a thing like Irish music. Here are all these lovely old tunes kept in the old people's heads, and they could all easily be forgotten and allowed to die if we didn't care. When you think of those unique rhythms in Gaelic poetry—some of that poetry extending back beyond Europe's Dark Ages, almost to the time of ancient Rome—well, we don't want that to die out, do we? And it's all worth preserving; it's not just a matter of being stuffy young academics. Both the music and the verse are worth keeping—certainly worth not losing."

"This is where you have the Puck Fair, isn't it? What actually happens?"

"Well, if you turned up here when Puck is on, you'd soon find out that we're far from being a lot of young fogies here. I don't suppose there's anything wilder if more good-natured anywhere on earth than Puck Fair. It lasts three days–Gathering Day, Puck, and Scattering Day. In that time, over seventy thousand gallons of stout are drunk and over £10,000 changes hands. What we do is put a goat up there on a platform fifty feet high, crowned with bells and the whole thing festooned with electric lights and a big shamrock. We've roulette, fiddlers in the street, dancing, and a big fair going on without stopping for three days and three nights."

"What's the origin of it all?"

"Well, some say it's a hangover from pagan days; others that a herd of goats warned the townspeople when Cromwell's troops were coming to attack the town. It could be a mixture of both, of course. After all, you'd describe Cromwell as a pagan at least, or even worse, wouldn't you?"

Whether I would or not, it gave me something to think about as I left Killorglin and headed north. I hastily skirted the Lakes of Killarney, which are now simply tourist bait, and eventually found myself in county Clare, where I wanted to find the famed Willie Clancy, one of the greatest of living Gaelic musicians. Clare is different from any other Irish county–but then each Irish county is different from the next, as though the natural features, rather than arbitrary administrative boundaries, have been the determining lines. Clare is not mountainous, but an open, wild, breezy county of dipping and rising hills and a strange region called The Burren, about fifty square miles, composed of bare limestone hills where hollows and crevices support a truly extraordinary diversity of flora.

The great Willie was, unfortunately, "up in Dublin" (Dubliners, it seems, generally are to be found in the country, just as all the countrymen are to be found in Dublin!). But I did manage to meet Martin Tetley. another gifted Gaelic musician. Martin, who is also a farmer, lives in a neat modern cottage about a mile outside the town of Miltown Malbay, whose chief claim to fame is that its population of 650 supports twenty-seven pubs. He plays the Uileann pipes, which are a development of the Celtic war-pipes, more widely known as Scottish bagpipes.

"Uileann pipes are the only pipes in the world that have a bass accompanist," explained Martin. "They're different from Scots pipes in that they're bellows-blown rather than mouth-blown. They were developed from the proper war-pipes, but have a bigger range so as to give better expression to Irish music."

I asked him how he got interested in piping. "Well," he recalled easily, "when I was a youngster, my Grannie used to be always singing these old Irish songs–Gaelic songs, that is. Then, when I was about eight, my mother took me into the town one day. She told me to stand outside while she went into the shop, and as I stood there an old Scots piper passed by, blowing for all he was worth. Well, it was like the Pied Piper of Hamelin—I followed him. Finally my mother caught up with me at the church and, ah well, let's say she gave me a scolding. But that night I couldn't sleep for the sound of the pipes. The next day I got an old sack and rigged up a whistle and a pair of fire-tongs over my back. Then the next year I began to study the tin-whistle—taking lessons from a local man here who teaches it for nothing, of course. No one charges money for teaching Gaelic music. In Ireland until the English destroyed it, all education was free. The older generation automatically passes its knowledge on to the new. For instance, I had twelve pupils myself before I got married. But my wife couldn't stand the racket, so I had to let them go.

"The great Willie Clancy and I both learned all we know from his father, who had thousands of tunes in his head. *He* had got them from an old, blind, itinerant musician who died sometime in the 1890s. Wasn't it from old, blind, and itinerant musicians like these that the airs of 'Danny Boy' and 'The Last Rose of Summer,' and all the rest were rescued from oblivion? Anyway, Willie now has between fifteen hundred and two thousand tunes in his head, and I've got about six hundred. It's very intricate and formalized music when you understand it—as artistic and certainly as profound as German Lieder. It's extraordinarily expressive, and whenever you get the original words—remember, all ancient Gaelic poetry was set to music—you can see how words and music fit perfectly. I think it's extremely expressive. Take this line for instance:

> There's a tree in the garden
> On which grow leaves and yellow flowers
> When I leave my hand on it
> It's as though my heart explodes.

"And, of course, we've got thousands of love songs. But the Celts or the Gaels were never a sentimental people. All that rubbish came in with the sentimental Saxons, who have never understood the true Irish mind.

"You know, there's this impression that we're all a bit stiff and straitlaced in Ireland, that ever since Saint Patrick arrived with the Catholic religion we've been almost puritans. None of it's true, of course, and you've only got to look at our old music or poetry to understand what we're really like. Take the songs 'The Little Bunch of Rushes' or 'The Bonnie Bunch of Roses.' The first is about a fellow who attempts to seduce a girl he meets on the road one morning. Both the rushes and the roses, of course, simply mean pubic hairs.

"The saddest thing in my own life is that although my wife's very keen on music, she won't listen to anything but symphonies or opera and won't let our children learn Gaelic music. So think of it–I won't be able to pass on the music to my own children."

If time had permitted, I would have headed north from Clare, aiming for Galway Bay. I had wanted especially to visit the Aran Islands, those rocky bits of land off the coast of Galway where Robert Flaherty, the classical documentary filmmaker, made *Man of Aran.* I had heard that all the islanders now spoke English with a "Kennedy sort of accent." Apparently they learn most of their English in Boston, which is where most of them go. "You'll find each part of the country has a different part of America or even Britain that it patronizes," a teacher on the mainland told me. "What happens is that one fellow goes away. Then when somebody else has saved up enough money, he'll follow the first. Actually, here along the west coast they're always coming and going between here and Britain or America, so half the time they're talking about Broadway or Picadilly instead of Eyre Square in Galway city. It's a strange sort of feeling. And it's not even as if they're just tourists! Actually, there was a fellow who came from a Gaelic-speaking district around here who'd gone to England and who came back and was asked by the local newspaper what his impressions of home were, now that he had been away for a while. 'Ah,' says he, 'I think everything here's gone to hell a bit. It's just like being back in Clapham Junction!' "

Rural Ireland, it seems, is becoming the breeding ground for a new race of tinkers: itinerants who, instead of traveling the roads of Ireland, will travel the airways of the world.

III

KATHLEEN

MAVOURNEEN

Ich am of Irlaunde
Am of the holy londe
Of Irlande;
Good sir, pray ye,
For of Saynte Charité
Come and daunce wyt me
In Irlaunde.

Fourteenth-century Norman song

"The really remarkable thing about Ireland is that a small country which has done so little should have had such fabulous myths established about her—particularly in America," says the Dublin actor Michael MacLiammoir.

Any definition of the Irish mystique is hampered by the fact that Ireland and the Irish mean entirely different things to different people. I am reminded of the American who got lost in the Wicklow Mountains and stopped his car to ask a local the way to the Sally Gap. The Irishman thought about it for a few moments, then asked the American if he knew of a few reference points, such as the Military Road. When the latter shook his head, the native said in despair, "*Your* trouble, you know, is that you're *starting* from the wrong place."

To an American, the Irish mystique probably has something to do with the Irish involved in the Democratic political machine—a mixture of Joe McCarthy, Eugene McCarthy, Mayor Daley, Boss Prendergast, the Kennedys, Honey Fitz, and Spencer Tracy in *The Last Hurrah.* It has something to do with factory signs declaring "No Irish need apply," and Irish boxing champions such as John L. Sullivan, James J. Corbett, Jack Dempsey, Gene Tunney. It involves high Catholic churchmen in America, many of whom are unquestionably Irish; also Fordham and Notre Dame; and writers such as Eugene O'Neill, F. Scott Fitzgerald, John O'Hara. And finally it has to do with lace-curtain Irish and shanty-town Irish. To get the full flavor of Irish America, one used to be able to collect all of these together in an annual jamboree called the Saint Patrick's Day Parade—for which the streets were closed by New York's finest, who were nearly all Irish.

Sloan Wilson, the American writer whose views, I suspect, mirror those held by most Americans, has written: "Despite the fact that I had never been to Ireland, I assumed, like many Americans, that I knew a good deal about the place. After all, I had seen *Finian's Rainbow* and *The Quiet Man,* Barry Fitzgerald had been one of my favorite character actors, and I was a devout admirer of Brendan Behan. Ireland, I was sure, was a land of emerald-green lawns where most girls looked like Maureen O'Hara and everyone was full of witty remarks. I also assumed that I knew a good deal about Irishmen, probably because I had known so many Irish-Americans. To me the stereotype of the Irishman was a handsome, sentimental rake who was great fun to have around, though he had to be watched carefully when he got into city government. Those Irish-Americans I had known in college and in the Navy had reinforced my impression that the Irish laugh, fight, drink, and wench with more dedication than most people." Needless to say, when Wilson actually went to Ireland, "the first thing I realized was that the Irish are, for the most part, the direct opposite of Irish-Americans."

My own conception of the Irish mystique centers on Ireland's antiquity, on early medieval Irish achievements, on the national fight for liberty, and on the character of the country people of Ireland, who to me are the most charming and innocent people in the world. I remain suspicious of Irish townspeople, particularly Dubliners. Dublin undoubtedly possesses its quota of magnanimous and brilliant people; the problem is that everybody in the place appears to be convinced that he belongs to this elite.

In certain moods I have only one concept of the Irish mystique—and I recommend it. It is of the land itself. A rough, peasant, primitive, simple, innocent land—a place where you can feel yourself at one with peasant France, Italy, Spain, Greece. This is not the Ireland of Joyce's *Ulysses,* which is about the Dublin of the British; nor the Ireland of *The Informer,* Liam O'Flaherty's vivid reconstruction of "The Troubles"; nor the Ireland of Sean O'Casey's plays, which often diminish a lovely country into little more than a city slum.

I hear, perhaps, a few echoes of this genuine Ireland in the words of Raja Rao, the Indian philosopher-novelist: "Ireland is like no other country in the world. It's a gem apart, something historic and holy that man has set aside for his imagination. . . . Sometimes of an evening you can lie by Innisfree and feel India in your bones. . . . What could an Indian philosopher do in Ireland? He could see nature—men as only ancient Greece has perhaps seen them in Europe—the natural man. . . . There's a breath about Ireland that is holy, and I was carried away by this etheric fantasy that seems such an ancient part of man. . . ."

What each of us must settle for is that we all have "this faculty for abstracting from the land their eyes behold, another Ireland through which they wander as in dream," as the Irish poet George Russell, who wrote under the signature AE, once put it.

Ireland, of course, is both blessed and damned. No one can hope to be totally right about the country, and no one can be surprised at the words once uttered by the brilliant Lord Curzon: "I do not understand Ireland. I know now I never shall—and that nobody else ever will either." Nor can Irishmen feel any resentment when foreigners such as the Swedes label the country "The Impossible Isle," which is no more than an attempt to sum up their paradoxical, ambiguous, contradictory, ambivalent, and elusive natures. Disillusionment and enchantment walk side by side in Ireland. Dominic Behan, one of Brendan's brothers, once said to me: "People say the Irish are always laughing. But if you tapped an Irishman on the shoulder and asked him what he was laughing about, he'd tell you it was 'because otherwise we'd be crying.' Sure, what the hell is there to laugh about in Ireland?" Dominic may have been in a maudlin mood when he answered my question. Certainly his brother found—and gave—plenty to laugh about. Indeed, the Irish are on the whole rather an entertaining lot.

They may never be quite the same as the popular images expounded in books, plays, films, and tourist brochures; nor is the country quite the "Disneyland run by the Pope" that the London actor Robert Morley says he found it.

The Irish, in fact, seem to oscillate wildly between various extremes, "struggling through century after century with this imaginative domination, seeking for a synthesis between dream and reality, aspiration and experience, a shrewd knowledge of the world and a strange reluctance to cope with it, and tending always to find the balance not in an intellectual synthesis, but in the rhythm of a perpetual emotional oscillation." For this reason, as Sean O'Faolain has observed, they tend to baffle people. But the results—the contrasts between light and shade—remain half the magic of the land and its people.

To say what Ireland is, one must admit that it is sometimes one thing, then the opposite; then something in between, and then something in between the in-between. Irishmen themselves are constantly confronted with paradoxes; aware at one moment of the beauties of Ireland and at the next of its obvious defects; constantly contrasting their high hopes and aspirations with the disillusioning realities. They satisfy themselves by recalling that the country is still slowly dragging itself up from the depths, still facing an almost insurmountable economic problem, the result of which is that its standard of living is never likely to be as high as that of the United States, Britain, Germany, or France. After all, it is less than one and a half centuries since the Duke of Wellington could say, "There never was a country in which poverty existed to so great a degree." Nineteenth-century Ireland, according to Cecil Woodham-Smith, presented "the extraordinary spectacle of a country in which wages and employment, practically speaking, did not exist. There were no industries; there were very few towns; there were almost no farms large enough to employ labour. . . . Greens were unknown. The butcher, the baker, the grocer did not exist; tea, candles, and coals were unheard of." A century later Eamonn de Valera, then Prime Minister of Ireland, announced that the country he envisioned was one which "would be the home of a people who valued material wealth only as a basis of right living, of a people who were satisfied with frugal comfort and devoted their leisure to things of the spirit." It was, perhaps, no more than Irishmen could reasonably hope for; and they settled down to make the best of it—aware that a moderate prosperity was better than enslavement, paternalism, or famine.

In their desire to attain the spiritual tranquility de Valera spoke of, many Irishmen have tended to equate the possession of a good suit with yet another attempt to grind the faces of the poor. As a result, a flashy motor car, a large house, or any ostentatious display of wealth was and still is, to some extent, frowned upon. Even regular habits, or efficiency, tend to be seen, if only subconsciously, as the stuff which could create class divisions in Irish society. In this context, *chassis*—the Irish penchant for carefree chaos—has come to be viewed not only as a desirable state in itself, as answering the needs and gratifications of the moment, but also as a kind of prescription for preventing the spread of evil influences that might harden Irish society into rich and poor, affluent and non-affluent; that might introduce a value system in which money counted for more than it ought to. Thus, to some extent Irish society became, and in some ways remains, a "maybe" society—going to work maybe, maybe taking the bus home at the end of the day or maybe not taking the bus home, but instead, maybe going into a pub for "a jar," and maybe getting home sometime, or maybe not getting home at all. All this, indeed, leading to a state of uncertainty which largely relieves the tedium inherent in a land that Sacheverell Sitwell has called "an unhappy paradise"—to which he added, "and so it must forever remain, far away from the stream of life and with the sadness of all things that are a little remote from reality. . . ."

This sadness and the reason for it undoubtedly have helped to embitter Irishmen. The most gregarious people in the world, they find themselves condemned to exist on the periphery of the world, with nobody but themselves to talk to. Yet the sheer "maybe-ness" of life, which can often exacerbate the bitterness, has become such an ingredient of Irish life that in an increasingly conformist world, it has become a tourist attraction. An American professor, in Dublin to research nineteenth-century Anglo-Irish literature, told me: "It's why I'm hooked on this country. It's the difference, if you like, between a California motorway and an ordinary road. On the motorway, you put your foot down and just drive, and nothing ever happens; in Ireland, you're constantly navigating bends, crossroads, and so to speak, getting mixed up with the donkeys and carts; so that you feel there's this nice, slightly lunatic quality about the whole place."

In the end, of course, what Ireland and the Irish really add up to all depends on your definition of *civilized values.* To M. Robert Poinset of Paris, whom I met in the county Cork, it is "the little things that have been forgotten everywhere else." It had seemed odd to me that a Parisian, who could drive to Provence in a few hours and laze in the sun, should brave the uncertainties and hazards of Irish weather instead. "But, my friend," he said, "one good day here is worth ten in the south of France! Think of the crammed Croisette at Cannes. The railway viaduct at Saint Maxime. The cars belching fumes everywhere! And here it is so peaceful. You are not overwhelmed. I can leave my car in the middle of the street and nothing will happen to it. I don't even need to lock it. Nobody, after all, locks anything. My car is a convertible, and if I leave it open and it rains–*zhut*!–someone will say, 'Ah, Monsieur Poinset is not here, let's put up the top for him.' And they do, just out of kindness. That's what *I* mean by civilized values."

It is not unknown for foreigners to feel rather surprised at the quality of Irish life. They are often surprised that they can find small justification, if any, for their vaguely subconscious antipathies to anything Romish. Despite what they may have expected, Irishmen, it turns out, are not observably priest-ridden. Nor, despite the drunken and pugnacious reputation of the Irish overseas, is the country one vast, brawling barroom. A few visitors even appear put out that the Irish community on the whole seems to be one where politeness counts for as much or even more than in their own. When they land in Dublin and check in at the Shelbourne, the Royal Hibernian, or the Gresham, and lunch at The Russell–possibly among the first dozen of Europe's best restaurants–they may have trouble equating all this with pervasive folk-memories of starving peasants trooping off coffin ships in Boston Harbor or with Liverpool's squalid, child-teeming council flats.

Dublin, naturally, will seem very Irish to begin with–at once enchanting and disenchanting–which is, at least, typical of everything and everybody they are going to run into on the rest of the island. Having drunk an Irish coffee in a hotel lounge on Saint Stephen's Green, they may sense soft magic stealing over them as they gaze out at the great spreading elms and chestnuts in the park opposite. At about this point they often begin to feel that they have been maligning the Irish–when crash! their eyes suddenly behold the stone enclosure built to surround Edward Delaney's statue to the patriot Wolfe Tone, an affair so hideous that Dubliners immediately christened it The Berlin Wall. They will probably infer from this that the natives have learned nothing from the Anglo-Irish and that given another half-century or so, Dublin will look like an enlarged cowshed, or series of cowsheds. They may then stroll around the five great Georgian squares of Dublin, and having admired the domes, pinnacles, and Palladian facades that are a monument to that brilliant half-English society of the eighteenth and nineteenth centuries, may pause for a moment on the quaint Metal Bridge over Mother Liffey–there to get a shock at the sight of a great phallic skyscraper flaring up from the riverside, totally blocking one of Ireland's few architectural treasures, James Gandon's graceful Custom House. The discerning visitor will at once reach the opinion that Irish artistic pretensions are yet another myth. Dublin will go on in this way, exploding point and counterpoint for them: trying to tell them of its noble past but instead being forced to put forth its rakish present; showing up the native Irish for what thev basically are–an emergent nation.

The city is not without color and vitality, however. It throbs with life much the way Barcelona does. Well-known faces from stage or screen pass along Grafton Street while down-at-heels wander along Westmoreland Street. Friars or nuns glide past in a holy trance, to be followed by a brace of tall, beefy-faced, horsy men who, like almost everybody who attends Ireland's great annual social event, the Dublin Horse Show, assume a proprietorial air toward the Irish capital, as though the years 1916-21, when the country won its partial independence, had never happened. Visitors, however, may be forced to contrast the good manners of the indigenous inhabitants with those of these relics of the Ascendancy. The former usually talk quietly and with gentle brogues; the latter invariably emit harsh braying sounds in accents rather more British than the British and so loud, even when they are addressing someone a mere six inches from their noses, that an Irish wit once said, "They wouldn't need a telephone to call up Galway."

Most visitors, particularly those from Britain, may be startled by these evidences of a residual arrogance belonging to a bygone age, even as they continue to be aware that a certain knobbly democracy is at work. For despite the generations of menials with which the Irish have supplied the world, despite all the hidalgo pretensions of the horsy crowd, on the whole the indigenous population still refuses to knuckle under to anglicized ideas of class distinctions.

By dinnertime on his first evening, the stranger will have begun to have a fair idea of what he has let himself in for. One or two Irish meals will be enough to get him into the habit of approaching every table warily. He will be aware that if he begins by anticipating delight, he is due for disappointment. If, on the other hand, he has prepared himself to cope with the awful, he may find himself in for a surprise.

The Irishman, of course, has invented no recognized international dish. Irish stew, for what it is worth, originated in Liverpool, and Irish coffee saw the light of day in San Francisco, on a theme suggested by the Viennese. In the past, Anglo-Irish aristocrats used to simply roast whole sides of beef for their guests, while the peasants had to make do with oatmeal, maize, potatoes, and the odd bit of pork. Regrettably, the rich never felt the need to invent culinary subtleties, and the poor never had an opportunity. There is some evidence that garlic was used centuries ago, but strangely enough, although the Catholic Irish—or at least those of them who could afford it—were sometimes educated in France, and although Irishmen fought in the French armies, French cuisine would appear to have been unknown to them. Or perhaps the conditions of Ireland were such that nobody cared to introduce refinements of this nature.

Most Irish dishes are simple improvisations on a theme of salmon, trout, woodcock, plover, pheasant, beef, steak, corned beef, chicken, or ham. Corned beef and cabbage is *not* a very typical Irish dish. Indeed, in rural areas meat, apart from bacon, is seldom eaten. On the other hand, great amounts of butter are used. Mushrooms and greens, potatoes, a little fish, and large quantities of either ordinary milk or buttermilk are drunk daily.

Until a decade ago I would have confidently recommended my countrymen and countrywomen as the worst cooks in the world. Usually, when steaks were served in ordinary households, they were cut thin and then fried until they had the consistency of old saddlebags. Vegetables were served in such an ooze of moisture that an Italian might have felt he was being served minestrone. As for the wild boasts that are often uttered about the world-beating quality of Irish salmon and trout, few in Ireland ever ate fish willingly—except on the one day of the week when church obligation demanded it, and even then the eating of fish was regarded as a penance. As for shellfish, I believe there was a vague feeling that they were mammals. On the whole, however, food habits were largely a matter of the purse. The well-to-do ate rather like their English counterparts, enjoying good plain cooking ornamented with oysters and Guinness beforehand, perhaps. The poor, the vast majority of the population, ate whatever they could afford, tending, as I say, to either fry or stew everything.

Today the average Irish home-cooking is not necessarily bad; nor necessarily good, either. In the past couple of decades, a major revolution has taken place, and there is usually at least one good little hotel or restaurant in even the smallest town where one can eat pretty well. But eating in Ireland, I think, still has a spice of danger attached to it.

One may have to exercise patience on occasions. Good food still continues to be equated with plenty of food, the idea seeming to be that the more stuff piled on your plate, the better the cuisine. Generally, at lunch or dinner the single biggest item will be a great tureen heaped with boiled and jacketed potatoes, set on the table by the help with the same manifestation of satisfaction that one imagines Nero's chefs must have shown when they served their master *pâté de chrétien.* Decades must pass, I fear, before Irishmen cease to regard the humble spud as their staple diet. The service, too, is apt to be a bit hit-and-miss. Intentions are usually excellent, of course. In the small out-of-the-way places, the waitresses are too often country girls who seem to be trying out their hand for the first time. In Dublin, some restaurants take it for granted that the client simply wants to bolt his food down as fast as he can—presumably in order to get back to the drinking. In one rather large hotel on the outskirts of Dublin—and an extremely popular one, judging by the crowds who patronized it—the stuff was whipped in and out so fast that when I was asked, "Now, did you enjoy that?" (you are always asked in Ireland, "Now, did you enjoy that?" and everybody, I notice, always answers with a polite yes, even when they've left most of it on their plates) I shook the place almost rigid by saying no. The red-jacketed waiter rushed away at once, and within seconds there were two or three important-looking fellows in different sorts of uniform around me.

"Now did you enjoy that, did you not?" began the chief fellow.

"No." I said.

There was a huddle.

"Was it that there was something wrong with it that maybe you'd like another dish?"

"No."

Another huddle.

"Now, couldn't you be the good chap yourself, sir, and tell us what it is that's troubling you?"

"Very well. I was asked if I enjoyed the meal. First of all, I object to having the waiter or waitress place it on the table and let out a big 'Now!' at me, as though I'd been fasting in the desert for forty days and was glad of anything. Secondly, the food was neither marvelous nor not-marvelous. It was passable. I ate, was fed, am not now hungry—but by no stretch of the imagination could I say I enjoyed myself. Lastly, I didn't like the way everything was served at a gallop."

Still, at their best, Irish food, Irish cooking, and Irish service can be good. In some respects, I believe, the postwar boom in Irish food had both good and bad effects on Irish cuisine. In the years immediately after the Second World War, Ireland, by simply producing unlimited quantities of steaks, oysters, Dublin Bay prawns, Cork lobsters, and so on, seemed a veritable cornucopia to many of the starving peoples of Europe, particularly the English. Many of the hotels and restaurants which then enjoyed a boom have allowed their standards to drop, I fear, basking in the repeated assurances of everyone who dined there that they had "never tasted food anywhere like this." (Well, they hadn't—not for five years anyway.) On the other hand, as Ireland began to enjoy a tourist boom, it was quickly realized that the old slapdash methods that had existed almost everywhere outside Dublin would no longer do. The great eating revolution, therefore, has taken place not so much in Dublin as in the small towns, where standards have been raised to a remarkable extent.

One has to remember, of course, that even the Irish sometimes find it difficult to spoil the magnificent natural foods produced by the Irish soil, which by and large has not been destroyed by chemical fertilizers or by the Irish seas, which do not have polluted rivers running into them. Most gourmets would be forced to express satisfaction with the mallard, snipe, and woodcock at Dublin Airport's restaurant; the lobster and other shellfish at Glenbeigh in Kerry; the flounder *à la meunière* and the salmon-trout with almonds at Ballylicky House, Bantry. Certainly there are moments when, in a typical Irish state of euphoria, one is forced to pound the table and declare with that awful conviction that sits, Lucifer-like on the Irish soul: "Is there anything better than this in the entire world?" Irishmen, note, are never satisfied to ask, "Can there be anything better than this in Kerry?" Or in Munster? Or in Ireland? Always, when carried away by the sheer glory of living, the demand is: "Is there anything better than this in the entire world?" There are moments when the Irish, I think, see themselves as the friends of the friends of God.

When everybody has at last sobered up, however, it has to be admitted that things often go wrong. Of one fashionable Dublin eating place, a critic recently complained, "As the same diluted tomato ketchup appeared below the prawns in their cocktail, over the sirloin steak, and unbelievably, around a Chicken Maryland, none of the party had the courage to order a Pèche Melba."

Often, the Irish themselves do little or nothing to help the aspiring restaurateur. Many a small place has opened up, certain that business would boom as soon as the locals tasted the delights of continental cooking. Most Irish, however, say they don't want "all this fancy stuff." No restaurateur, especially those in small, out-of-the-way places, can hope to survive without some sort of a steady home trade. The wonder is that Irish cuisine is not, in fact, worse than it is.

So there it is. Elegance and monstrosity rubbing shoulders. High skill and a kind of bungling-out-of-this-world amateurishness often intermingled in the same person. The perceptive visitor sauntering through Dublin may soon begin to appreciate both the joke and the tragedy. This, after all, is the city of Jonathan Swift, the first of the Anglo-Irish "patriots," who left his money to found a lunatic asylum "to show by one sarcastic touch no nation needed it so much;" of the poet W. B. Yeats and AE (George Russell), who once decided, at the same time, to call on each other–and, of course, passed each other on the way, Yeats with his head in the air, AE with his in his beard; of the famous sporting surgeon who, when dragged from the racecourse bar to attend a jockey who had just broken his neck, announced after a swift examination: "Well, boys, he's dead–but I'll do the best I can." It is also, of course, the city of Bishop George Berkeley, the philosopher, who gave his name to California's Berkeley; of Hamilton, who discovered the Quarternion Theory; of Edmund Burke, who pleaded impassionately for American liberties; of Fitzgerald, whose discovery of wireless waves before Marconi helped the development of radio and television; of Dominick Corrigan, the great heart surgeon, and Sir William Wilde, father of Oscar, who gave his name to that incision which begins a mastoid operation.

The visitor who succeeds best in this society is the one who understands that he is treading upon a carpet of glass marbles. Not all the characters he is likely to meet in Ireland—particularly in Dublin—are admirable ones. Shaw once said after reading something by James Joyce, "If such characters really do exist, there should be a commission to inquire, Why?" The visitor has to recognize that beneath the surface charm of Dublin, at any rate, the place "is a cauldron of enemies and people who are temporarily not speaking to each other." You will constantly be warned, "You don't want to talk to that fella" or "Watch out for him!"

Nor can the visitor easily reconcile what he has been told about "Catholic Ireland"—about the politeness, good manners, chastity, and the lack of swearing and so on (*Fielding's Guide to Europe* once warned Americans that they should avoid swearing in Ireland)—with what he often finds. He may be sitting quietly in a smart restaurant when a handsome, well-dressed, flamboyant character storms in, and amid a fever of good-will and general bonhomie, abruptly yells out to a friend, "Ah, ye whoor's bastard, so there ye are!" The astonished visitor, informed that this is a man with an international reputation in artistic circles, will conclude that the Dublin idiom is a naturally coarse one—until he comes to realize that the swearing might be just another ploy in what is obviously a very convoluted game. I personally deplore much of the coarseness in Dublin talk—the constant flow of "bejasuses," "damns," "bloodies," and worse which seems to have become the natural idiom not only of the working class but also of the better-off.

I can, of course, understand some of the reasons for this linguistic phenomenon. With the better-off, I think, it bespeaks a wish to show disdain for petty bourgeois values. There is also obviously an intention to spread *chassis* and confusion among visitors, who are usually looked upon as lambs to be led to the slaughter, while possibly at the same time serving notice on the world at large that neither smugness nor pomposity will be tolerated in Ireland.

As Irishmen discover the delights of commerce, industrialization, technology, and all their ancillary processes, some of the old haphazard qualities are dying out. A whole new breed of Irishmen "on the make" is being generated as the nation fights for economic survival. A decade or so ago, trying to do business in Ireland was like trying to have an argument with a Trappist monk. What Irish businessmen wanted to do was to talk about golf or fishing or horseracing—that is, when they were *there* to talk about anything at all. Foreign businessmen used to complain that nobody could do business in Ireland unless he was prepared to spend two or three days at the races first.

Much of this attitude is, or was, a hangover from the days when Ireland was regarded by the better-off English and Scotch, as well as the local gentry, as one of the best "sportin' countries" in the world. The native Irishman—if he can afford to—now likes to follow in the footsteps of his erstwhile master. By one of those paradoxes I keep talking about, while the Irish consume less fish per head than anyone else in Europe, they have more fish-bearing waters, relative to size, than any other country in the world. There are more than 950 miles of fresh water lakes and hundreds upon hundreds of fishable streams and rivers, the vast majority as clear as nature intended. The country, indeed, produces no less than a fifth of Europe's total salmon harvest. Irishmen as well as visitors also go in for brown-trout fishing, while between mid-May and mid-June one can "dap the Green Drake"—fish with mayfly—upon the lovely waters of that most haunted of Irish lakes, Lough Corrib. Nor is there anything to stop anyone from doing some coarse fishing—the country teems with pike, perch, bream, rudd, carp, roach, and dace, while off the coast mullet, wrasse, sea bass, flounder, pollock, shark, tunny, broadbill, skate, swordfish, top, and halibut are easily caught.

Sport, in fact, preoccupies the Irishman to such an extent that the country ought to be producing world champions at almost every pastime. However—and as they say in Ireland, thanks be to God!—even sport isn't gone at in too serious a fashion. In a relaxed country, sport is regarded as merely another method of becoming even more relaxed. People play games and do things for enjoyment, rather than with that spirit of do or die that is as necessary to success in sport as in any other walk of life. Most Irishmen are addicted to golf; Dublin alone has no fewer than twenty-seven golf courses within or just on its city boundaries. There are several water-skiing centers, and yachting has become an increasingly popular sport. Although there is nothing quite so dramatic or bloody as bullfighting, there are those who will tell you that hurling is an excellent substitute if it's just blood you're after. Actually, hurling—easily the fastest field game in the world—is well worth watching, although the Irish themselves are becoming less fond of it, preferring a game called Gaelic football, which is a rather crude cross between soccer and rugby. Soccer, rugby, cricket, hockey, lacrosse, handball, tennis, badminton, and other games are played with varying degrees of enthusiasm.

Above and beyond everything else, of course, preoccupying many Irishmen much more than it ought to, is "the horse." The position of the horse within Irish society, however, is like most other positions within

Irish society—simply the starting point for an argument. Brendan Behan once summarized the horsy position by declaring that "Anglo-Irishmen are only Protestants with horses." Or put another way, the cult of the horse is basically an Anglo-Irish pursuit. A large section of the Dublin and Cork populations has a vested interest in "the horse." These are the rather pathetic people, often the shiftless or unemployed, who spend their days in bookmaker's shops, their only interest in the horse being whether it will make "a bob or two."

Dublin itself boasts no fewer than three racecourses—one right in the heart of the city, in the Phoenix Park. A half-hour's car drive from the city is Naas racecourse, and only a little further away is The Curragh, once the headquarters and training ground of the British army in Ireland and still a unique place—an enormous plain of more than five thousand acres, heavy with that deep-green grass Irishmen like to believe incomparable. There are more than two dozen other racecourses scattered throughout the island, and even this is probably no more than the tip of the iceberg, for in fact almost every small town has a regular meeting. Three- or four-day meetings are common at Tramore, Killarney, Tralee, and elsewhere. In Listowel, the profits made during the first three hours of a three-day racing festival are said to be enough to pay every shopkeeper's annual rates. Many of these festivals produce uproar. Supreme above all others is the one in Galway, which is legendary even in Ireland. For three days and three nights nobody sleeps. Racegoers bed down in bathtubs or on billiard tables or sleep out under canvas. In Dublin itself nearly everything stops during the annual jamboree known as the Royal Dublin Horse Show Week, which, paradoxically, is really a part of the "London Season." During Horse Show Week, Dublin is a very good place to stay away from; the best hotels are filled with horsy devotees, and at night reckless young aristocrats, both British and Irish, pelt each other with bread and pour champagne over each other's heads in a way that recalls the worst excesses of the eighteenth century.

It is in the hunting field, of course, that the real spirit of the Anglo-Irish gentry is still kept alive. John Huston, the American film maker who has become an Irish citizen, insists that his basic reason for living in Ireland is "because of the hunting here.... Fox hunting is responsible for producing the great courage of the Irish people." Huston was on firmer ground when he said "Nobody has lived until they've seen an Irish woman, sixty-five or seventy years old, sitting sidesaddle on a horse and taking one of the great Irish banks. Every year a half-dozen oldsters fall out of their saddles and are dead before they hit the ground—literally dying with their boots on!" He insists that the world "owes an enormous debt to Irishwomen and to fox hunting": "Irishwomen are the mothers of Ireland's greatest export—Irishmen; and stout and fox hunting are responsible for most of the good characteristics in Irishmen." Huston's remarks, in fact, are of the kind that can easily lead to a further misunderstanding of the Irishman's basic nature. Hardly any of the indigenous population are or have ever been involved in fox hunting, although if by Ireland one means principally Anglo-Ireland, then Huston is undoubtedly correct. However, leaving all that aside, one could still wonder whether Irish hunting is really as marvelous as it was said to be.

Huston said, "Yes–because of the magnificent horses, magnificent country, and magnificent companions. Every obstacle, you see, is a natural one. The great limestone walls of the West or the terrifying double banks of Kildare are like nothing you've ever met anywhere else. Hunting in America doesn't even begin to compare. There you have to put up with big holes in the ground, rattlesnakes, hard ground, paneled fences, and wire. In Ireland, on the other hand, the going is always beautiful, with the ground more like a cushion than a part of the earth. In my own county, Galway, you can take the walls anyway you please and take any line you like, and as one of our fellows put it, 'You'll be seasick with the leppin.'"

Hunting, of course, like everything else, is always good for a story. One told me by another huntsman was about the day an Irish hunt stopped short, faced with what appeared to be an insuperable obstacle. Finally, a hard-bitten farmer rammed his hat down hard, kicked his heels into "his game little mare," and thundered at it. Through a flooded ditch he charged, then up and over a jungle of whitethorn, and finally up and over an enormous double bank. As he vanished over the bank the entire hunt waited the result with bated breath. Finally the master, his nerves stretched to breaking point, yelled out, "Hey, Paddy Slattery, what's behind that?" "Thanks be to God, I am!" yelled Slattery.

During the tourist season, one sees the visitors sitting in the hotel bars all over Ireland, wearing slightly bemused expressions on their faces, obviously trying to find out where the holes are in the Irish bucket. Everything seems too good to be true. Anyone with a nodding acquaintance with history or economics knows, in fact, that the island is not even viable. Yet, in some crazy, inexplicable way, the inhabitants continue to go about their daily lives as though they had personal access to a crock of gold. Nobody seems short of the "readies"–either in material or spiritual coin. Yet a half-century ago Dublin was still something from a Victorian print: beggars accosted visitors everywhere; old women tottered about with black shawls clutched round their heads; there was a depressing atmosphere of ingrained and ineradicable poverty. Now the only beggars are likely to be priests, nuns, or members of lay orders such as the Legion of Mary or Saint Vincent de Paul, rattling their collection boxes.

There are all the obvious signs, too, that the Irish have not given up the practice of works of charity. A bustling businessman up to his ears with problems will be still seen taking his time to stop an old lady, grab her gently by the hands, and listen sympathetically as she pours out news about a sick daughter. Nobody can expect to make much headway unless the word is passed around that "he's a daycent sort," for charity is the oil in the gearbox of Irish life. That fellow speeding out the door, apparently risking a coronary, is as likely as not rushing off to see a sick friend as to back a winner. Visiting the sick and burying the dead still remain the cardinal ordinances of the Irish social scene, and few men pass a week without attending at least one funeral.

Even in Dublin, funerals are still occasions of splendid solemnity. A man's importance is not measured by his expensive coffin or many wreaths of flowers but by the long line of mourners who follow his cortege to the graveyard. And whereas other great cities of the world hasten to hurry away their dead in an almost unseemly rush to be rid of such reminders of mortality, Dubliners take a pride in dressing up in their best and joining in long processions which often hold up traffic for considerable periods.

Slowly, perhaps, a perceptive visitor may begin to appreciate that the deep spiritual qualities usually associated with the Irish race actually have a practical application. An unbiased observer must agree that they enhance and enrich daily life. Nor are the surface impressions of a good-natured and by and large not ill-intentioned community in any way belied by the statistics. Ireland, on the whole, remains remarkably free from crime.

During the sixties, the murder rate was almost non-existent, ranging from two murders a year at its lowest to six at its highest. In 1970, the rate rose to eleven, but fell again to nine in 1971. In common with most countries, however, Irish crime seems to be on the increase. There were 24 cases of rape in 1971 against 15 the year previously, while sex assaults of every kind, many of which the police dismiss as "mainly charges of a technical nature," rose to 139 in 1971 as compared with 124 the previous year. Arson was up from 132 cases in 1970 to 151 in 1971 but manslaughter fell from 7 to 4. General assault cases were up from 734 to 848.

The year 1971 saw the publication of separate statistics for armed robbery and attempted murder—the figures being, respectively, 30 and 3. For years, the majority of robberies with arms were believed to be the work of the IRA or splinter organizations, seeking funds in the approved revolutionary way and were therefore regarded as basically political in intent. Some armed robberies are still politically motivated but more and more it would seem that criminally-inclined gangs are carrying out holdups under the guise of patriotic ideals—in one instance, at least, going so far as to murder an unarmed policeman. It is also clear that English criminals, faced with a security tightening in their own country, are taking advantage of the relatively crime-free atmosphere of Ireland and the less stringent precautions in operation there to carry out armed bank robberies—a spill-over, in fact, of the crime wave now reaching record proportions in

Great Britain. At the time of writing, the Irish authorities are seeking the extradition of three London men held by the British police on charges of robbing an Irish bank. The Irish authorities insist,–and this is somewhat surprising–that the troubles in the North (that is, that part of Ireland still lying within the United Kingdom) have had no appreciable effect on Irish crime statistics. This attitude is likely to undergo some change when the statistics for 1972 and 1973 are considered–for the militant Protestant extremist organizations in the North have publicly claimed "credit" for the few minor bomb incidents along the Border between the Republic and Northern Ireland. Only one person in every 175 members of the Irish public ever gets into trouble with the police for drunkenness.

Ireland's relative tranquility does not exist without exacting its price. It is paid in terms of relative backwardness. The majority of Irishmen remain farmers. There are still nearly a quarter of a million farms in this small country, and a quarter of these have less than twenty acres, while two out of three have less than fifty acres. It is not an existence that would appeal to everyone. To city dwellers it might even appear a life of unutterable boredom. But a day passes pleasantly enough, and everybody takes his chores at a comfortable pace, stopping to chat or gossip unless there is urgency about the work. When it is a matter of getting in the hay–cutting it, putting it up in cocks, and so on–or digging the winter's turf, the last charge one could lay against an Irishman is that he is lazy. Then everybody works like demons–including the women and children. There are the daily milking chores, often carried out by the women, and the feeding of pigs; there is the spraying of the potato and other crops to prevent blight. But there is also time for fishing, for a little shooting, perhaps, or if one belongs to the more prosperous farming class, a bit of hunting. Fair Day is a time for getting drunk; but usually the only time the bottle is taken out otherwise is when a visitor calls. In many parts of the country the men still go "rambling" at night; that is, they will call in at neighboring houses and either sit down and chat, if there is enough company present, or play cards. Most rural homes now also have television. The family rosary is still said every night before bed.

For the young, much of the beauty of country courtship has disappeared with the ending of the traditional crossroads dancing, or "kitchen dances." Neither the lay nor clerical authorities favored these unlicensed entertainments, with the result that dancing, which used to be a natural diversion, has been transformed into big business. All over rural Ireland now a series of cavernous, ugly buildings has been erected, into which the young pour nightly to listen and dance to pop music and pop singers. The result, in effect, has been largely to destroy traditional Irish values and to replace them with shoddy and trashy ones.

The tastelessness of these dance halls notwithstanding, one cannot help but notice how Ireland, on the whole, has remained remarkably free of some of the seamier forms of exploitation which we usually associate with modern life. Neither Dublin nor Cork, for instance, assault the unwary with garish nightclubs or strip clubs. The nude or semi-nude female body is rarely exploited in advertising; the visitor never finds the nocturnal delights of Hamburg or Amsterdam or Copenhagen. Ireland is not about to lead any revolution in favor of the Permissive Society. The whole country is incorrigibly old-fashioned—or, as the Irish themselves see it, sane. Since Independence, the country has indeed leaned rather more toward a conservative outlook than a mature people might be expected to do, so that there now exists a whole corpus of written works dealing with the iniquities of the Irish Censorship Board, which has at some time or another banned every Irish writer of note, or even of unnote (including myself), and which used to scissor films in such crude fashion that what remained often tended to look like some avant-garde experiment in incomprehensibility. Most reasonably intelligent people in the country accepted the antics of the Board with a degree of tolerance, even apathy; for Ireland is a country with so many bees in her bonnet that the existence of a band of self-righteous individuals sitting in judgment upon what the Irish people should hear or read hardly appeared much out of place. In fairness, however, it should be noted that they did represent what the mass of the people wanted—a "clean" society. If a referendum had been held, most people, I believe, would have voted in favor of censorship. It was not, after all, political censorship, but simply an expression of a consensus of opinion dealing mainly with the narrow issue of sex.

Sex, so far as the Irish are concerned, is best done in the dark. I don't think the people as a whole ever lost much as a result of the Censorship Board and although it meant that many fine writers went unread, the more salacious offerings of the popular British press (which any civilized society could well do without) were the chief sacrificial lambs. Nor did the Irish become a hard, intolerant, puritan lot as a result. Everything tended to get laughed away, and the antics of the Board were at least always good for a discussion lasting another round of drinks. Dublin's O'Connell Street still boasted its three great monuments to adulterers—to Charles Stewart Parnell, Horatio Nelson, and Daniel O'Connell (of whom it used to be said that you couldn't throw a brick over a wall without hitting one of his bastards). A few years ago, however, the IRA blew old Nelson down (nobody was ever clear, anyway, why he had been put up in the first place, as he never had anything to do with Ireland), but even the most vociferous supporters of the Permissive Society never got around to suggesting that the IRA had done it on the grounds that its continued presence offended their chastity.

Involvement, it could be argued, is the real stuff and guts of Irish society, although you'll never hear an Irishman use the word. Clearly, any society—e.g., America—where people sit around in solemn enclave, discussing ways and means of achieving involvement, has little idea of what life is all about. To the Irish, after all, such notions are a natural way of life. What on earth, exactly, is there to discuss? Irishmen are used to the friendliness of their own country; to the fact that people talk to each other at the drop of the hat; to the fact that they are invariably involved in all the illnesses, strokes of good and bad fortune, deaths, and marriages of their friends and acquaintances. Almost nothing is private in Ireland, and this fact causes Irishmen to feel rather more at sea than they ought to be when they are forced to emigrate, for they are never quite able to understand how men came to veer so far away from what seems to them the only way to live. So often they suffer acute loneliness.

Cynics, of course, may point out that the Irish penchant for involvement is a result of dire necessity. There are long, interminable stretches of time when nothing seems to be happening in Ireland, and it is precisely because these long stretches of nothingness are a normal state of affairs that the Irishman is ever willing, whatever the hour or the circumstances, to take part in something. "This hole!" is how you often hear them decry a reasonable-looking town although there are many Irish towns, indeed, where it is fairly clear that nothing exciting has happened since Parnell spoke there during an election campaign in the 1880s.

Yet the attraction of Ireland, after all, is that it provides a refuge, a place of balm and peace and tranquility, to those used to the bustle of large modern cities. Vincent Mulchrone, a London journalist, told me: "I suppose you could be driven mad with boredom in Ireland as easily as anywhere else—if you stayed long enough. But what I like about it—apart from the sea, the golf, the swimming, and all the rest of it—is the way everybody gets involved with everybody else—not in the sense of sticking their noses into your business when it's unwanted, but in the way there is this marvelous interest in you *as a person.* Englishmen like me are simply left boggling. When an Irishman or woman meets you, they want to know all about you—in the sense that they want to know if you've got any 'good crack' in you or if you'd be good for ten minutes' worthwhile talk. Any Irishman, for instance, is delighted to give you a lift anywhere—not because he's a kind fellow, but because he hopes you'll provide *him* with an experience. Ask an Irishman to go three miles out of his way to deliver meat to Mrs. Nolan and he'll do it, knowing he'll get a chance of a chat."

The Irish seem so eager for personal encounters that anyone who is a natural talker, a wit, an extrovert with a quick intelligence, anyone with a reservoir of ideas, cracks, jokes, witticisms, will do very nicely there. Provided you do not insult anyone, or allow arrogance or pompousness to creep in, then you're safe enough. Indeed, when a visitor first arrives in Dublin, for instance, he often quickly comes to feel that all the more or less derogatory tales he has heard about the place are simply not true—not true in his case, anyway. How, he may ask himself, did these charming people ever gain such a reputation—a reputation largely based on Samuel Johnson's famous remark: "The Irish are a fair people—they never speak well of each other"? Where is the famed malice? the famed uncharitableness? How nice everybody is!

The innocent, in fact, is likely to find himself feted at first, listened to as though he were an oracle—his opinions and ideas weighed and considered as though they were Papal Encyclicals. He might even be encouraged by the smiles and ready laughter that greet his remarks to consider himself witty. Warned beforehand that he ought never argue religion or politics with an Irishman (and he should not in the North of Ireland), he will be astonished to find himself drawn to expound his opinions fully upon these topics. At this point he may suddenly discover where the Irish reputation for verbal vitriol comes from. There is something in the very air of Ireland that makes even a casual visitor want to condemn everything in sight. The pure malt of freedom and democracy welling within him will spur him to hurl anathemas at Irish politics, morals, churchmen, capacities, and incapacities—indeed, Irish *everything*—until, teetering his way into "the gents," he may stop to wonder exactly what is it that has got him so worked up about Ireland and the Irish. After all, he is enjoying himself hugely.

Only when he has been in the country for a month or more does he discover that he has been the victim of a well-known confidence trick. Almost everyone new who promises to provide some "divarsion" is immediately taken up. What the innocent chose to believe was a genuine and permanent liking for him, a genuine pleasure in his company, was never, he discovers, anything more than a mixture of self-interest on the Irishman's part coupled with ancient laws of hospitality. He has been sacrificed to what is really a veneer of politeness only slightly less ritualistic than that of the Japanese. He may suddenly remember that Ireland's national motto is A Hundred Thousand Welcomes—that hospitality is an old *geis,* which nobody wants to break. To his horror, he may even discover that the Irish have been making fun of him behind his back. In the end, he may quit the green shores convinced that its people are a two-faced lot.

If he has had time to see the Janus-gods of Boa Island in Lough Erne, he may be reinforced in his opinion. These statues are stone images of a pagan god with two faces growing from a single neck. Yet even this certainty will quickly turn to confusion when he sees others with three or even four faces growing from the same neck and comes to realize that nothing in Ireland is ever quite what it seems; that no words ever mean what they appear to; that the Irish, in a very deep sense, are always trying to hide themselves.

They are in fact a people who for centuries have been afraid—more often than they would have wished, about the natural world; more often than they could have desired, about what lies beyond.

IV

THE NATIONAL REPUTATION

Full oft hath honest Teague been here displayed
Any many a roar have Irish blunders made.
The bull, the brogue, are now so common grown
That one would almost swear they were—your own!
But, lo, to-night what you ne'er saw before,
A tragic hero from Hibernia's shore,
Who speaks as you do, both of men and things,
And talks heroics just like other kings.
"Irish heroics" yonder Cit exclaims,
Who's been to Hackney and has crossed the Thames,
Who forms his judgment from a few dull plays,
And thinks a Porter's is a Nation's phrase.
To hold forth nature once the stage was meant:
'Tis strangely altered from that first intent.
Were we by it to judge Ierne's sons,
They all are honest, but they all are clowns.
Yet truth hath said, and I shall take her word,
That some have graced a court—and some a cord.
Know yet what part I act who speak so well—
I'd lay my life not one in ten can tell.
So many lines without an Irish howl,
Without "By Jasus" or "Upon my shoul,"
'Tis strange indeed, nor can I hope belief,
When I declare myself the Irish Chief.

Prologue to "The Irish Chief" by

FRANCIS DOBBS, *1773*

The clash and clatter of opinion about the Irish—particularly by non-Irishmen—has often seemed to me to reach levels of sheer incoherence. Some, indeed, would maintain that the "real Irishman" was long ago buried under a fictionalized character largely invented by everybody but Irishmen. Dominic Behan, for instance, who has himself been known to leap onto the counter of an English pub and jink about like a *lióprachâin,* insists, "What's funny about the Irish, what's sentimental about them, what's romantic about them is what has been said about them—and that's it."

What has been said about Irishmen certainly has contributed in large part to the myths that now surround them. Even rational statements often merely turn out to be paradoxes. The judgment of the nineteenth-century French critic, Emile Montegut, for instance, was: "This race is at the same time inferior and superior to the rest of humanity." That of the London *Times*: "While the best Irishman is perhaps the highest type of man the civilised world produces, so the worst is about the lowest."

Irishmen, in fact, have been called everything any people could be called—wild, savage, feckless, irresponsible, idle, comic, sad, garrulous, conceited, hypocritical, mild, shy, gentle, amorous, desexed, drunken, religious, superstitious, envious, learned, stupid, virtuous, honest, unteachable, poetic. One could go on, but it is clear that the Irishman is really much like everybody else—perhaps even a little more so.

Certainly, one cannot escape from the continual aura of paradox that surrounds the Irishman. G. K. Chesterton, for example, once described the Irish as "romantics," only to contradict himself elsewhere by declaring that they made "such excellent lawyers and soldiers because they were such hard-headed realists." He unconsciously summed up his sense of paradox in a verse:

> . . . The great Gaels of Ireland
> Are the men that God made mad,
> For all their wars are merry,
> And all their songs are sad.

One can reel about if one wants to, picking up such nice remarks about the Irish as William of Malmesbury's comment in the twelfth century: "The Irish are of genuine simplicity and guiltless of every crime." Or Professor Arland Ussher's "I believe the Irish to be a mild and gentle race." Even President John Kennedy's "this is an extraordinary country." But then one can turn right around and find the typical member of this "mild and gentle race" described as:

"Blackguard, bully, drunkard, liar, foulmouth, flatterer, beggar, backbiter, venal functionary, corrupt judge, envious friend, vindictive opponent, unparalleled political traitor." Thus Bernard Shaw once lashed his countrymen; but as Chesterton pointed out, Shaw was an "anti-Irish

Irishman"—which was perfectly all right, he hastily explained, "because every Irishman is an anti-Irish Irishman."

One would have thought that at least the one thing everybody could agree about was Irish courage. Yet not at all! Thus Louis XV: "My brave Irishmen!" James II: "I had often been warned that Irishmen, however well they might look, would never acquit themselves well on a field of battle; and I have now found that the warning was but too true. I will never command an Irish army again." After watching the Union Irish Brigade battle against him at Fredericksburg, Robert E. Lee declared, "Never were men so brave." Voltaire, as one might expect, put such contradictory views into perspective when he noted that "the Irish, who have shown themselves the bravest soldiers in France and Spain, have always behaved shamefully at home!"

The range of epithets hurled against the Irish is all the more remarkable because, as a whole, they are a people of classic gentleness who have hitherto responded without demur to paternalism; a people delighting in gentle anarchy but with a natural gift for keeping to the center of the road; creators, in fact, of a society where the noisy and violent stand out more strongly than they would in almost any other Western society, simply because of the tender backdrop. Perhaps the right note was that once struck by the poet Louis MacNeice when he said "It is never safe to generalize about the Irish."

What, indeed, can one really say about the national reputation, if only because it seems so difficult to be clear about exactly what that national reputation is. Does it rest on the title "The Isle of Saints and Scholars"? On Jonathan Swift with his penetrating ironies or Oscar Wilde with his epigrams? Is it something to do with a poor, drunken, lazy, superstitious idol-worshipping mob or with Irish-Americans crooning *toor-a-loor-a-laddy*? "Is it John MacCormack warbling "I'll Take You Home Again, Kathleen"? or John L. Sullivan boasting "I can lick any man in the world"? Is it Henry Ford inventing mass assembly industrial methods? or is it an incorrigible raconteur? or even, perhaps, a Nobel Prize winner for literature, such as Yeats, Shaw, Beckett? Is it a fellow with mud on his boots and drink on his breath, or is it Brendan Behan? Is it Victor MacLaglen helping John Wayne save the U.S. Cavalry in a film made by Irish-American John Ford? Is it a rake-hellion, sprinkling garrulous absurdities and Irish bulls right and left while weeping maudlin tears into his cups and muttering about dear old Ireland? Is it Michael Collins, the daring Pimpernel of the War of Independence, or is it James Cagney, daring Pat O'Brien to get him to go to Confession? Or is it a member of the IRA blowing up an English-owned shop in Belfast? There is, it has to be said, an Irishman to fit all and every occasion.

This difficulty in pinning down the Irish national reputation ought to come as no surprise if we realize that there is no real consensus of opinion as to what actually constitutes an Irishman. The Irish, after all, are made up of almost as many ethnic groups as are the Americans. They are not a homogeneous people. Nor has there been a real synthesis among all the races that make up the island's inhabitants. Many of the paradoxes and ambiguities that surround the national character are due simply to the fact that a single character, as such, has yet to be formed. The country thus remains a motley collection of people of various racial and even cultural strains, hardly even loosely collected together—and, indeed, sundered violently at several points by what ought to be cohesive forces, such as religion. Consider, for example, that by the end of the Neolithic period in Ireland (circa 2000 B.C.) at least five distinctly separate races of invaders or settlers had colonized the island.

By the time the Normans arrived in the twelfth century, the figure of invaders or settlers had probably reached the round dozen, and since that time the country has been asked to assimilate the Normans themselves (some of whom, for example the Fitzgeralds, originally came from as far away as Florence); their Welsh and Flemish auxiliaries; large numbers of French; the English, bringing their own mixed Celtic-Roman-Saxon-Angle-Jute-Frisian-Danish-Norse-and-French blood; then Scots (an intermingling of old British, Picts, Danes, Angles, Saxons, Normans, and old Irish); then Cromwellians (whatever mixture they were); Williamites, which included Dutch; Spanish—not, as popularly supposed, due as a result of the destruction of the Spanish Armada on Ireland's west coast, but as a result of normal port-to-port trading; more French (descendants of various French contingents despatched to Ireland); Germans from the Palatinate; Huguenots; and Jews. By the Middle Ages the Irish population—leaving out the Normans entirely—had already come from Scandinavia, Scotland, France, England, Wales, the Netherlands, Spain, Portugal, North Africa, and the upper reaches of the Danube; possibly also from Egypt or the Near East or from somewhere near Asia.

Visitors have often criticized the Irish for the way they go on about "their Gaelic ancestors" or "their Norman ancestors" or "their Norse ancestors." Michael MacLiammoir has pointed out that more sensible races such as the English never go around declaring "I'm Anglo-Jute-Danish-Norman on my mother's side but Saxon-Celt-French-Frisian-English on my father's." The histories of England and Ireland, however, are not the same. William the Conqueror's victory at Hastings enabled a Norman monarchy to forge a single nation out of the mixture of Romanized Celts, Angles, Saxons, Jutes, Danes, and Norman-French that made up England; but Ireland never experienced such a welding together. When attempts were made in this direction, they came too late, for a battle, not yet ended, had already commenced between Celt (or those who thought they were) and invader.

It is, sadly, precisely these invaders who are largely responsible for the Irishman's national reputation. For over seven centuries England has fought to kill off Irish culture and replace it with "the civility" of English order. She has taken up an attitude toward the Irishman and toward his religion that has veered between the extremes of an outright determination to exterminate everything Irish and an amused and perhaps even enlightened tolerance. To this day she has remained basically anti-Irish and, of course, anti-Catholic. Few English either know much about the modern Irishman or want to know much; and what they *think* they know is invariably prejudiced. Indeed, in the year 1970 a young Manchester journalist was able to tell me frankly: "I've always been prejudiced against Irishmen. All I ever saw of them, to be quite honest, was a rough, drunken lot being hauled up in front of the judge at Manchester assizes. People used to try to tell me that they were a different lot in Ireland itself, but the last place I ever wanted to visit was Ireland. Then I had to go there on a job recently, and I found it an incredible place—southern Ireland, that is. The kindness and the courtesy. The good manners. They *were* a different people! Complete strangers would nod to you in some little town and courteously wish you good evening. Once, a man who was only a laborer insisted on jumping into my car and showing me the way, although I know he lost about a quarter of an hour's wages as a result. Another time, when the landlord caught my English accent in the bar, he stood me a drink. And then when he had officially closed the bar—which, as you know, is often a bit of a joke in Ireland—we all sat drinking and talking *at his expense* until 2:00 A.M. Everywhere I went—and I'm not exaggerating a bit—I found manners perfectly marvelous and the country itself astonishingly beautiful after being locked up in the dustbin that's Manchester."

The Irishman's image in Britain today obviously has been colored by events that have taken place in Northern Ireland since August 1969. Once again, to some extent, the Irish Catholic is in direct conflict with the British army and is, therefore, seen as a traditional enemy. Yet because of the complexities of English society itself, no Irishman can be certain that he will not be admired in England for qualities he is only assumed to possess or that he will not be treated with an unconcealed hostility and contempt which he feels he does not deserve. There are English who can see no Irishman except through the most colorful of rose-colored spectacles; who exclaim at once upon being introduced, "Oh, how lovely! My grandmother came from Ireland." Yet there are also those who automatically regard Irishmen as little more than white Negroes. The actor Peter O'Toole told me that both he and his sister were once refused flats in London when they gave their names. Patrick O'Donovan, a London journalist, admitted to me: "There's a pub just around the corner here which refuses to admit Irishmen. I only get in myself because I was once an officer in the Irish Guards." I once had to deal personally with a suspicious Chelsea landlady who quite clearly did not trust me in her flat, when she discovered where I came from.

Few Irishmen are insufficiently arrogant to feel a sense of injustice about this sort of treatment, but they rarely see any need to protest about it. Like the Welsh, I suppose, we have never quite lost our Celtic belief that the Anglo-Saxons are basically an illiterate, uncultured lot, and what more can you expect from them?—which, I suppose, is an equally obnoxious prejudice and only proves that we are, perhaps at heart no better than they.

Considering the long battle between England and Ireland—and the former's ascendancy in the matter—it is hardly surprising that the Irish character that appears to have gripped the imagination of the greater part of the Anglo-Saxon world is largely an Anglo-Saxon invention. The national reputation which began with the Anglo-Saxons, however, was very different from that which has gained currency in the English-speaking world over the past four hundred years. To the Anglo-Saxons before the Norman Conquest, Ireland was an almost legendary place: quite holy ground. The Venerable Bede, "father of English history," described her as "a land of wholesomeness and serenity of climate far surpassing Britain"—a land "flowing with milk and honey, full of vines, fish, fowl, deer, and goats." No reptiles were found there, he noted, "and no snake can live there, for though often carried thither out of Britain, as soon as the ship comes near the shore and the scent of the air reaches them, they die." Anything brought from Ireland, he added, was a sure "charm against poison."

When a Saxon chief had the temerity to raid the Irish coast, Bede recorded the act with horror and lamentation, as though it were sacrilege. William of Malmesbury followed with his famous opinion that the Irish "are of genuine simplicity and guiltless of every crime." Even when Pope Adrian IV, an Englishman, issued a bull to the Norman king of England, Henry II, instructing him to invade Ireland "to reform the Celtic Church," the Empress Matilda, Henry's aged mother, put her foot down fiercely, insisting that it was out of the question for any Christian monarch to desecrate a land so long regarded throughout Europe as holy ground. Thus the Norman invasion was postponed for several years.

Although Norman and Gael eventually were to clash bloodily, the Normans in fact never treated the Irish in the same infamous way they did their Saxon subjects. They readily intermarried with the families of Irish "lords," or chieftains, and became so enamored of Irish aristocratic customs and manners that many finally came to be described as "more Irish than the Irish themselves." The Irish indeed still have a noteworthy capacity for mentally colonizing the minds of invaders or even temporary settlers; there are cases of Africans from the emergent nations, who, having studied in Dublin, return to their countries with their heads full of Irish problems instead of their own. As the novelist Elizabeth Bowen, herself descended from Cromwellian settlers, says: "Ireland makes Irish."

Although a great deal of legislation passed by the "Irish Parliament" set up by the Normans was undeniably anti-Irish, the main purpose of most of this was not so much to interfere with the Irish themselves as to prevent Normans living in Ireland from going native. The intentions of monarch and Parliament were, instead, to bring "the wilde Irish" to a knowledge of English law as it was developing in England. Perhaps the Irish could be brought to follow the example of the great Norman barons who had been placed among them and who began to open up Ireland to commerce and trade. Unfortunately for Ireland, however, many of the great Norman barons preferred the Irish way of life, and so Ireland never did get to be quite like the Home Counties.

Despite a Norman insistence that they were more or less magnanimously out to elevate the Irish character, we ought not to forget that they were also out for conquest and loot. Bringing the Irish to "civilite and order" was only another way of saying "We've beaten you; now lie down and accept defeat." Nor did bringing the Irish into the fold extend to giving them the benefits of the protection of English law. Despite pleas, and even bribes, offered by Irish chieftains, the so-called Irish Parliament blocked all attempts to give the natives equal status and protection in their properties. English law was merely used by these colonial barons to justify and legalize seizures of lands by the sword and to justify their treatment of the "mere" or common Irish. As English and Irish interests thus began to settle down to a state of war, the Irish became "enemies" and subject to war propaganda. Thus began the series of wars that laid waste southern Ireland and amounted to an early attempt at settling the Irish Question by genocide.

In the reign of Elizabeth I, large numbers of "mere" (as distinct from aristocratic) Irish fled to England by way of Cork and Bristol, and we hear of them as peddlars and beggars, consorts of gypsies and wandering riff-raff, and even as leaders of London thief gangs. In 1572, London Irish were held to be so undesirable that an Act of Transportation was passed to reduce their numbers. One of the greatest ironies of history, indeed, is that as the English moved into Ireland the Irish moved into England—thereby satisfying no one. Those allowed to remain were employed as footmen or chimney sweeps—a filthy job few Englishmen cared to tackle; others sold coal, coming out of the East End and into the City and Westminster with "good Newcastle coal," which had been landed on the Lower Thames from barges. There was a colony of Irish seamen at Wapping. Most, however, made a living as apple vendors—sellers of custard apples (costermongers) and pippins: "The Irishmen cry Pippe, fine Pippe, at Mercer's Chapel." They are described as wearing saffron-colored linen tunics, close-fitting bright blue trews worn so tight as to be offensive to English ideas of decency, and the famous Irish mantle, which originally was colored red or blue and from which developed the Scottish kilt. In Ireland, trews were the garb of the "lower orders" only.

There was fresh influx of Irish into England during the Civil War in the seventeenth century, many being recruited to serve the king or as batmen to cavalier officers. With the king's defeat they found themselves jobless and wandered about the country, mingling with refugees from the troubles in Ireland itself. Some became butlers or valets and their women maidservants. Others became barmen or tavern keepers. All were nicknamed "Teague," from a character in a play—a word that survives in Northern Ireland as a term of abuse for Catholics. Despite their obviously desperate plight, few elected to learn a trade. "Bububbuboo a trade! An Irishman scorns a trade, that he does!" cries another stage character. They sought for jobs, it appears, where wit or cunning were the prerequisites, and fled from anything involving monotonous or steady application. By the Restoration, however, they had become popular entertainers. Irish wakes were fashionable, and boxing matches between Irishwomen drew big crowds. Irish ability to tell any kind of a story in a witness box—and to tell it with artifice and subtlety—led unscrupulous English solicitors to import cargoes of professional witnesses, accompanied by suitable consignments of usquebaugh (from the Irish *uisce-beatha,* meaning "water of life," anglicized to *whiskey*).

Already, by the end of the seventeenth century, the Irish reputation in England could hardly be described as admirable. Twice—in 1641 and again in the 1680s—Londoners were terrified at the thought of retribution for English behavior in Ireland, and tales of an impending massacre of the population by Irish armies led to violent demonstrations. When they were not being half scared to death by the Irish, the English population appears to have regarded them as fit only for menial jobs. Ireland itself they looked upon as a wild and untamed land, full of dangerous and unpredictable enemies—a country which consumed English armies and English money with frightening rapidity. (It never seems to have occurred to anyone that they could have solved the problem by simply getting out of Ireland altogether).

The general portrait of the Irish was hardly helped by the biased picture of them presented on the London stage. Political propaganda clearly was not invented by Herr Goebbels. Several scurrilous anti-Irish plays were performed during the seventeenth century. In one, Irish soldiers are described as "glaggard, and wild, unruly, careless, vain." Irish "rabbles" were shown "following a prey of cattle, the men with swords and clubs, the women with *skean dhus* (Irish knives) and a piper before them as was their custom"; their conversation was "rough and ignorant, made up of priests, politics, and travestied history." A line in one play has a rabble declaim: "There's Father Dominic made a swear that [this] was all our country five thousand years before the new moon was made, and the English thieves only came over the year after the flood." (There is just enough truth in that to make it a travesty of what the Irish actually believed.) Priests were usually depicted as sly rogues always on the lookout for "a cheese or a flitch of bacon," and Irishmen did little else but drink usquebaugh—as American Indians drink firewater, one presumes. The Irish were the constant butts of knockabout humor. A "barrel of gunpowder" would blow up among a bunch of "poltroonery Irish soldiers," who would then fall about the stage amid gales of laughter.

In periods of stress, however, the comic image gave way to savage caricature. When the Ulster Irish, ruthlessly dispossessed of their lands and rights by the Plantation of Ulster in the reign of James I, took a bloody revenge in 1641 on the English and Scotch settlers who had moved in, tales of atrocities swept England, and the Irish quickly became objects of the kind of treatment handed out to the Germans some centuries later. Indeed, the stories circularized then about the Irish came to be repeated almost word for word in regard to the German invasion of Belgium in 1914: newborn babies were allegedly speared (bayoneted), women subjected to mass rape, fat Protestants (Belgians) boiled to make candles, and so on.

By the middle of the eighteenth century, however, Irishmen had won themselves a considerable popularity in London. Their stage appearances had always been occasions for mirth; but by this time audiences had begun to laugh with them instead of at them. The Irish "bull," in particular (whose greatest exponent, Sir Boyle Roche, was of Norman descent), had them roaring in the aisles. As G. K. Chesterton has explained: "A proper Irish bull is only a paradox which people are too stupid to understand. It is the rapid summary of something which is at once so true and so complex that the speaker who has the swift intelligence to perceive it, has not the slow patience to explain it." Thus Sir John Mahaffy, Provost of Trinity College, once was asked by a lady, "Pray explain to me an Irish bull" to which Mahaffy replied, "An Irish bull, Ma'am, is always pregnant."

The Irish, it seems, were always good for a laugh. Captain O'Blunder, a character in a play by the Anglo-Irish playwright Thomas Sheridan, father of Richard Brinsley Sheridan, declares: "Give me this lady's lily-white hand and I'll take her stark-naked without a penny of money in her pocket but the clothes on her back." In another play an Irishman comes on stage to a full house, looks at the audience in rapture, and exclaims, "Isn't it great to have the house full before the doors are open!" An Irishman tells a landowner who is thinking of improving his dilapidated mansion, "It must cost your worship a great deal of money to keep those ruins in a continuous state of decay." An Irishwoman, married to a baronet called Fallal who wants to correct her brogue, cries: "I would not part with anything I brought from my own dear country upon any account whatever, and I'd have you to know that I think my brogue, as you call it, the prettiest feather in my cap, because it tells everybody without their asking it that I am an Irish woman and I assure you that I am prouder of that title than I am of being called My Lady Fallal—and I don't believe there's a Fallal to be found in all Ireland except myself, and I'm out of it." The alleged baby-spearing of 1641 was soon forgotten.

A process had begun, however, that was to be carried to its ultimate with the invention of the "stage Irishman." M. Bourgeois in *John Millington Synge and the Irish Theatre* has written:

> The Stage Irishman habitually . . . has an atrocious Irish brogue, perpetuates jokes, blunders and bulls in speaking, and never fails to utter, by way of Hibernian seasoning, some wild screech or oath of Gaelic origin at every third word. . . . His hair is of a fiery red; he is rosy-cheeked, massive and whiskey-loving. His face is one of simian bestiality with an expression of diabolical archness written all over it. . . . his main characteristics are his swagger, his boisterousness and his pugnacity. He is . . . always anxious to back a quarrel and peerless for cracking skulls.

The stage Irishman was more the creature of simple commerce than of politically-motivated propaganda. As G. C. Duggan in *The Stage Irishman* has emphasized:

> It was the degeneration of stage writing itself that began to produce the first embryo of the Stage Irishman. . . . The last half of the eighteenth century saw the coming of sentimental and humanitarian drama, followed by burlesque, farces, romantic comedies—an era of spectral shapes, of mountaineers living in operatic scenery, of mechanical stage effects and of *fêtes champêtres.* Even good plays became artificial and forced. Playwrights who were Irish might introduce a live Irishman (and, indeed, such very often saved a play from complete dullness), but the temptation to repeat what succeeded became a danger. At

> their best such characters had . . . undoubted courage, buoyancy of disposition, a natural simplicity. But these characteristics began to be travestied by writers who knew nothing about Ireland. . . .
>
> The *penchant* for blunders is overstressed, wit degenerates into mere verbal effects, the true nature of the "Irish Bull" is misunderstood, and the misapplication makes the Irish reader curse the Saxon writer with curses loud and deep.

As Duggan points out, one of the extraordinary things about all this image-making was that it had very little to do with the genuine article. The writers who wrote Irish characters into their plays or the actors who portrayed them on the London stage were invariably either Englishmen or Anglo-Irishmen. The position of the Anglo-Irish had always been highly ambiguous. To the "native" Irish, only a man with an *O* or a *Mac* in front of his name was a real Irishman; indeed, the distinction between Gael and Gall lingers even to this day. To the English at all levels of society, however, the Anglo-Irish in the course of time simply became "the Irish"—a situation which aroused controversy whenever an Anglo-Irishman such as Swift or the Duke of Wellington achieved distinction and *both* countries wanted to claim him.

Forced to consider themselves Irish in England and English in Ireland, the opportunistic Anglo-Irish made the best of both worlds. In England they played up the comic and lovable aspects of the stage Irishman, establishing precedents which Bernard Shaw, among others, was happy to follow. Permitted the license of sly and amusing clowns, they went on to exaggerate those qualities which the English became more and more convinced belonged to the genuine Irish. A wild, feckless, hard-drinking, and hard-wenching lot, the Anglo-Irish helped to create a myth about Irishmen that still largely continues to be perpetrated:

> Beauing, belling, dancing, drinking,
> Breaking windows, damning, sinking,
> Ever raking, never thinking,
> Live the rakes of Mallow.
>
> Spending faster than it comes,
> Beating waiters, bailiffs, duns,
> Bacchus' true begotten sons,
> Live the rakes of Mallow.
>
> When at home with dada dying,
> Still for Mallow-water crying,

But where there is good claret plying,
Live the rakes of Mallow.

Living short, but merry lives,
Going where the devil drives,
Having sweethearts, but no wives,
Live the rakes of Mallow.

Racking tenants, stewards teasing,
Swiftly spending, slowly raising,
Wishing to spend all their days in
Raking, as in Mallow.

Then to end this raking life,
They get sober, take a wife,
Ever after live in strife,
And wish again for Mallow.

While the Anglo-Irish, pursuing their rakish ways amid the social whirls of Dublin, London, and Bath, trod merrily on the national reputation, the London stage continued with gusto its profitable task of inventing Irishmen whose images bore little resemblance to the poor and desperate creatures then struggling to stay alive on the land of Ireland itself. Throughout the eighteenth century, audiences continued to howl with laughter at an interminable procession of absurd Irish wooers, philanderers, and fortune-hunters–Sir Callaghan O'Brallaghan, Sir Lucius O'Trigger, Sir Larry MacMurrough, and others. In a play given at Stratford-on-Avon in 1769, at a time when the vast majority of the Irish in Ireland were still speaking Gaelic, an Irish "tourist" is made to lament: "I had never an intrigue since I left Chester and that's about a week now, and for an Irishman to be so long without one is a burning shame. Och, 'tis a business we are all famous for"–lines, it is hardly necessary to add, that were not written by an Irishman, but by David Garrick. It was all a long way from the realities of Catholic Ireland, empty of stomach and with the fear of hell in its mind. Invention after invention poured out, not without protest from Irishmen. Indeed, a riot marked the first performance of Sheridan's *The Rivals* at Covent Garden in 1775, for the London Irish, much to Sheridan's mortification, protested that Sir Lucius O'Trigger was a national libel.

Yet the juggernaut rolled unheedingly on, often aided and abetted by Irishmen bearing the indubitably Gaelic names of O'Kelly or Murphy. Chesterton once wrote: "All the real amiability which most Englishmen undoubtedly feel towards Irishmen is lavished upon a class of Irish which does not exist. And, unfortunately, all the time that we were creating a comic Irishman in fiction, we were creating a tragic Irishman in fact. The more the oppressor looked down with an amiable pity, the more did the oppressed look down with a somewhat unamiable contempt."

If the Irish had been a successful nation, the chances are that they would have grown as thick-skinned as the English, who are renowned for their ability to laugh at themselves. The Irishman, however, has been the butt of other people's amusement a little too long to wear it all that easily. To make the Irishman an essentially comic figure was to take away from him the last shreds of his remaining dignity, though he would not have minded so much if only his true sense of humor had been presented or understood. Irish writers have argued about the matter and have never really decided whether the portrait was deserved or not. In a statement which may not earn him the gratitude of his countrymen, the writer George Birmingham once said: "The fact is that in spite of the protests, in spite of the ignorant caricatures which have well deserved the title of Stage Irishman, this type . . . is an authentic presentation of what we are." This view is echoed by Duggan, who adds the sociological explanation that "the irresponsible outlook on life was indeed a way of escape from tragic thoughts, from drab surroundings." By the nineteenth century the Irish as a race were being savagely attacked by the English government or its adherents as "reckless, ignorant, improvident, drunken and idle," which drew from Sir Robert Kane, in his *Industrial Resources of Ireland,* this comment: "We were idle for we had nothing to do; we were reckless, for we had no hope; we were ignorant, for learning was denied us; we were improvident, for we had no future; we were drunken, for we sought to forget our misery."

Stephen Gwynn, the Irish writer, thought that the playwrights and novelists who between them had created this "mythical" figure "merely magnified an irresponsible type found oftenest among boatmen, carmen and gentlemen's servants into the type of the whole nation."

Personally, I incline to the view that art—as always, exaggerating and distorting life—was undoubtedly followed by life, which, as Oscar Wilde observed, tends to imitate art. Faced with an impressive body of "evidence" as to the "real" nature of their national character, many Irishmen, I believe, decided to emulate the characters of literature—to "give the jintlemin what they expect." There is no doubt that the desire to please is an innate part of the national character, or style, even if on occasions it is simply used to exploit the gullibility of the stranger. The Irish, it ought to be said, have an overriding sense of possessing an ancient and profound wisdom, so that they tend to see other nationalities as largely made up of gullible people. The success of such exaggerated characters, too, has strengthened the imitative inclinations of the Irishman and has provided a way by which he can secure praise; for, as Edmund Campion noted as early as 1633, "greedy of praise they be." The result is that today, certainly in Dublin, there are Irishmen leading lives—or at least giving themselves "characters"—that are largely artificial.

In much the same way that a whole generation of Americans and Europeans allowed themselves to be, either consciously or subconsciously, influenced by Hollywood, many Irishmen have elected to re-create, and if necessary embellish, roles that originally have been created by someone else. The actor Peter O'Toole admits: "I think we Irish do tend to react to what's expected of us, and ham it up a bit at times. I think we all do it when we get the right encouragement." Bernard Shaw spoke of the advantages of adopting the literary conventions about Irishmen when he admitted that although he preferred the English to the Irish as people, he would never call himself English "because the Englishman is always gaping admiringly at the Irishman as at some clever child prodigy." And Brian Inglis, an Irish journalist who now lives in London, says, "All I had to do was to indicate Irishness at a cocktail party to find myself the center of attraction." He adds, "When you know you're going to be liked a bit more because people call you 'Paddy,' you can't help but trade on it."

Patrick Murphy, a retired London journalist now living in the county Cork, summed up this whole complex dimension of being Irish when he said: "Much of the Irish image is simply *not* of our making, however much we might try to take advantage of it at times. I remember one St. Patrick's Day going along to interview Shaw. Rather innocently, I said 'There's no sign of it being St. Patrick's Day with you, Mr. Shaw?' Shaw nearly jumped down my throat. 'The trouble with you, Murphy,' he said with immense passion, 'is that you've become anglicized. You imagine that a sign of St. Patrick's Day would be if you could see me walking down the Strand with coals of fire on top of my head, a shillelagh in my hand, and me gloriously drunk! Well, that kind of Irishman doesn't exist. There is no such person!' I could understand what he meant, of course. I remember when I first went to school in England, a boy coming up to me and asking my name. When I told him, he at once jumped at me, shouting 'Oh, so you'll want a fight, then!' I simply couldn't convince the fellow that I wasn't pugnacious. So I used to pray at nights that I'd grow up to be seven feet tall, so that I could bash his bloody brains out. When I got to Fleet Street I again found out that 'the national reputation' had preceded me. Time after time I was forgiven things for which any Englishman on the staff would have been booted out. 'Ah, Murphy, I suppose you'll carry the bog around with you wherever you go,' the editor used to say. When an Irishman finds he's expected to fill a certain role—that he's expected to be a harum-scarum, devil-may-care, irresponsible, sentimental dreamer, well, I suppose he can't help trying to live up to the image—particularly if it's going to be to his advantage."

And yet, as they say, there's never smoke without a fire. No Irishman reading over his history, particularly the stories concerning battling tinkers, ne'er-do-wells and "faction" gangs—the rootless, unemployed men who were such a feature of Ireland in the late eighteenth and early nineteenth centuries—can deny altogether that the prototypes for the Stage Irishman did, to some degree, exist.

Much of it, too, is tied up with the cult of personality, which is such a striking feature of Irish life. There is a strange paradox here too, vis-à-vis English society. While the English tend to see great national events in terms of personality—"the wars against Napoleon, against the Kaiser, against Hitler," Winston Churchill "leading us to victory," and so on—the Irish see both world wars simply as conflicts between contending national interests, with both sides in the part of villains. Conversation generally tends more toward the philosophical and the abstract than in England, where everything, particularly politics, is usually reduced to an interplay of personalities. On the other hand, what makes a man important in Ireland is the sheer power or magnetism of his personality. And personality has been equated with the ability to give a good performance, to amuse your audience, to hold it with stories and anecdotes and drolleries. This has to some extent necessitated the enlargement of personality; it helps if you can become a larger-than-life character—become an actor, in fact. The national reputation, it seems, has grown out of a complex of circumstances—with life and art constantly interplaying and reacting on each other.

In *John Bull's Other Island* Shaw drew three recognizable Irish types—the eccentric saint; the Irishman who played to the gallery, trading on the national reputation; and the Irishman who hated the national reputation and did everything exactly opposite. Shaw's account explains a lot about Irish behavior, but in fact by far the larger proportion of Irish people fall into none of these categories. They are shy, gentle, and often inarticulate, the prey of immense personal difficulties and feelings of inferiority, which do not necessarily derive from any sense that their country is inadequate but simply from the fact that the general nature of the Irish cannot stand up to the psychological batterings it has had to take from dominant personalities. In any gathering of Irishmen today there will be one or two outstanding individuals totally monopolizing the conversation, "and refusing to pass it," as one American lady complained to me. They plunge into conversation with the same recklessness that became part of the whole Irish scene after the ancient Gaelic society had been shattered by the Cromwellian invasion in the middle of the seventeenth century.

The "raking" Anglo-Irish, in fact, brought a new spirit into Ireland—one that assisted in no small measure to change the whole meaning of the words *wild Irish.* They may or may not have been influenced by the fact that they found themselves in a land where order, as they knew it in England, had always been lacking, where men lived easy, come-as-you-go lives to some extent. They also knew themselves to be conquerors who could be as arrogant as they liked among an abject people. They suffered, too, from the worst excesses of the newly enriched. Maurice Craig, who has written a definitive history of Dublin city, describes them as "immigrants who, had they stayed in England, would have behaved like normal Englishmen, [but] who found in Ireland an almost rootless society of speculators and go-getters. Many individuals adopted a violent habit of behaviour which brought them closer to the dispossessed helots than might have been possible [otherwise]."

They did not come to full flower until the eighteenth century, by which time these descendants of Cromwellian captains had had full time to forget their puritanical background and to grow attached to what they conceived to be aristocratic living. In the cases of some individuals this consisted of displays of incorrigible arrogance and rascality. They were typified by the Dublin Bucks and the gentleman-hoodlums called *pinkindindies*—a group of night wanderers, often practiced swordsmen, who got their name because they earned their living by "pinking" their victims in order to recoup at swordpoint what they had lost at gaming tables. Their behavior was execrable; they seized women in the streets and rioted in the theaters, often climbing onto the stage to interrupt the actors, so that, as V. S. Pritchett has written, "In Sheridan's time, the theatres were a mixture of beer-garden and brothel." The Bucks, for their part, were an even more ferocious bunch. Tiger Roche and Buck English cut a savage swath through society with shootings, riotings, woundings, and thievings both in Dublin and in London, where they were forced to spend some time in a debtor's prison. Buck English and Buck Whaley helped to organize the unspeakable orgies that took place at the Hell Fire Club in the Dublin mountains. They were rakes, rogues, and hell-raisers who would do anything for a dare or a bet, from stealing an heiress to leaping out of a window onto a hackney carriage fortuitously passing below. To a man they were of the new race, the Anglo-Irish Protestants. As Pritchett further remarks, "In so far as the rioters were of immigrant stock, one can remark that, outside their own country, they were able to liberate the strong, suppressed theatrical capacities of the British." If anybody created the myth, if myth it is, of the wild Irishman, it was these Anglo-Irishmen.

They moved about, too, in a dazzling world—an Irish world that was gradually becoming a land of fine glass, fine silver, fine Italian stucco and plaster, fine carriages, fine furniture, fine silks, fine fireplaces, fine libraries, and fine gardens. For wit and pleasure, observed Lord Cloncurry, the Dublin of their day could be compared to Paris. In the mid-eighteenth century a Commission for Making Wide and Convenient Streets had been set up in the capital, resulting in a city that "might have been built out of the poetry of Pope." The avenue now called O'Connell Street was 154 feet wide; two others were 100 feet wide, and another 96 feet wide. Beautiful buildings such as the Custom House, the Parliament House, and Trinity College—with a library containing one of the largest reading rooms in the world—rose side by side with town mansions of the most imposing dimensions and decorative motifs. In London, Horace Walpole told Sir William Pitt's sister Anne that "all the spirit or wit or poetry on which we subsist comes from Dublin." Indeed, some of Europe's most eminent writers, artists, architects, sculptors, wits, scientists, philosophers, and military and political figures walked its streets within a few short decades.

This was a world in which dinners were magnificent, gambling was incessant, and claret was guzzled as though Dublin had made up its mind to drink all Bordeaux dry. A more reckless, rowdy, euphoric world would be hard to imagine. And the rowdy ebullience of Dublin high-life was mirrored, as it were, in the sullen rowdiness of Dublin low-life. Amid all the splendor of increasing trade and wealth, of fine houses, fine public buildings, and fine words, the landless Irish continued to flood into the city slums—stinking, sewerless places made even more degrading than those of Hogarth's London because the inhabitants were plunged into an even deeper despair. More than two thousand ale houses, three hundred taverns, and twelve hundred brandy shops flourished in Dublin alone. Slum dwellers downed such cascades of whiskey that even today the term *drunken Irish* hangs around the national reputation like a millstone.

Outside Dublin and at a respectable distance from the Italianate mansions and the melting parklands with their wild deer and their exotic shrubberies lay the teeming, ragged "plague-driven, poverty-stricken shiftless, thriftless, desperate world of rural Ireland." In the countryside, "the savage old Irish," as Swift described them, were forced to lurk in the bogs and hills, living, as another Anglo-Irishman, Bishop Berkeley, put it, "in a cynical content in dirt and beggary to a degree beyond any other people in Christendom."

Irish roads swarmed with landless, jobless beggars, traveling from house to house looking for scraps of food, mingling on the way with peddlars, packmen, horses laden with goods, wagons, carriages, coaches, and bands of highwaymen called *Rapparrees* and *Tories* (the latter usually dispossessed native aristocrats). Plague and other sicknesses had caused blindness everywhere. Blind poets, blind beggars, and blind ex-prisoners all tap-tapped their way along the teeming Irish roads, making their way from one "Big House" to another. The more fortunate common people lived in incredibly wretched hovels with dungpits steaming at the door and hordes of children scrambling about on earthen floors by day and making room at night for the family's few poor beasts, brought inside to prevent them from perishing.

All this chaos, anarchy, and desperation produced conditions which, some authorities insist, were worse than those existing in France just before the Revolution. If the Irish had survived without a few twists, distortions and warpings of their attitudes and character, it would certainly have been remarkable. They undoubtedly learned to hate the English, and they unquestionably learned to become more shiftless and idle and devious than they had ever been—although it is clear that many of them had always been pretty content to take life easy. Of course, their scorn for their rulers was not unmixed with a measure of grudging admiration for what Anglo-Irish society proved able to do. Indeed, there seems little doubt that many of the more energetic and dominant of the native Irish were influenced by the rakish, reckless behavior of the Bucks and the other wilder spirits of the new aristocracy. Conduct that was good enough for the lads from the "Big Houses"; that even aroused the admiration of members of more orderly and disciplined English society, was clearly worth imitating.

Irish society, roughly until the middle of the nineteenth century, lacked a strong middle class occupied with making money through trade and commerce. The Anglo-Irish largely had their rents to live on, so that the old rural Irish, moving into the towns, found that Ireland had not yet provided them with any great commercial or industrial dynamo to drive them on. Law, medicine, and tavern keeping became their principal occupations. In such a society there was little to hamper anyone inclined toward extreme behavior.

In addition to the example set by sprigs of the Anglo-Irish aristocracy, relics of tribalism, with its strong elements of paternalism, continued to permeate Irish society. Paternalism, after all, had been the natural order of things in Ireland for at least four thousand years. The old Irish had always submitted themselves entirely to the head of the family—the clan chieftain—and to their spiritual leaders who, after the downfall of Gaelic Ireland, became largely the heirs of the chieftain's authority. To this day the ordinary Irishman finds it difficult to get used to doing without paternalism. Thus it is hardly surprising that much of the rebellious Irish spirit in the eighteenth and early nineteenth centuries emanated from members of the new immigrant society rather than from native stock. The great figures such as Henry Grattan, Henry Flood, Wolfe Tone, Robert Emmet, and others were all Anglo-Irish, all Protestants.

Irish society, in short, was a society where a slight anarchy—sometimes a wild anarchy—became almost part of the natural order of things. In such an atmosphere there were opportunities for people to assert themselves, to usurp authority, to bully, to run wild. Ireland, indeed, bore many resemblances to the much later American Wild West. Personality was able to flower in a way that would be difficult in better ordered societies, where conventions tend to dampen natural impulses.

In Ireland, the maverick became a familiar figure—in some circumstances even an admired figure. He had to fulfill certain essential conditions: He had to be colorful and lovable. Provided he added color either to the local or national scene, he was allowed to get away with almost anything short of murder. Brendan Behan, for example, provided this color; he was "a broth of a boy." The point about Behan is that in the eighteenth century he would have been hardly noticed. But as Ireland grows slowly away from being a society not unlike the American frontier, fewer and fewer Behans are likely to arise. They are still there, of course, and on the whole, whatever their faults, they are perhaps more admirable than the kind of figures who emerged from the saga of the American West. Behan summarizes, in a sense, the extremes in Irish society, a society which is still in its emergent stage, but which still likes to look back over its shoulder to the "wild Irishman."

V

WHO ARE THE IRISH?

Without a fault of his, beat not thy hound; until thou ascertain her guilt, bring not a charge against thy wife.

Two-thirds of thy gentleness be shown to women and to children and to poets, and be not violent to the common people.

Utter not swaggering speech, nor say thou wilt not yield what is right; it is a shameful thing to speak too stiffly unless that it be feasible to carry out thy words.

So long as thou shalt live, thy lord forsake not; neither for gold nor for other reward in the world abandon one whom thou art pledged to protect.

Be no tale-bearer, nor utterer of falsehoods; be not talkative nor rashly censorious. Stir not up strife against thee, however good a man thou be.

Be no frequenter of the drinking house.

Dispense thy meat freely; have no niggard for thy familiar.

Be more apt to give than deny.

Maxims of the FIANNA

Proud possessor of the oldest vernacular literature in Europe after classical Greece and Rome, the Irishman inhabits an island whose historical origins are lost in antiquity. A blob of land on the periphery of Europe, Ireland twice in its history has somehow or other managed to vitalize the West in art and learning without ever quite developing a Caesar, Aristotle, Shakespeare, Michelangelo, Beethoven, Darwin, or Einstein. She is also a land haunted by war, famine, invasion, and tragedy for the past one thousand years.

The early medieval Irishman found himself tucked away in a pastoral society behind a formidable barrier of sea, mountain, quagmire, and wooded fastness, which had preserved him from invasion since before the time of Christ. Conditioned to undisputed military and cultural eminence, he never dreamed of what was coming. At a time when Europe was still forming its modern self from the chaos of the Dark Ages, Irishmen, for two centuries the torchbearers of Christianity, civilization, and learning in the West, suddenly found themselves assailed first by the ferocious and formidably armored Vikings, and then while they were still reeling from this attack, by the Normans, the most advanced military society then known to Europe. Their struggle to disentangle themselves from the culture that resulted has been, as we have already noted, "one of the noblest and most touching things in all history."

The native Irishman, therefore, has been badly savaged, and his character and his society have to be considered in this light—although it hardly explains everything. He has been often crushed and degraded, and sometimes near to extinction. Yet he has somehow survived and gone on assimilating invaders to some extent even while being very definitely assimilated himself.

From the last Ice Age until Columbus' discovery of America, Ireland lay at the end of the world. Early waves of migrating people, seeking less vulnerable pastures, were driven to the rim of the Continent and ultimately to the final island. The first were hunters from Scandinavia who walked through the forests and swamps that now lie beneath the North Sea into Yorkshire, thence across northern England to the tip of southwestern Scotland, and from there by *coragh* or dugout canoe to the coast of Antrim, where they landed a few miles from Belfast. This was in 6000 B.C., and for the next three thousand years they lived peaceably, an experience that ever since has eluded Irishmen.

Sometime between 3000 B.C., when the first farmers arrived (they came from the Pyrenean region and spread from Ireland into Scotland), and the arrival of the first men who understood metals, a creative people about whom we know little except that they have also left monuments in Brittany, landed in Ireland to give it its first artistic objects and architectural monuments. These great mounds are vaguely reminiscent of Egyptian pyramids and were built for the same burial purposes. Broken into and stripped of their treasures by Vikings, they lie on the north bank of the River Boyne, and until Christian times were the great burying places of the High Kings of Ireland.

By the time the Normans arrived to disrupt a native culture, Ireland had become a loose fragmentation of subject peoples—with varying abilities, skills, and qualities; differing physical and facial characteristics—some already intermingling; some living entirely distinct existences in vastly separated areas. Travel was difficult because of thick woods, impassable bogs, rough mountains, and savage wolves. The country—staggeringly—was a great deal wetter than even now.

Among these races was a brilliant pre-Celtic race to whom Ireland owes a great deal. Probably a small, dark, Mediterranean people, they may have reached her from Spain or Brittany, either directly or through Britain. These men gave Ireland her first Golden Age—a term which in this case is not hyperbole. They were a quiet, well-behaved, and unwarlike race of herdsmen, tillers of the soil, and above all, artificers. They had skillful fingers and imaginative, if patient, minds. Utilizing the enormous vein of gold that once made Ireland the richest producing land west of Greece, they fashioned an incredible legacy of golden lunulae, or moon-shaped neck ornaments, sun-discs of pure sheet gold, torques of twisted bar gold, bracelets, brooches, pins, fibulae, and ornamental boats whose working parts still function to this day. To this they added (by working the great copper vein that accompanied the gold and mixing it with the raw materials they imported from Crete, Mycenae, and the Baltic) another treasure of copper halberds, bronze trumpets, engraved bronze knives, sword scabbards, daggers, and necklaces of delicate metalwork embodying faïence and amber.

At this stage, Ireland had become the primitive industrial powerhouse of western Europe and evolved a sophisticated society in touch with the civilized cultures of the Near East. The country's prosperity lay not only in her fantastic deposits of gold, whose abundance, measured by existing relics, astonishes modern metallurgists, but also in her position along the great sea route between the civilizations of the Near East and the producing countries of the Baltic. For a thousand years she flourished, a rich land with great herds of cattle roaming unfenced pastures; the home of industrious craftsmen working glowing designs onto metals or developing the processes of mining and smelting copper and gold; finally exporting these metals, either in their manufactured or raw ingot states, first to the British tribes centered on Stonehenge and Avebury and then to the eastern Mediterranean, particularly to Crete, which in turn was the major supplier of gold and gold ornaments to the Pharaohs of Egypt and the ancient Greeks.

After 950 B.C., ominously, swords and spears and ornate shields of bronze, leather, and wood began to be produced in increasing numbers, and merchants and metal founders buried treasure in the ground. Envious eyes were being cast on the golden isle, and soon invaders from Britain and the Continent arrived. Over the next few centuries plunderers appeared intermittently, and the cumulative effect of their depredations was enough to overthrow the existing society. Whoever they were or wherever they came from, by 500 B.C. the dominant race in Ireland were the Priteni (in Irish, *Cruithin*), from whom the British Isles obtained their first name, the Pretanic Isles. Descendants of these people, soon to be overrun themselves by new and more powerful invaders using iron weapons, probably still form an important element of the common people of Ireland. They held on, indeed, in small independent states, particularly in northeast Ulster, and were the dominant people of the greater part of Scotland until the ninth century A.D., by which time they were known as Picts.

In the third century B.C. the first Celts, equipped with iron weapons and a culture based on ideas and influences imbibed from the Etruscans, descended on the British Isles. These first Celtic invaders have made a considerable contribution to the Irishman's cultural background. They have left a highly sophisticated art, beautifully worked sword scabbards and horse-trappings, and the first stone carvings to show an advance on the work of the early farmers who built the great burial mounds. They are almost certainly the people who built the extraordinary stone fortress of Dun Aengus, eleven acres in extent, that still clings to the clifftop of Inishmore in the Aran Islands. But by far their most important contribution—and one that still exerts its influence today—is their literature. No one knows for certain when the great tales of Ireland were first fashioned, but it is now generally accepted that the *Tain Bo Cuailgne,* probably the greatest indigenous literary work before James Joyce's *Ulysses,* was originally created in primitive form by these invaders—and that the story, in however many glorified and oft-revised forms, reflects something of real historical events. These Irishmen, hardy and warlike, established two capitals—one at Emain Macha (Armagh) in Ulster, which is marked on Ptolemy's map of the second century A.D. as *Isamnion,* and the other at Cruachan in Connacht. The two factions, alongside whom smaller independent kingdoms continued to exist, waged continual war with each other.

Like some Irish Punic War, the rivalry continued for almost five hundred years, until finally the Connachtmen completed the drama in the correct classical fashion by wiping out Emain Macha forever—although its configurations, a mile outside the modern town of Armagh, can be still seen to this day.

On top of all these peoples, by the time the Normans arrived in the twelfth century and despite the inroads of the Vikings, stood the Scot, otherwise known as the Gael (a fifth-century A.D. name bestowed on him by the ancestors of the Welsh, the original being *Gwyddel*). He appears to have arrived in relatively small numbers in Ireland about 100 B.C. He was a true Celt, a member of the warrior caste of the Celtic peoples, who were themselves no more than a mixture of different ethnic groups held together loosely by a common language and culture. He was an aristocrat and did not, for instance, wear trews like the common people (according to the Romans, most British Celts wore trews). Saint Patrick made a very clear distinction between the Scot and the indigenous Irish peoples, whom he called Iberians. The Scot imposed his version of the Celtic language, now called Gaelic, on the native populations; this must have been a gradual process, for it was not until the third century A.D. that Gaelic became generally spoken throughout Ireland. Previously, a variety of languages, including the lost Pictish, was spoken; that used by the first Celts was probably P-Celtic, similar to the language spoken by the Celts in Britain.*

The Scot was probably "tall, large-limbed and with fair or reddish-blonde hair." This is a description given of the Celts by the Romans, and Professor Carlton Coon's findings in this century bear out this description. The Scot was very aggressive and warlike, a great boaster and lover of feasts, a womanizer of herculean proportions, and incredibly superstitious. He made human sacrifice before an idol called Crom Cruach (he was no worse than his cousins in Britain or France). However, like the German, he responded profoundly to music and poetry, and from the earliest times appears to have had a deep desire for learning and an admiration for it. He claimed to have come from Spain directly to Ireland, and although modern scholars are inclined to doubt this (although the Celtiberians of northern Spain are known to have been mercenaries employed by the Romans), his own chieftains right up until the seventeenth century persisted in this belief. Indeed, until the end of the Spanish monarchy in the early 1930s, Irishmen could lay claim to—and were always granted—special privileges in Spain, being in fact treated as natives.

The Scot had established a strong kingdom in Munster by about A.D. 100, and from the middle of the fourth century he ruled from a capital fortress built on the great Rock of Cashel in Tipperary, where eight hundred years later, hot-tempered Henry Plantagenet, whose vast domains

*The Celtic languages, it should be explained, are divided into P-Celtic and Q-Celtic. This linguistic distinction is based on the fact that in certain etymologically related words a *p* sound in one language is matched by a *kw* or *q* sound in the other. Thus the modern Welsh word for "head" is *pen*, whereas the equivalent Gaelic word is *ceann*.

included the kingdom of England, would receive the feudal submission of the majority of Irish kings and princes. By the middle of the third century, another invading force of Scotti, moving farther to the north, had established themselves on what to this day is still the most haunted and hallowed place in Ireland–Tara. Here, on an ancient acropolis, rose wondrous halls whose magnificence, according to the early medieval chroniclers (who regrettably were given to flamboyant exaggeration) rivaled the glories of Solomon's Temple. From here the first attempts were made to establish a central monarchy and a line of titular High Kings.

The Scotti of Cashel, however, continued to rule independently, so that Tara was forced to concede the point and agree with her sister kingdom of Cashel to divide Ireland in two–north and south–on a line roughly drawn from Dublin to Galway. Although the Tara kings eventually called themselves High Kings, it was a claim that seems never to have amounted to much more than a courtesy title. Indeed, the life of royal Tara, for all the fame and mystique that surrounds it and the hold it has on the Irish imagination, lasted for less than three hundred years.

The Scot, or Gael, although never actually forming more than a relatively small proportion of the Irish population, put his stamp firmly upon it. He was king and warrior and priest-bard, and it is doubtful if either he or his family or his followers ever did any useful work. They were simply an aristocracy, possessing exactly the same ideas and prejudices as other aristocracies. They abhorred trade or industry and they loved pedigrees. Their role, as they saw it, was to raid and plunder petty chieftains who failed to pay tribute and to plunder and raid the decaying provinces of Rome, particularly that of Britain. They feasted, listened to tales and poetry and music, and squabbled among themselves while the earlier peoples–many of whom they had actually enslaved–tilled the soil, tended the great cattle herds (which, as in parts of Africa still, were the only form of money), and worked in the smithies, making those exquisite examples of Celtic Christian metalwork which we can still enjoy today.

By Roman standards they were unquestionably barbarians, although certainly not savages. They loved childish display; indeed, everything that gave brilliance and a sense of drama to life appealed to them. Their weapons were richly ornamented in bronze and enamels, and their garments decked in gold, even in battle. They rode home, however, with their victims' heads dangling from their horses' necks, seemingly because they believed that this would help them inherit the brains and virtues of their opponents to add to their own. (And if this seems barbaric, there are contemporary illustrations showing Elizabethan English soldiers returning from forays carrying the bloody heads of their Irish enemies; and the war in Vietnam has produced similar pictures.) Their temperament was so similar to a modern Irishman's that it is worth recalling what the ancients had to say about them. Aristotle had an ambivalent regard for their bravery. "We have no word for the man who is excessively fearless; perhaps one may call such a man mad or bereft of feeling, who fears nothing, neither earthquakes nor waves, as they say of the Celts." In 222 B.C., Polybius said, "I say not usually, but always, in everything they attempt, they are driven headlong by their passions, and never submit to the laws of reason." After watching them at the battle of Telamon, he speaks of their necklaces and bracelets, of their vanity and bravado, their head-hunting, their use of trumpets, their reckless courage and self-sacrifice in battle—and their mass suicide when defeated. Cicero treats them harshly, describing the Celtic peoples (of Britain) as "stupid and unteachable."

The Greek historian Diodorus Siculus has left us one of the best accounts of them:

> They were terrifying in appearance with deep-sounding and very harsh voices. [In conversation] they frequently exaggerate with the aim of extolling themselves and diminishing the status of others. They are boasters and threateners and given to bombastic self-dramatization, and yet they are quick of mind and with good natural ability for learning. They have also lyric poets whom they call Bards. They sing to the accompaniment of instruments resembling lyres, sometimes a eulogy and sometimes a satire. They have also certain philosophers and theologians who are treated with special honor, whom they call Druids. They further make use of seers, thinking them worthy of praise. . . . [The Celt's] custom is that no one should offer sacrifice without a philosopher; for they say that thanks should be offered to the gods by those skilled in the divine nature, as though they were [the only] people who can speak their language, and through them also they hold that benefits should be asked. And it is not only in the needs of peace but in war also that they carefully obey these men and their song-loving poets, and this is true not only of their friends but also of their enemies. For oftentimes as armies approach each other in line of battle with their swords drawn and their spears raised for the charge, these men come forth between them and stop the conflict, as though they had spell-bound some kind of wild animals.

A parallel is found much later in Christian Ireland, for there were occasions when monks achieved similar results by placing themselves between warring clansmen and holding aloft the "Staff of Saint Patrick." Indeed, the Catholic Irishman's reverence for his priests—often sneered at and condemned by Ulster Protestants—obviously does not have its roots in the "Roman" religion, but in the most ancient traditions and customs of the Celtic race.

Caesar himself found the Celts of Gaul "valorous and eager for battle," but—and perhaps this is significant—"easily dashed by reverses." He also discovered that they were great gossips. (As late as the sixteenth century, the poet Edmund Spenser wrote that the Irish "use commonyle to send up and down to know newes, and if any meet with another, his second woorde is, What newes?") But Caesar thought them "too easily influenced" and also "sanguine, credulous, fond of change, and wavering in their counsels." They were quick and intelligent, however, and swift to seize on somebody else's good idea and imitate or even improve on it. Of the Druids he said, "They are generally freed from military service, nor do they pay taxes with the rest. . . . Encouraged by such rewards, many of their own accord come to their schools, and are sent by their friends and relations." Finally, many observers speak of the chivalry of the Celts and note particularly that when they gave their word, they kept it—and expected the same treatment in return.

Two things ruled the Scot—his ego and his priests. In this we find one of his enduring legacies to modern Ireland. His ego was so enormous that he employed poets or bards to tell him what a great fellow he was. Like the Angles, Jutes, and Saxons of England, he could listen all day to verses and songs lauding his deeds, in a manner that would have made Nero blush, and to a catalog of his ancestors that literally never stopped until it reached Adam.

The ego of the Scot startled even Alexander the Great. In 334 B.C., when he was about to go into Asia, Alexander entered into an alliance with Celts living on the Ionian Gulf to protect his rear. When negotiations had been concluded and he was drinking with the plenipotentiaries, described as men of "haughty bearing and great stature," Alexander asked pleasantly what it was they most feared. "We fear no man!" they answered. "There is but one thing we fear; namely, that the sky should fall on us; but we regard nothing so much as the friendship of a man such as thou."

"What a vainglorious people!" remarked Alexander, when they had departed (many have said the same about their descendants).

Several reasons have been advanced as to why it was such an easy job to Christianize the Scot. One is that he already had accepted the immortality of the soul; another, that he already had reversed the Roman conception of deity, and in line with Judaeo-Christian tradition, had created men from his gods. With typical Celtic extravagance, however, he went even further than Jews, Christians, Arabs, or anyone else by creating a whole race of allegedly historical people from his gods. The Scot's capacity to humanize natural forces or to personify skills or qualities such as science, poetry, or artistic ability was so powerful that he invented the *Tuatha de Danaan,* powerful magicians who once—or so he claimed—physically ruled Ireland and whom he had had to overcome in a great battle at Telltown, outside Dublin. By a use of their magic arts, the Danaans, following defeat, threw a veil of invisibility over themselves, which they could put off and throw on again as they chose. Ousted from the physical domination of Ireland, they became masters of the Unseen and vanished from human sight below those great green mounds and raths that still dot the Irish countryside. Here, within fairy palaces, they held—and still hold—revels in eternal sunshine, coming forth from time to time to mingle with mortal men. Gradually this great race, at first regarded as people of normal stature, were reduced into fairies and líoprachāin, the People of the *Sidhe* or *Shee.* To this day, they live in a Land of Youth in enchanted palaces, and most Irishmen, whatever their education or experience of the world, like to suspect that they are still there. Sean O'Faolain relates how an old Cork woman, once asked if she really believed in fairies, replied indignantly, "I do not!—but they're there!" Not so many years ago, an entire Irish building project was held up because workmen refused to bulldoze a lone thorn bush, believing that it marked the site of a dwelling place of the *sidhe.*

Allied to the Scot's superstitiousness was his preoccupation with the sky, which Caesar considered "extreme." This early evidence of how intensely religious the Celts were gives us a glimpse of the origins of that zealous faith which has made Irishmen such a power in the Catholic world; their history of concern for the spirit rather than for material things is older even than the Church of Rome itself. It is this deep obsession with the otherworld that has given the Irishman, absorbed in the values of eternity, a certain contempt for the ephemeral and created in him an impatience with the minutiae of living. It was probably this attitude among his Celtic fellow-countrymen that led George Bernard Shaw to suggest that they were "unfitted for reality."

VI

TALES TOLD
BY THE
FIRESIDE

Perished is every law concerning high fortune,
Crumbled to clay is every ordinance;
Tara, though she be desolate today,
Once on a time was the habitation of heroes.

There was no exhaustion of her many-sided towers
Where was the assembly of storied troops;
Many were the hands whose home was
The green-soiled grassy keep.

When Cormac was among the famous,
Bright shone the fame of his career,
No keep like Tara could be found,
She was the secret of the road of life.

From the DINDSENCHUS
Eleventh century

For all Irishmen, their ancient literature still holds a wonder and enchantment. Even in the twentieth century there remains a magic in this compound of romance, faerie, religion, and unquestionably, real history. Although there are elements in both Irish and Welsh literature indicating a common Celtic origin, Ireland possesses by far the older and fuller body of work. The Scottish cycle of Fionn and Ossian, unlike the Welsh stories, derives directly from the Irish.

It is a literature that still permeates every Irishman's imagination and, subconsciously, still colors his attitudes toward the outside world. It is a constant reminder to him that he comes of the oldest nation at his end of the world. What is more, it provided the inspiration and material for the great Irish Literary Revival of the late nineteenth century, which in turn gave impetus to the political nationalism that triumphed in 1921.

Ireland's ancient literature existed originally in oral form only. Irishmen had managed to develop writing long before the Christian Era, but it was a crude system, called Ogham, as cumbersome as Chinese and almost as difficult to decipher. Examples of Ogham writing still can be seen chipped into old memorial stones all over Ireland and in those areas of Britain–Scotland, Wales, and western England–where the Irish once ruled. It was so profligate of space, however, that it has been estimated that today a modern novel of eighty thousand words would need a surface over a mile in length. The Irish began to adapt the Latin alphabet when converted to Christianity about A.D. 432. Almost at once, their Druidic classes began setting down all that they considered worthy of preservation. Although their first efforts were in Latin, the vernacular quickly followed, thus providing us with the oldest writing in any vernacular in Europe. It was a body of writing embracing both religious and secular material, and included Saint Patrick's Autobiography and the Life of Saint Columcille, as well as secular poems, topographies, law collections, the great sagas, and a compilation of fact and fiction offered as *The History of Ireland,* which modern scholars politely call "synthetic." Between the fifth and twelfth centuries these old materials were copied again and again so that, in fact, the earliest extant copy of any writing in the Irish language dates only from the twelfth century. However, by a study of the language used, it has been possible to date the works to a much earlier period. The great *Cattle Raid of Cooley* epic, therefore, has come down to us in exactly the same way that we have received our present versions of the New Testament.

Sadly, the body of Irish manuscript literature we have is only a fraction of what once existed. Apart from the natural erosions of time, there were two periods when a tremendous destruction of Irish books was wrought. The first occurred during the Viking raids, when hundreds of priceless Irish manuscripts were vandalized in acts called "the drowning of the books." The second, in the late sixteenth century, was carried out as a deliberate act of English state policy, in an effort to wipe out native culture. Some idea of what has been lost can be deduced from a study of *The Book of Leinster,* which was compiled in A.D. 1160, making it the second oldest surviving collection of native-language manuscripts. This book lists only 187 sagas, but indicates that 120 already had been lost. In addition, it is now known that before writing was introduced at all, every chief poet had to know 350 of the sagas, each committed to memory.

The relatively late development of a sophisticated system of alphabetic writing in Ireland was a result of the failure of the Romans to invade the country. In A.D. 81, Julius Agricola, Governor of Britain, established posts along the British west coast as a prelude to an invasion. He had even welcomed a rebellious Irish prince to his court, apparently with the intention of setting up a puppet. For one reason or another, the invasion was called off, and thus Ireland was left isolated from the benefits of early Romanization. (Extraordinarily, though, Irishmen, who have always fiercely resented the invasion by the Normans, sigh over the lost opportunities an injection of Roman learning and Roman discipline might have given them.)

Ancient Irish literature is divided roughly into three sections: the Mythological Cycle–stories dealing with the earliest invaders of Ireland; the Red Branch Cycle–dealing mainly with the Cuchulain legends and the wars between Ulster and Connacht; and the Ossianic Cycle–dealing with the exploits of Fionn MacCool and his son Ossian, or Oisin (pronounced *Awsheen*), and the professional army they led, called the *Fianna.* During the eighteenth century James MacPherson, a Scottish writer, published what he pretended were translations of the latter, and they became the favorite reading of Napoleon and Goethe. MacPherson's work stemmed mainly from his own imagination, which he let play freely with some borrowed names and "genuine" episodes. However, in Ireland we still have the original tales, which have been told and retold down the centuries in fortress, castle, and cottage–and which are still told today round Irish country firesides by *shanachies,* the descendants of the old poets and storytellers.

It is probably this extraordinary link with the ancient past that gives the Irishman, among western races, a unique perspective on life. He still tends to identify himself to some extent with kings and warriors who lived two hundred years before Christ. An Englishman, for example, has difficulty identifying with the shadowy King Arthur, the sixth-century British warrior, because Arthur was a Celt who fought against the Englishman's ancestors, the Saxons. The Irishman, however, has lived on his same land for over two thousand years, in some instances longer; has his stone monuments still about him, raised by his ancestors; has his ancient literature and histories. He is not unique in possessing a body of ancient saga—but he is unique in that it has perhaps more meaning for him because of the intense efforts made to wipe out the culture that created it. The heroic image of a warrior caste has persisted, therefore—honed and sharpened by centuries of resistance to Britain.

The Cattle Raid of Cooley remains highly significant, also, because it takes one right to the heart of the authentic Irish mind—hard, diamond-bright, unsentimental; totally at variance with the sham-Irish image which had its apogee during the nineteenth century and which still turns up in films or Broadway musicals today. The tale can be also enjoyed simply as a good story—or, more to the point, seen as a great moral tale about the futility of war, for it is a narrative full of classic irony.

There is a good deal in *The Cattle Raid*—indeed in all of the Irish epic literature—to astonish anyone who imagines that the idea of chivalry was the invention of medieval Europe. The lofty courtesy shown by enemies; the tremendous pride, which prevented a warrior's taking advantage of an adversary's wounds; the punctilio with which each man observed the duties of his caste or station in life were all anticipated by Irishmen. There is one striking difference, however, between the great Gaelic tales and the Romance literature of medieval France and Germany; this is an absence of "love"—love, that is, as an ideal. "It would have seemed absurd to the Irish Celt to make the plot of a serious story hinge on the kind of passion with which the medieval Dulcinea inspired her faithful knight," wrote T. W. Rolleston, the eminent Irish scholar. Woman-worship and the idealization of the female play no part in Irish literature. On the contrary, in the two great Irish love tales—of Deirdre and of Grainne—it is actually the women who do the wooing. Irishwomen clearly were always a handful, and the Irishman's wariness of sex is clearly of long standing. Obviously Irishwomen were never soft playthings or toys to be petted and idealized. It has to be remembered, of course, that Celtic women were liable for military service up until the seventh century.

It is women, however—women with strong physical desires and ambitions—who both inspire and dictate the course of events described in *The Cattle Raid.* Yet the epic never actually takes on the character of an antifemale tract. The figure of Deirdre, for example, is undeniably as sympathetic a portrait of a tragic heroine as has ever been drawn in literature. To understand *The Cattle Raid*—in which magic, gods, and supernatural wonders all play a part and are related in the original in a mixture of prose and poetry—it is necessary to go back to earlier stories telling of Queen Nessa of Ulster and Deirdre, the latter the subject of famous plays by Yeats and J. M. Synge, another ornament of modern Anglo-Irish literature.

Nessa, an attractive widow, was mother to Conar, a youth for whom great things had been predicted. She was ambitious for him, and when Fergus, king of Ulster, wooed her, she agreed to marry him on one condition: that he step down from the monarchy for a year and allow Conar to reign in his place. The enamored Fergus, archetype of that Irishman who prefers "the feast and the chase" to the onerous exercise of responsibility, willingly agreed, and Conar MacNessa became king. He proved himself such an able one that the Ulstermen decided after the year was up that they preferred him to Fergus. Fergus accepted the decision and settled down with Nessa to live with honor at Emain Macha (Armagh). Some years later, however, he was among the guests, who included Conar and his chief Druid, Cathbad, attending a feast given by a nobleman called Felim MacDall. During this feast it was announced that Felim's wife had borne him a daughter. Then, as was the custom, Cathbad was asked to predict her future. At first he refused to cast a horoscope, but eventually revealed that "the infant shall be fairest among the women of Erin,"

> With blonde hair, eye-blinding,
> Green-irised, stormy eyes,
> Cheeks blood-tinged like foxglove,
> Like to a flash of snow,
> The flash of her teeth's treasury
> Between crimson lips' treasure.

She would even wed a king. But—and here Cathbad's face grew dark and troubled—"because of her, shall death and ruin come upon the Province of Ulster." This led to immediate uproar, during which the Red Branch warriors voted that she should be put to death; but Conar had no stomach for such a measure and suggested an alternative solution. "I will avert the doom," he insisted, "for she shall wed no foreign king. She shall be my own mate when she is of age." He ordered that she should be handed over to the nurse Levarcam and kept hidden away in a *dun* (stone fortress) in a deep wood until she was of age to marry.

The years passed, with the lovely Deirdre allowed to see no one but Levarcam, and from time to time, the Druid Cathbad or the king himself. By the time she was of marriageable age, Conar himself was no longer young. One morning, after a night of heavy snow, Deirdre looked out and saw a raven sipping the blood of a calf which had been slaughtered for meat. "Such," she remarked to the nurse, "and not Conar, would be the man I would love—his hair like the raven's wing, and in his cheek the hue of blood, and his skin as white as snow." Levarcam, sympathizing with the girl, revealed that there was just such a man among the Red Branch warriors–Naisi, son of Usna. Deirdre pleaded to be allowed to see him, until finally the nurse arranged for Naisi and his two brothers to hunt near the dun. On seeing Naisi, Deirdre immediately fell in love with him. The nurse was induced to arrange a meeting, during which Deirdre begged Naisi to save her from Conar. At first the warrior, reluctant to betray his king, refused; but under the spell of her beauty he finally agreed to flee with her. The lovers eloped, taking with them Levaram and Naisi's brothers, Ardan and Ainle. Hunted and harried all over Ireland by King Conar, the party finally sought refuge in Alba (Scotland), where the brothers took service with the king of Picts. Later, after the Pictish king tried to tempt Deirdre away, the little party fled to "lonely Glen Etive," where in a hut by the lake, they lived by hunting and fishing.

Many years passed before Conar discovered their hiding place. He then thought up a trick to induce them to return. He dispatched Fergus, an old friend of Naisi's, with the promise of forgiveness if the party returned to Ireland. Deirdre scented treachery, but Naisi argued that they would be under Fergus' protection, and Deirdre finally gave in. Once they set foot in Ireland, however, Fergus was detached from the party through an invitation to a feast given by a local lord–the latter putting him under a *geis* (a sacred vow, bond, or taboo) to attend, which Fergus could not honorably refuse. Fergus, however, made his sons, Illan and Buino, continue the journey with Deirdre and the sons of Usna, as a sign that they were still under his protection.

Deirdre remained fearful, however, and as the party approached Emain Macha she again warned Naisi to beware of treachery. If they were admitted to the Royal House, where Conar and his nobles were feasting, all would be well–for Conar would dare not abuse the laws of hospitality. But if they were sent elsewhere, it meant danger. In fact, when they entered Emain Macha they were led straight to the House of the Red Branch–the hall where Conar's warriors normally assembled, each sitting in his appointed place at table, under his own device, and with his back to the wall for fear of being taken at a disadvantage (for the frequent arguments were often followed by swordplay). The king sent for Levarcam and asked her about Deirdre. "She is well," the wily nurse answered, "but she has lived many years in the wildwood and toil and care have changed her. Little of her beauty of old now remains." Conar, disappointed, dismissed the nurse and went on with his drinking, brooding over the matter. Finally, he ordered a servant named Trendorn to go to the House of the Red Branch and then come back to tell him what he had seen. Trendorn, finding the door of the house locked, climbed up a ladder and looked through a window. Inside he saw Naisi's brothers and Fergus' sons cleaning their weapons. Sitting at a chessboard with Naisi himself was the most beautiful woman he had ever seen. Naisi happened to look up at that moment, and sighting the spy, flung a chess piece, which struck Trendorn in the eye. Face streaming blood, the servant returned to inform Conar that he had seen "the fairest woman in the world." Conar at once summoned his guards and ordered them to seize Naisi and his brothers and to bring Deirdre before him. The guards were met by Buino and his retinue and in the ensuing fight were at first driven back. While the battle raged Naisi and Deirdre calmly continued to play chess, Naisi remarking, "It is not seemly that we should seek to defend ourselves while we are under the protection of the sons of Fergus."

Fortunes changed suddenly, however, when Conar, angered by the delay, appeared on the scene. Faced by Buino's obstinate resistance, Conar offered him a bribe. Treacherously, Buino gave way, but at once his brother Illan rushed into the gap left by this desertion. Illan, however, was swiftly slain, and at last Naisi and his brothers were forced to fight. They fought so desperately and so successfully that Conar finally had to ask Cathbad to cast a spell, which the druid was glad to do when his king assured him that he would do the little party no harm. Deceived by this promise, Cathbad cast his spell, and at once Naisi and his brothers believed that they were standing in a lake of slime into which they were slowly sinking. Chivalrously, Naisi sought to protect Deirdre. Dropping his weapons, he lifted her upon his shoulders, and as he did so the king's guards leaped upon the whole party and overcame them. They were at once led to the Royal House, where Conar called on a Red Branch warrior to slay the three brothers. The first man refused, and indeed warrior after warrior stubbornly declared he would have no part in such a deed. Owen, Prince of Ferney, advanced, and with one sweep of his sword beheaded all three. Deirdre, her hands roped behind her back, her head bowed in sorrow, thus stood before Conar, at last at his mercy.

Conar then took her against her will and kept her for a year, during which time she "did not move her lips in a smile, she took no food nor sleep, her head held bowed to her knees the sheaves of her downstreaming hair." Conar several times tried to lull her grief, but Deirdre remained inconsolable and continued to mourn Naisi.

> I do not sleep
> Staring through half the night
> My head aches with too many people
> I can neither drink nor eat.

Again, she declared: "I do not tint my nails any more. There is no one to prepare for."

When Conar made a final despairing bid to win her round, she reproached him.

Conar, you are foolish, or blind
To this tiredness, to woo,
When such hate and sorrow find
Biding place between us two?

Furious, Conar demanded, "What is it you hate most of all on earth, Deirdre?"

"Thou and Owen, Prince of Ferney," she answered.

"In that case," replied Conar cruelly, "thou shalt go to Owen for a year."

The next morning, therefore, Deirdre was led captive to the king's chariot, and Conar and Owen stepped up beside her. As they drove off Deidre's eyes remained fixed on the ground. Even when Conar taunted her, "Deirdre, the glance of thee between me and Owen is the glance of a ewe between two rams," she refused to look up. A little later, as the chariot swung into a rocky defile Deirdre saw a rock projecting from the side of the road. As the king's chariot breasted this rock, she flung herself onto it, and thus smashed her head and killed herself.

Afterward—so it is said—two yew trees sprang up from her grave and that of Naisi; when full grown, they met each other and intertwined in such a way that no man could part them.

The king's treachery, however, did not go for long unpunished. Fergus, learning of what had happened, gathered all his followers and launched an attack on Emain Macha. In the battle that ensued, he not only killed Conar's son and grandson but also three hundred of his warriors. The quarrel at once sundered the sympathy of the warriors of Ulster. Many felt inclined to take Fergus' side, but they had, after all, sworn an oath of loyalty to Conar, their king. Some, however, decided to follow Fergus, determined to exact further vengeance. The hero led them into Connacht, where he offered his services to Queen Maeve and her husband, Ailill. This is the point at which the *Tain Bo Cuailgne—The Cattle Raid of Cooley*—begins.

Maeve, tall, with "masses of hair yellow as ripe corn," comes down the centuries as a strong-minded, wild, and self-willed woman. Although her husband titularly was monarch, Maeve had become the real ruler of Connacht, which she bent to her impervious will. She took lovers as and when she pleased and dismissed them with equal arrogance. Upon entering her service, Fergus was at once led to the queenly couch, where after an amorous interlude, the two decided on a plot to attack Conar. Maeve had her own excellent other reasons for wishing to attack Ulster. Among her herds was the famed White Bull of Connacht, a great animal that had an obstinate habit of straying away from her herds and into her husband's. On one occasion, while she and Ailill had been counting what they each owned, her husband had taunted her that the White Bull was too proud to stay with a woman. Infuriated by this boast, Maeve had called her steward and asked if there were a finer beast anywhere else in Ireland. Yes, replied the steward: the Brown Bull of Cooley, in Ulster, which "had a back so broad that fifty children could play on it. It is the mightiest of all beasts." Maeve pondered this and finally sent an emissary to the owner of the Brown Bull, asking him to rent her the animal for a year, at the end of which time she would duly return it. The bull's owner, however, had refused, and the arrival of Fergus, therefore, had proved opportune. Having made their plans, Maeve ordered a hosting of warriors.

She had little reason to doubt victory, because Fergus had told her of a curse that hung over Emain Macha: In their time of direst need a great weakness, similar to that which afflicts women in childbirth, would fall on the men of Ulster. Yet even as her host prepared to set out, Maeve received a prophetic warning. A woman of the sidhe (a *ban-sidhe*) appeared to her. Fearfully, Maeve inquired, "How seest our host?"

"I see them all becrimsoned," replied the ban-sidhe. "I see a man of small stature, but the Hero's Light is on his brow. He is a stripling, young and modest, but in battle a dragon. By him your slain shall lie thickly." Despite this dire warning Maeve and her host set out, starting from her capital at Cruachan, crossing the Shannon above Lough Rea, and marching by Longford and Westmeath right up to the borders of Ulster. Because the sickness predicted by Fergus had fallen upon its warriors, Ulster at this moment was guarded solely by one man—the great Cuchulain, the Hound of Ulster—magically exempt from the curse because his real father was "a man of the Tuatha de Danaan" (that is, a member of the sidhe).

Although he had been warned of Maeve's approach, Cuchulain displayed a brand of coolness scarcely surpassed even by fictional nineteenth-century Englishmen. Having dispatched a messenger to warn Conar of the host's approach, he then went to a love tryst. Before going, however, he put the enemy host under geis not to pass a large pillar-stone. He did this by twisting a bundle of oak saplings into a great ring, hanging it on the pillar, and then leaving a message in Ogham, warning Maeve that neither she nor her men must pass the spot until one of them had succeeded in making a similar ring. Upon reaching this stone, several of Maeve's warriors attempted the feat, but none could match Cuchulain's strength, and so they were forced to camp for the night—a night, presumably, spent by Cuchulain in happy dalliance.

Next morning Maeve resumed her advance, having decided that the geis lasted only for a night. But as her army approached the burial place of the kings at Brugh-na-Boinne she suddenly perceived the first sign of Cuchulain's presence. Two scout chariots returned "and their cushions very red on them." When they reached the Boyne itself, she and her men were greeted by an even more gruesome sight. Someone, at a single blow, had severed a tree fork from its trunk and planted it in the river; and from the four arms hung the heads of the two scouts and their two charioteers. Here also Cuchulain had put them under geis: Until the tree fork was lifted from the river bed, the host must halt. Fergus at once attempted the feat but broke seventeen chariots under him before he managed to hoist the fork and enabled Maeve to resume her march.

Now Cuchulain himself appeared. In a bewildering series of hit-and-run attacks, his chariot again and again swooped from the blue as he picked off men in twos and threes with his slingshot. He flashed into the attack, only to vanish before the host could strike back, so that no one could be sure where he might spring from next. Maeve herself was almost killed when his slingshots first slew a pet squirrel and then a pet bird which she had perched on her shoulders. Finally, Cuchulain became possessed with his great battle-rage–a supernatural fit that came upon him and distorted him out of all human shape. He grew into a monster whose feet and knees turned back to front; one eye receded into his head, while the other protruded abnormally; and his mouth widened to meet his ears. The beat of his heart became as loud as a lion's roar, and a jet of dusky blood shot up from his head, tall and rigid as a ship's mast, while a magic light blazed about his head. At the sight of this paroxysm, a hundred of Maeve's warriors fell dead. As long as the battle-frenzy lasted, Cuchulain was able to kill hundreds with every charge. Night and day he allowed his enemies no rest. Indeed, he himself rested only "a little while against his spear after midday, with his head on his clenched fist, and his clenched fist on his spear and his spear on his knee."

Finally, through the good offices of Fergus, Cuchulain and Maeve agreed to a compact. Cuchulain would stop harrying the host if each day they sent out a champion to meet him in single combat at the ford over the River Dee. In return, Maeve agreed to limit her daily march to the time it took Cuchulain to slay her champion. One after another the warriors of Connacht strutted forth to face the great hero, only to be cut down. Maeve, meanwhile, finding herself short of supplies, decided to send out raiding parties to seize them from the petty states neighboring Ulster. In the course of one of these raids the Brown Bull, which, ironically, had been removed from its own pasture for safety, was accidentally discovered by the raiders, who with great joy drove it back toward Connacht. On the way they passed Cuchulain, still stoutly defending the ford at the river. Although the great champion made an attempt to rescue the bull, he succeeded only in killing the leader of the raiding party before being forced to return and defend the ford.

Although Maeve had achieved her main objective, she decided to continue her attack on Ulster in accordance with her pact with Fergus. Indeed, in her impatience to strike directly at Conar himself, she broke her word to Cuchulain and sent forward parties of twenty or thirty men at a time to engage him. In such circumstances, even the great hero was hard pressed to save himself.

In recounting the defense of the ford at this stage, the epic reaches its most dramatic moment–although the late Frank O'Connor, the short-story writer, has dismissed the episode as "lacking in artistry." Nonetheless, it remains one of the greatest and most poignant accounts of single combat in all ancient literature.

The warrior Ferdia, Cuchulain's oldest and dearest friend, at first ignored Maeve's blandishments and refused to fight him. The great queen, having failed with a succession of bribes, ended by offering him her daughter. Still Ferdia refused, at which point Maeve played trump card: If Ferdia refused the challenge, she declared, she would order a poet-satirist to compose verses against him. Satire was the most terrible weapon known to ancient Ireland; often men ridiculed and reviled by the poets died of shame. Ferdia, his brow black with misery, at last agreed.

Cuchulain, for his part, was dismayed when he saw Ferdia approach. He protested their friendship, but Ferdia cut him short, saying: "O Cuchulain, though we have studied poetry and science together and thou hast spoken of our friendship many times, yet it is my hand that shall wound thee. I beg thee not remember our comradeship."

The two champions commenced combat, and the battle raged for a full day without either gaining advantage. Toward twilight, each having suffered minor wounds, Ferdia suggested that they rest.

"They ceased. They threw away their weapons from them into the hands of their charioteers. Each of them forthwith approached the other, and each put his arms round the other's neck and gave him three kisses. Their horses were in the same paddock that night and their charioteers were at the same fire; and for the champions their charioteers spread beds of green rushes. . . . Of every herb and healing plant that was applied to the stabs and cuts and gashes, and to all the wounds of Cuchulain, he would send an equal portion westward over the ford to Ferdia, so that the men of Erin might not be able to say, should Ferdia fall by him, that it was by better means of cure he had gotten the victory over him. And of each kind of food and of pleasant drink that was sent by the men of Erin to Ferdia, he would send a fair moiety over the ford northwards to Cuchulain; because the purveyors of Ferdia were more numerous than those of Cuchulain."

On the second day the two men again fought chivalrously and again that night shared all things. On the morning of the third day, however, Ferdia's face was clouded over, and even Cuchulain could not help sneering at his friend for rising to the challenge–simply, he alleged, because Ferdia lusted for Maeve's daughter. "Had I not faced thee when summoned," answered Ferdia angrily, "there would be shame on me in Cruachan." That day the two champions fought with less chivalry and wounded each other more seriously. When night fell this time they neither shared nor helped each other and both were "mournful, sorrowful, disheartened."

The Cattle Raid was once considered no more than a glorification of war, a large-scale romanticization of the hit-and-run cattle-stealing raids that were said to have marked ancient Irish society. Today it is regarded as something markedly different. Seen as the natural consequence of Conar MacNessa's treachery and Deirdre's sorrowful death, its twists of fate and intricacies of motive all give it a grandeur that make it a compassionate statement of the human predicament in terms that are still being argued about today. As the fight progresses, for example, we see violence distorting friendship to a point where the antagonists contemplate each other's death; how the air between them becomes slowly poisoned; and how both are brought to the point where they are capable of the final degradation.

By the fourth morning the heroes were aware that the issue would be decided that day. Ferdia had the more formidable task, for he knew that if hard pressed, Cuchulain could always use his enchanted spear, the *Gae Bolg.* As protection against this weapon, Ferdia strapped a large flat stone over his stomach, on top of which he placed an iron apron. Then, prepared for the worst, he drew on his crested helmet studded with carbuncles and inlaid with enamel, girded himself with his gold-hilted sword, and lifted up his shield with its fifty bosses of bronze. Advancing to the river bank, he tossed his weapons in the air "doing wonderful feats." The two warriors closed, but although both fought mightily, neither could secure advantage. At midday Cuchulain decided to change his tactics. He laid aside his spear and took up his sword and tried to smite Ferdia over his shield. Three times he leaped into the air, seeking to reach over it, but each time Ferdia, a giant Firbolg, flung him off like a child. Urged on by his charioteer, Cuchulain became possessed by his great battle rage. His whole body became distorted, and he grew until finally he was taller even than Ferdia and "the Hero's Light blazed about his head." Together the champions struggled like giants in mid-river, while all around, creatures and demons and goblins gibbered with fright. Even the waters recoiled, so that they were fighting on the dry river bed. Slowly Ferdia gained the upper hand. Finally he gave Cuchulain a mighty wound and pressed him so hard that

Cuchulain, in desperation, called upon his charioteer to throw him the *Gae Bolg.* This deadly weapon, often called the world's first torpedo, was always launched upward. Ferdia instinctively lowered his shield to meet the new danger. In a flash Cuchulain struck with his sword over the top of Ferdia's shield, getting in a blow that caused the Connacht champion to raise his shield again. At once Cuchulain launched the enchanted spear. It passed upward through apron and stone and deep into Ferdia's body, where it exploded and sent its barbs into "every crevice and cranny."

" 'Tis enough," cried Ferdia, "I have my death of that!"

The lust of battle dying in him, Cuchulain caught his friend as he fell, and overcome with sorrow, carried him to the Ulster side of the river "so that the slain man might be on the north side," the side he had fought to gain. Cuchulain then spoke a lament over his dead friend before falling into a swoon himself. Believing him also dead, Maeve and her host marched into Ulster, "tossing their spears and singing their war songs."

The epic continues with Conar and his men recovering from the curse and giving battle to the invaders. Fergus, wielding the magic sword *Caladcholg* (*Excalibur* is a Latinized corruption of this name, so that here we see the genesis of the Arthurian sword), slew whole ranks of the Ulstermen at one blow, and the fiery Maeve charged thrice into the heart of the enemy. But when Cuchulain recovered and caught up with the battle, Fergus, who was under geis never to fight him, withdrew, and Maeve's host took flight. During the rout, Cuchulain overtook the warrior queen, whom he found hiding under her chariot. She pleaded for mercy, and the hero, observing disdainfully, "I am not wont to slay women," gallantly escorted her to the Shannon, the borders of her kingdom.

The epic ends on a note of magnificent irony, which is a reflex of a quality pervasive in all genuine Irish poetry, prose, speech, and song—a quality that many who think most things Irish excessively sentimental may find totally unexpected. It is also an extraordinarily modern comment on the nature of war and its futility. Frank O'Connor, perhaps in an effort to make amends for his criticism of the fight at the ford, once said that he knew of nothing in literature that expressed this ironic insight into the nature of war so well.

Despite their rout, the Connacht men led the Brown Bull back in triumph to Cruachan. But when the Brown Bull met the White Bull, the two locked horns in terrible battle. For a day and a night they fought in a Roscommon lake until finally the Brown Bull emerged victoriously, with what was left of the White Bull impaled on his horns. Maddened by his wounds and sheer homesickness, the victorious animal roared off toward his Ulster homeland. Bellowing and roaring all the way, he traveled the width of Ireland, tossing the fragments of the White Bull to the winds and vomiting black gore, until finally he reached Ulster. And there he dropped dead.

Thus ends Ireland's great national epic. Other tales, however, carry on the fortunes of Maeve and Cuchulain. The death of Cuchulain is a magnificent piece of writing; probably nothing else in Irish or Anglo-Irish literature quite surpasses it.

Despite Cuchulain's chivalrous behavior toward her, Maeve decided that he had to die. So she led yet another great army into Ulster, this time in alliance with Lewy, King of Munster. When they reached Ulster, she decided upon a trick: She sent a satirist to Cuchulain to demand his spear. By custom, if an Irish bard demanded anything, it had to be given him (in real history, an Irish king once surrendered his eye). Rather than hand over the spear, however, Cuchulain angrily threw it at the satirist, doing so with such force that it carried through the unfortunate poet and killed nine men beyond him! It was his last great feat. Lewy picked up the spear and cast it back. His aim was inaccurate, however, and the spear struck Cuchulain's charioteer, Laeg, who was standing near him.

Yet even as Cuchulain plucked the weapon from his friend's dying body, a second satirist stepped forward and again demanded it. Cuchulain refused, pointing out that custom bound him to grant only one request a day to a bard. The satirist retorted by threatening him with the most fearsome of all weapons–his verses; if Cuchulain refused to give him the spear, he would compose a poem reviling Ulster and putting it to shame. In despair, the great hero tossed him the weapon. A second time King Lewy cast it back–but again his aim was inaccurate, and this time he killed one of Cuchulain's two chariot horses. The second horse, taking fright, immediately bolted, leaving Cuchulain alone, ringed by his enemies. A third satirist now stepped forward, and once again, under the threat of satirical verses, the great warrior surrendered his weapon. This time Lewy did not miss; the spear struck home, piercing Cuchulain's stomach.

Gathering his entrails in his hands, the dying champion stumbled to a nearby lakeside as his enemies watched in awe and wonder. They kept a safe distance from him as he knelt at the lakeside and bathed his wound and drank for the last time. Finally he dragged himself to his feet, and lurching and stumbling, made for an upright pillar stone. Here he removed his girdle and tied himself to the stone so that he would die facing his enemies. The latter still stood off from him, unable to believe that he was dying. Slowly, death crept upon Cuchulain. Once, a few bold spirits crept near, but the second chariot horse returned to stamp the ground around his master and drive them off. The day waned, but still none dared approach, even when Cuchulain's head had slumped forward. Then his enemies saw a crow circle and eventually alight on the hero's shoulder.

Cuchulain, the Hound of Ulster, was dead. At once they charged forward and smote off his head.

The great tales of Cuchulain and the warriors of the Red Branch, clearly prototypes for King Arthur's Round Table knights, continued to be told in Ireland down through the ages. Despite the fantasy and the symbolism that circumscribe the tale, there is obviously some residue of genuine historical fact in *The Cattle Raid.* A famous Latin marginal note, written by a monkish copyist on the earliest manuscript extant, declares: "But I who have written [copied] this history, or rather fable, am doubtful about many things in this history, or fable. For some of them are the figments of demons, some poetic imaginings, some true, some not, some for the delight of fools."

Down the centuries of misery, deprivation, defeat, and humiliation, these tales have remained splendid symbols of a golden Ireland that supposedly once existed. Even today, most Irishmen and women believe that heroes like Cuchulain actually lived. Inside the General Post Office in O'Connell Street, Dublin–that most sacred shrine of modern Irish nationalism, the headquarters from which the heroes of 1916 fought the last of all Irish rebellions–there is only one statue. It is of Cuchulain.

VII

A TIME OF TRIUMPH

The strong fortress of Tara has perished with the death
of her princes; with its quires of sages, great
Armagh lives on.

The rath of Cruacha has vanished together with Ailill
the victorious; fair above all kingdoms is the majesty
in the city of Clonmacnoise.

The proud fortress of Allen has perished with her
boastful host; great is victorious Brigit,
beautiful her crowded city.

The fortress of Emain has faded away; only its
stones survive; crowded Glendalough is the
Rome of the western world.

Calendar of the Saints,
circa A.D. 800

Had the Irish Celt been left to develop his own society, then the twelve hundred years that elapsed between the arrival of the Gael in Ireland and the coming of the Normans might not hold the deep nostalgia it does for most Irishmen. His pride wounded, his sense of humiliation and hurt deep, the Irishman likes to remember a time when he cut a not inconsiderable figure in Europe; when his fighting prowess was unquestioned and his reputation for wisdom and learning unchallenged. In an age when he still tends to be dismissed as a dreamer, romancer, or comic, he does not mind reminding others that he was not always the loser.

The modern Irishman's strong sense of nationality–which some see as a rather obtuse decision not to avail himself of the riches and talents of Britain–stems from several disparate urgings: first, a tradition inherited from the eighteenth-century English colonists in Ireland who wanted their own independent legislature; second, republican ideas which were first voiced at the time of the American and French revolutions; third, a tradition of strife arising out of the economic and agrarian troubles caused by callous landlordism in the nineteenth century. In forming all of these and giving them their uniquely Irish character are the traditions deriving from the old and ancient battle for Gaelic independence. Curiously enough, it was the idea of Gaelic independence that inspired most of the men who between 1916 and 1921 won independence for twenty-six of Ireland's thirty-two counties. The declared aim of Patrick Pearse, leader of the rebels who "shook the British Empire" by seizing Dublin in 1916, was to create "an Ireland not free merely–but Gaelic as well." It was an extraordinary, phoenixlike conception.

To understand what Pearse meant, one must go back centuries, to the dawn of the Gaelic epoch in Irish history. On his arrival in Ireland, the Scot found the country divided into five ancient kingdoms or provinces and several smaller kingdoms. The number of kingdoms, in fact, was absurd–although it was to rise even higher by the time the Normans arrived in the twelfth century. Then there were four great provincial kings (one calling himself High King) and almost two hundred petty or over-kings ruling the country–so that when a modern Irishman claims to be "descended from kings," it is possible that he is not merely boasting. With two hundred kings to serve a population of just under a half-million, everyone has at least a sporting chance.

Gaelic Ireland, however, was anything but a classless community of all kings and no subjects. It has been described as "tribal, rural, hierarchical and familiar;" a society, though, with rigid stratifications, where the inequalities between man and man, based on birth and calling, were embodied in legal principle. Each local king (and kingship was confined to members of the royal family) had several grades of nobility under him.

Under these where the commoners, who were freemen. And at the bottom of the heap were unfree men and slaves. When surnames came to be adopted in the eleventh century, everyone took the name of his chieftain, whether related to him or not; so that even an English slave might bear a kingly name like O'Neill.

In its natural state, Irish society was not so dissimilar to the kind of society dissident students are aiming at today–less centralized, less bureaucratic, more personalized, and "free." Each petty king ruled his own small area, within which he was final arbiter. But he neither made laws nor enforced them and was himself also subject to them. These laws were based on the Brehon code, which had its origins in even more ancient Indo-European ideas. There was no machinery, however, for the enforcement of law, largely because it was thought unnecessary. Such was the normal harmonious balance of society that people usually obeyed the laws without question. Indeed, when the Normans introduced their law into Ireland, with its various punishments for misdemeanors–including hanging–the Irish were appalled, for such barbarity was beyond their comprehension. At every opportunity they immediately reverted to their own Brehon laws. "Agin the law" or "agin the government" meant "agin English law" or "agin English government."

Although the petty king owed loyalty and paid tribute to an over-king, and he in turn was vassal to the provincial king, each ruled so absolutely in his own territory that for most Irishmen, "the State" never meant more than his local petty king. He shared a common culture and language with the rest of Ireland, but he owed no loyalty to anyone outside the pillar stones marking the limits of the tiny kingdom in which he lived. There was never, therefore, a polity in Ireland, mainly because the society itself was never sufficiently complex to demand one. The glue that held the whole fabric together was simply art, culture, and learning. And it was the men of art, culture, and learning–the *aes dana*–who were reverenced above all others. They were the members of the Druidic class, and were poets, historians, seers, priests, lawgivers. The respect in which they were held was such that they were permitted to travel freely anywhere in Ireland, and it was entirely because of them that any kind of homogeneity existed.

Yet if conditions were hardly such as to force the development of a modern state, the idea of a unified Ireland under a single monarch took shape almost six hundred years before it happened in Britain. In the first century, when the Gaelic king Tuahal put down a rebellion launched against him by the more ancient peoples, he found himself the most powerful ruler in Ireland outside his Scottic kindred in Munster. One hundred years later his great descendant, Conn of the Hundred Battles, who had enlarged the territories passed down to him from Tuahal, claimed for himself the High Kingship of Ireland–a remarkable step, which as Irishmen like to point out, established a precedent for an immense area of western Europe. Neither the Germans, Franks, Gauls, Spanish, Scandinavians, nor British had then envisaged such a political development.

Under Conn's grandson, King Cormac MacArt, the Scotti flourished in Ireland. Cormac was the first Irish monarch to establish Tara as capital and to reiterate the claims that his father and his grandfather had made to the High Kingship of Ireland. Cormac has come down to us as a legislator and innovator of considerable power and wisdom (he introduced the water mill), and under him, indeed, a kind of Irish *Domesday Book,* called *The Psalter of Tara,* is said to have been drawn up. He codified the laws of Ireland, as expounded and interpreted by the Brehons, and this code remained basic Irish law until the seventeenth century, being one of the prime causes of friction between the native Irish princes and the British monarchy. But his real significance lay in what he did outside Ireland. According to the *Annals of Tighernach,* which are based upon ancient tradition, sometime about A.D. 240 Cormac "sailed across the high sea and obtained the sovereignty of Alba [Britain]." We now know that Cormac never quite achieved anything so impressive, but it is true that before this Golden Age ended, Irishmen were to control great areas of Britain. Irish tradition (backed up by the Venerable Bede) has it that from the second century onward, small bands of Irishmen began crossing the narrow strait between northeast Ireland and southwest Caledonia and effecting permanent lodgments there. By the third century they had also occupied Pembrokeshire in south Wales and had set up a kingdom there. Cormac's "three years out of Ireland with his fleet" very unambiguously started something. It was the beginning of an Irish military expansion that saw a Tara king die at the head of his army on the banks of the Loire and another fall dead at the foot of the Alps from a bolt of lightning. It was an expansion that threatened to give Irishmen sovereignty over the British Isles and dominion over parts of Gaul. At its peak, almost half Britain had fallen into Irish hands.

The advances of the rampaging Gaels were foiled by two things. At home, under the impact of the new Christianity, an amazing flowering of learning and civilization had begun, turning kingly thoughts away from predatory conquest. And in Britain a significant new foe made his appearance–a foe who appeared able to call on inexhaustible reinforcements of Angles, Jutes, and Saxons from the continent. Traditional accounts say that the Romans and Romanized Britons, informed by an Emperor who could no longer help himself that henceforward they must fend for themselves, hired mercenary bands of Angles to come to their assistance;

once in, these Germans decided to stay and brought in reinforcements. True or false, the outnumbered Irish fell back, and Roman Britain, to its dismay, found itself under a heel more barbarous than the Irish.

While the general outlines of the period are fairly well known, much still lies wrapped in mystery and confusion. Much of this springs from the origin of the word *Scot,* a Roman word meaning raider. The Scotti, of course, were the Gaels or Irish. Wherever they originated–in Spain or in Brittany–they were the ruling caste in Ireland when her checkable history opens. By the Christian era, the Romans, in fact, had begun calling Ireland *Scotia,* although earlier they also called her *Ierne, Ivernia,* and *Hibernia.*

The exact circumstances under which the Scots occupied Caledonia are not clear, but we do know that by A.D. 360–which is seventy-two years before Patrick arrived in Ireland–the Romans were reporting that bands of Scots and Picts had descended from Caledonia and were raiding their northern stations; so a third-century occupation seems valid.

By A.D. 364, Roman Britain was in a bad way. "Picts, Scots, Saxons and Attacotti prest the Britains with incessant invasions," declares the historian Ammianus. Four years later the Britons had been reduced to the "lowest extremity of distress," for the Scots and their allies had advanced so far into southern Britain that the fall of London was imminent. A new Roman army was hurriedly dispatched from Gaul under the command of the elder Theodosius. London was eventually relieved, and the "barbarians" driven from England. Claudian, the Alexandrian poet, sings of Theodosius, who "followed the Scots with wandering sword and clove the waters of the northern shore with his daring oars, [treading] the sands of both tidal seas," so that "icy Ireland weeps for the heaps of Scots slain."

Irish history is specific in naming four Irish kings–Eochay, Crimhann, Niall of the Nine Hostages, and Dathi–as leading a whole series of invasions into Britain. Irish attacks were carried out from a bridgehead in southwest Caledonia, and also directly across the Irish Sea. Tara Gaels, as well as those from Cashel, took part in these invasions, and at the peak of their power they held both north and south Wales, Cornwall, Devon, Somerset, and parts of Hampshire, Monmouth, Gloucester, and Wiltshire. Their power was particularly strong in Wales, and Welsh history itself provides much fascinating confirmation of the Irish influx; indeed, a race of Irish kings ruled in south Wales till the tenth century.

The precise extent of power and settlement by the Irish in south Britain, of course is a matter now impossible to determine. Cormac, King and Bishop of Cashel, writing of the period in retrospect from the tenth century, says, "The power of the Irish over the Britons was great, and they had divided Britain between them into estates . . . and the Irish lived as much east of the sea as they did in Ireland, and their dwellings and royal forthresses were made there."

More than one Irish king assumed the title of King of Alba: Muirchetach, son of Earca, who died in 533, claimed to be king of Britons, Franks, and Saxons. By the middle of the fifth century, however, Irish power in Britain was at its apogee. There is some evidence that it withered away more through intermarriage and alliance than as a result of the onslaught of the Saxons, and the subsequent history of Ireland and Wales would appear to bear this out; for the closest relations in art, law, education, and Christianity were maintained between the two countries for centuries.

Yet if Irish power withered in south Britain, it continued to flourish in the north. The little kingdom of Dalriada successfully contended with the indigenous Picts and in the eighth century eventually overcame them. Pictish culture vanished, its last traces disappearing completely, when following a crushing defeat inflicted upon the English Northumbrians by the Gaelic king Malcolm II at Carham, near Coldstream, in 1015, Malcolm's grandson joined Scots, Picts, Angles, Saxons, and Britons into one kingdom, thenceforward called Scotland. Today, wherever a man's name bears the prefix *Mac*—the Irish word for "son"—that name is of Irish origin. Indeed, one half of the fifty commonest Scottish surnames today are of Irish origin, and many lowland names—Bain, Dow, Ferguson, Grierson, Gow, Kerr, Scott, and Wallace—are altered forms of an Irish original; for example, Allison and Ellison were MacAlistair, Ferguson was MacFergus, and so on. The Irish language, called Gaelic (but pronounced *Gallic* in Scotland), is still spoken in many areas of Scotland.

The Coronation Stone kept in Westminster Abbey and used at the crowning of all English monarchs since Edward I is another legacy of Gaelic Ireland. The *Liá Faíl [lee-ah fall]*, or "Stone of Destiny," was originally the stone upon which all kings of the Scotti were enthroned. Early in the sixth century the High King of Ireland, Muirchetach I, sent the stone to Scottish Dalriada to ensure that kings of the Scotti would always rule there. The stone was kept in the castle of Dunstaffnage until the union of the Scots and Picts, at which point King Kenneth MacAlpin removed it to Scone, the old capital of the Picts. There it remained until Edward I captured it and brought it to London. British monarchs still sit on it at their coronations simply to "ensure" their rule over the Gael.*

* The Westminster Abbey stone is not, in fact, the original one, whose history is traced here; it is Scottish stone which at some time replaced the original.

Even now, it all seems an incredible time—that period from the sixth to the eleventh centuries that constitutes the Irishman's Golden Age. There he was—his days of military expansion over—teaching, evangelizing, baptizing, founding and building monasteries from the Aran Islands to the plains of Lombardy, overcoming illiteracy and savagery everywhere. What the devil were Irishmen doing buying furs in Kiev to help build a monastery at Ratisbon? What was an Irishman doing as bishop in North Africa? What was another doing, charging into the court of a great European king and overturning a laden table to show his displeasure with the monarch? How came an Irishman to discover Iceland in A.D. 795—three quarters of a century before the Vikings? What possessed Ferghil, Irish bishop of Salzburg, to argue in A.D. 774 that the earth was not flat, as supposed, but round; and that the Antipodes existed? What drove an Irishman to measure the pyramids of Egypt and tour the Red Sea looking for the precise spot through which Moses had passed? What was Saint Brendan doing scurrying around in his coracle, getting mixed up with icebergs off Labrador, visiting Iceland, landing on the back of a whale, and possibly discovering the Antilles and North America? There were the Irish, publishing their studies on geography and astronomy; producing theologists and philosophers who were the wonders of their age; ticking off Popes in Rome; making pilgrimages to Jerusalem and the holy places; writing the first European guidebooks; making contact with the monastics of Egypt and Syria; producing early chronicles of European history—and, of course, like all Irishmen throughout the ages, disputing and arguing everywhere and, on occasions, suffering the glories of martyrdom.

Such a display of energy and achievement might well seem laudable enough. On top of that, however, we are forced to pile more. First they contributed to Europe the whole glory of Irish illuminated manuscripts, of which *The Book of Kells* and *The Book of Durrow* are supreme examples. Then they created the beautiful metalwork that has given us the Ardagh Chalice, the Tara Brooch, the Cross of Cong, and a treasury of croziers and crucifixion plaques—not including innumerable silver reliquaries and caskets of Irish origin that even yet are being dug up from Viking graves. Then they made the sculptured stonework that produced such a magnificent tour de force as the high Cross of Muiredeach. To all this we must add their steady and impressive development of ecclesiastical building, progressing from simple wooden churches to mortarless stone oratories; thence to the charming and often elaborately decorated Celtic and Celtic Romanesque "cathedrals"; culminating, finally, in the Gothic majesty of Boyle Abbey and other now ruined holy places. Finally, as a kind of Irish Imperial Crown, heaped on everything, was their prose and poetry, sacred and profane: the annals, histories, and law tracts; the written versions of the great Irish epics; the lives of the saints, and the satires; and the oldest transcriptions into a European vernacular of the *Iliad,* the Civil War of the Romans, and other classical works.

Ireland's claim to have been "the storehouse of the past and the birthplace of the future", as Cardinal Newman once described her, or "The Lamp of the West" or "The University of Europe" or "The Island of Saints and Scholars," as medieval Europe called her, lay in an accident of geography rather than in some innate greatness in Irishmen themselves—although it is true that they had the ability and purpose to profit from the situation. Professor James Carney, in his essay "The Impact of Christianity," has written:

> Immediately after our adoption of Christianity our geographical position for once worked in our favour. . . . Ireland alone . . . remained immune . . . and for the first and so far, the last time, in her history, became the most vital civilising force in the West. This position, in the nature of things, could hardly last. . . . With the conversion of the Germanic peoples, the natural equilibrium of Western Europe was reestablished, and the great center no longer existed, paradoxically, on the outer perimeter. In the early period of the Irish missions the Irishman brought Christianity and civilisation to the backward parts of Europe. In the late ninth century it becomes very obvious that the Irishman coming to the Continent has at least as much to learn as he has to teach.

The Irish, in fact, had burst upon the international scene in typically dramatic and controversial fashion. Fifteen years before Saint Patrick set foot in Ireland in 432, Saint Jerome writes of "an ignorant calumniator . . . full of Irish porridge" who had been impertinent enough to criticize him. This was Pelagius, the heresiarch, who appears to have been an Irishman born in what is now Wales. The founder of Pelagianism and the great antagonist of Saint Augustine's teachings on free will and grace, Pelagius was a man who proclaimed the doctrine of the freedom of personality and "man's power to make his own soul unaided"—a man whose ideas persist to this day in Catholic thought through Pascal and Jansenism. It was Pelagius' ideas, ironically, that led to Patrick's mission. His views had swept through the Christians of Britain to such an extent that Pope Celestine was forced to send Germanus, Bishop of Auxerre, to bring "the Britons back to the Catholic faith." This, in turn, drew the Pope's attention to the condition of Ireland, which officially still lay outside Christendom. As a result, Palladius was appointed bishop to win the island, and when he died in 432, Germanus then appointed Patrick, who had been hopefully waiting his chance for fifteen years.

The Irishman's self-assurance and enthusiasm at this time reached a peak when Columbanus disputed with Pope Gregory the Great on the dating of Easter. Irish scholars—speaking not only their own tongue but Latin and Greek as well—at that time were more learned than any at Gregory's disposal in those dismal days when the European continent was barbaric. Dr. Heinrich Zimmer has written: "While on the mainland and in Britain, budding Christianity and the germs of western culture, such as it was, were effectually trodden under foot . . . when the entire West threatened to sink hopelessly into barbarism, the Irish established several seminaries of learning in their own country. The standard of learning [in Bangor, Armagh, Clonmacnoise, Lismore] was much higher than with Gregory the Great and his followers."

Christianity and the ferment caused by the arrival in Ireland of a handful of refugee Gaulish and British scholars were undoubtedly the causes of the great intellectual flowering that distinguished Irish life during the Golden Age. Still, any idea that one day Ireland was savage and the next—through the medium of Christianity—civilized is obvious rubbish. Indeed, long before the arrival of Patrick, Ireland hummed with indigenous learning. Each petty kingdom had its own bardic school, under a chief poet, where law, history, poetry, music, and other studies were pursued. Within a century of Patrick's death, no fewer than a third of the men of Ireland belonged to the poetic order. At the Synod (or parliament) of Drumceat in 575—a great affair presided over by the High King and attended by Saint Columcille and King Aidan of Dalriada, who both came from Scotland for the event—a decision was made to drastically reduce their numbers. Legend has it that the politicans wished to "banish all the poets from Erin," but that Columcille, a poet and writer himself, pleaded with the Synod and saved them. Thus Irish poets continued to enjoy extraordinary respect and exact great fear. Of course, to be a poet was to escape drudgery. Yet, in their defense it should be said that poets boarded and educated their pupils free and in conjunction with the clergy undoubtedly inculcated in the Irish people an abiding interest in matters of the spirit.

According to tradition, Ireland became Christian through the work of Patrick, although the saint himself, in the scraps of his autobiography that have come down to us, clearly states, "In the days of old the law of God was already well planted and propagated in Ireland; I do not wish to take credit for the work of my predecessors." Even so, paganism survived for a long time after Patrick's death. In every country where Christian missionaries spread the gospel, they never fussed too much over pagan superstitions and customs. Old fertility rites, often connected with wells or springs were quickly translated into Christian terms, so that in Ireland today there are still holy wells–in particular, wells dedicated to Saint Brigid–patronized by women.

Irishmen, of course, have long resented the sneer that they are a superstitious people. Yet it is impossible to discount the importance of supersition in making their conversion to Christianity so easy. Even today there are people living in remote parts of Ireland who have retained an almost superstitious belief in the powers of the clergy. The explanation of what happened is put forward by J. F. Kenney in his *Sources for the Early History of Ireland,* when he says of the state of the Irish mind at the beginning of the Christian era: "It was fundamentally the product of countless ages of paganism. . . . Irish paganism seems to have consisted of a lower stratum, deep and wide, of magical belief and practice, and superimposed thereon, an upper section of mythology. Myth and magic were ejected from their positions of supremacy by the coming of Christianity, but the evidence does not indicate that the sphere of operation of either was extensively diminished." Some would argue that this is still largely true of Irish religion.

When Patrick began his missionary work, therefore, the miracles of Christ and his Apostles placed little strain on Irish credulity. Indeed, Irish Christianity tended to become more and more a "magic" religion as time passed; and Kenny emphasizes that in the later medieval texts we see the survivals of paganism more and more marked–as though Christianity had been turned into something else. We also know that when the Irish monks began flooding on to the Continent "they found a receptive audience for their tales of the fantastic miracles wrought by Saint Patrick and other Irish saints." Wherever they went, in typical Irish fashion they made extravagant claims for the greatness and the wonders wrought by these men, to such an extent that the continentals were eventually forced to censure them. Yet the propaganda undoubtedly had its effect. As early as the seventh century, Saint Patrick's Day was being celebrated at Luxeuil, Peronne, Fosses, Echternach, Corbie, Nivelles, and Reichenau. By the tenth and eleventh centuries it was also being celebrated at Treves in Germany and Landevennec in Brittany. Even the old myth that Saint Patrick banished the snakes from Ireland still finds a reflex in the ancient Breton saying that anyone killing an earwig with his finger will have the blessing of Patrick.

The Irishman's ability to mingle old pagan magic and exciting new Christianity–thus creating fresh legends and myths around his new heroes, the saints–is seen vividly in the legend of Patrick's joust with the messenger of God on top of Crochan Aigli:*

> Patrick went to the Crochan Aigli on Saturday, the Vigil of Pentecost. The angel came to him and said: "God does not grant you everything that you ask, because this seems excessive to Him, and your requirements are very large"—"Is that His will?" said Patrick. "Yes," said the angel. "Then this is mine," said Patrick. "I shall not move from here until either I am dead, or all my requests are granted." So Patrick stayed for forty days and forty nights on the mountain, which then suddenly became covered with blackbirds which prevented him seeing the sky or earth. The saint sang "psalms of cursing" at them, but they refused to leave. In his anger, he rang his bell so that all the men of Ireland heard it, then he threw it at the birds, which disappeared. Then the angel reappeared and he and Patrick bargained.

Patrick finally obtained a long list of privileges, one of which was "that Ireland, alone of all nations, will be spared the torments and tortures of the Last Day." Seven years before the awful event, "a great sea will cover Ireland. . . ." On the Day itself, Patrick, it is believed, will be permitted to judge the people of Ireland. As Professor James Carney of the Dublin Institite of Advanced Studies has written:

> The early Irish Church never lapsed into formal heresy, but there were always curious ideas abroad that in Rome, or indeed anywhere else in Christendom, would be looked upon as somewhat bizarre. . . . A certain number of these ideas had to do with a strong nationalistic spirit. . . . if the early Irish had questioned the ways of providence, they would have asked:
>
> "How did God fail
> To choose the Gael?"

—a play on Belloc's odd little verse:

> How odd
> of God
> to choose
> the Jews.

* Now called Croagh Patrick, this peak is today a "holy mountain" in county Mayo and the center of a great and impressive national pilgrimage every last Sunday in July, when thousands, many barefooted, climb a stony path to the 2,510-foot summit to hear mass.

Even during Ireland's Golden Age, however, Irish scholarship never quite reached the level of learning represented by Saints Ambrose, Jerome, or Augustine. The role of the Irish scholars was essentially that of preserver, a bridge between the ancient and modern worlds. They played a vital part, along with Byzantium and the Latin Church, in preserving a fragile link with Greece and Rome. And if they cannot claim to have been the instigators of the Carolingian Revival, they clearly played a large part in conducting it. Turner, in his *History of Philosophy,* has written: "Although it was Italy that inspired Charlemagne with the idea of founding schools throughout the empire, it was Ireland that sent him the masters who were to impart the new learning. . . . Throughout the ninth century, [they] were found in every cathedral and monastery of the empire as well as at the court of the Frankish kings, and were so identified with the new intellectual movement that the teaching of the newly founded schools was characterized as Irish learning." In the ninth century such was the intellectual prestige of Irishmen that one of Charles the Bald's ministers hailed them as "rivals of the Greeks," and it became the fashion of the educated classes at Laon to study the Irish language and Irish literature, even while at nearby Rheims Irish teachers, the only masters of Greek in the West, taught the language and literature of that classic land.

The greatest ornament of both Irish and Western learning at this time was John Scotus Erigena, who from 845 onward, lived at the court of Charles the Bald, who appointed him head of the palace school. He first came to the notice of Charlemagne's grandson through his remarkable knowledge of languages and paleography. But it was in philosophy that his claim to real greatness lay.

Unlike the majority of the peripatetic Irish teachers, John was not a monk. He was, however, a man of prodigious learning and of great charm and humor. He is best remembered in Ireland today for the reply he is alleged to have made to the Emperor, who when they sat across the table from each other one evening, essayed to match wits with him by asking, "Tell me, John, what is the difference between a Scot and a sot?" To which the Irishman flashed back, "Why, the width of a table, sire."

De Wulf, in his *History of Medieval Philosophy,* says of John: "While his contemporaries were only lisping in philosophy, and even his successors for centuries did no more than discuss a small number of disconnected questions, Erigena in the ninth century worked out a complete philosophical synthesis. Apart from those incredibly daring speculations which make him the *enfant terrible* of his time, he reads like a pantheistic contemporary of St. Thomas [Aquinas]." Indeed, his most important work, *De divisione naturae,* was placed on the Papal Index in 1685 and confirmed by Leo XIII in 1900. He has been accused of being a freethinker and rationalist, as well as a pantheist, yet his views are probably nearer to agnosticism.

John's intellectual daring is typical of the whole Irish movement of the Golden Age, a classic example of the Irishman's persistent enthusiasm, self-assurance, and egotism. (Centuries later, Pope Benedict XV was to declare, "What Ireland lacks is humility.") Although they were the great ornaments and decorations of Christian thinking in those ages, fighting the battle for orthodoxy against Arianism and the other great heresies, Irishmen were so sure of themselves that they continually fell foul of the authorities. "They drew back from no inquiry; boldness was on a level with faith," wrote the Comte de Montalembert. "Their strength lay in those exercises of pure reason which go by the name of philosophy or wisdom," noted Cardinal Newman. John himself declared, "I am not so browbeaten by authority nor so fearful of the assault of less able minds as to be afraid to utter with fearless forehead what true reason clearly determines and indubitably demonstrates." Obviously the national character has not changed all that much.

One key to this extraordinary flowering of Irish learning was the monastic system. Saint Patrick himself introduced it along with episcopacy, personally placing the veil on Saint Moninna, who founded seven monasteries in Ireland, seven in Caledonia, and others in south Britain. Shortly after Enda had founded a settlement on the Aran Islands, Brigid founded her famous establishment at Kildare. In 520, Finnian, known to history as "the teacher of the saints of Ireland," founded Clonard, on the river Boyne, and among his "twelve disciples" were several famous Irishmen. There was Columcille, who founded the monasteries of Durrow and Derry and one of the most influential of all Irish monastic foundations, Iona. There was Ciaran, who founded the most evocative of all Irish monasteries, Clonmacnoise, whose ruins still stand along the Shannon banks, with rows of burial inscriptions of Irish Christian kings. There was Brendan, who founded Clonfert. His story is one of the most astonishing in the history of Christian Europe; he sailed far into the Atlantic—Columbus himself inquired about "Saint Brendan's Island," a land to the *west* of the Azores—and judging from descriptions of the places he visited, might have been the first known European to reach America, three centuries before Leif Erikson.

Between the fifth and seventh centuries, no fewer than thirty-two major seats of learning were established in Ireland. From them spread the *peregrini,* an astonishing band of itinerants who painted their eyelids and colored or tattooed their bodies and tonsured their hair in front from ear to ear, carrying staffs, leathern wallets, flasks, and books—"wanderers for

Christ," who spread the name and fame of Ireland throughout early medieval Europe.

Of this movement, still thought of by many Irishmen as their greatest contribution to the world, the French writers, G. and B. Cerebelaud-Salagnac have written in *Ireland, Isle of Saints*: "These saints with strange names have no place in our calendar. . . . How many Christians of our day know that they came from Ireland or could say to what age they belong? Only the old Breton women of our Armorica can still tell the beautiful and surprising stories of those saints of old time who came from the North, carried across the wild seas by the wind of the Spirit, and won their land for Christ, Saint Gildes, Saint Brieuc, Saint Guenole and many another."

The peregrini descended on Britain and Europe–sometimes as individuals, sometimes in small groups, often merely as pilgrims or travelers–seeking voluntary exile "for love of Christ." Exile, for most of them, was the supreme penance.

These wandering Irishmen have left their traces all over Europe. Saint Goar, on the Rhine, not far from the famed Lorelei rock, is named after an Irish saint who passed that way. Some German authorities insist that Brandenburg, near Berlin, is named for Saint Brendan. In the cathedral of Cefalu in Sicily, there is a picture of Saint Cataldus, whose memory is still venerated in Puglia and in Sicily; he was an Irish monk who was shipwrecked in the Gulf of Taranto while returning from a pilgrimage to Jerusalem and who then was made Bishop of Taranto by the Pope. At Pinerolo in Italy, Saint Brigid is copatron of the city and has a fourteenth-century church dedicated to her. Saint Fiacre, from whom that famous horse-drawn Parisian "taxi," the *fiacre,* derived its name, is the patron of gardeners and agricultural workers in France. Rudpert is still remembered in Carinthia as the man who started the salt mining that gave Salzburg its name. Scores of cities and towns, from the Irish Sea to the Adriatic, owe their origins to the peregrini–Saint Bees, Malmesbury, Saint Gibrian, Saint Gobain, Saint Die, Saint Ursanne, Dissentis, San Columbano, San Cataldo, Altomunster, Saint Desibod, and Beatenberg. Restless Irishmen roved from Iceland to the Azores, Greenland (and possibly America) in the west to Kiev in Russia in the east, teaching and exploring.

Easily the most attractive and most fascinating of all these early Irish saints is Saint Brendan the Navigator, described recently as "an Odysseus behind his time, and in some ways a [James] Bond before." Certainly, Brendan's story was an early European best-seller, having been translated into no fewer than nine languages. The tale of his voyages–which lasted seven years, and in the course of which, some experts are satisfied, he reached the Everglades around Miami–is highly ornamented in the Celtic tradition; yet few scholars doubt that it has a basis in reality. All attempts to plot Brendan's itinerary have failed, however, for the vogages appear to have taken a zigzag course, and Brendan's currach returned each year to precisely the same spot for Holy Week. The little boat has been described as "more like a floating monastery," tossed hither and thither by the Atlantic winds and currents. Brendan, born in 484 near Tralee, led a party which landed on various islands, including one where there was no grass. Here some monks who had gone ashore to boil fish lit a fire and put on a pot. As soon as the pot boiled, however, "the island moved as if it were afloat." The monks raced for their boat, and the island submerged, but Brendan declared, "My dear sons, have no fear; it was not an island on which we landed, but a gigantic fish, the largest in the ocean."

On another occasion they were becalmed for days in a stretch of curdled sea, thought to have been the Sargasso Sea, a weedy mass in mid-Atlantic. Again a furious monster with "boar's tusks and fuzzy hair upon him"–evidently a walrus–chased them until it was diverted and killed by a whale. Later they passed over a clear sea, so shallow that they could see great shoals of fish "like flocks of sheep." This sea has been identified as the waters off Bermuda or Jamaica. One sight in particular could have owed nothing to Celtic imagination, especially in the sixth century, and it sets Brendan and his monks clearly among the Arctic currents that sweep down the eastern seaboard of the North American continent. "One day they saw a column in the sea, which seemed not far off, yet they could not reach it for three days. When they drew near, St. Brendan looked towards its summit, but could not see it because of its great height, which seemed to pierce the skies. It was covered over with a rare canopy, the material of which they knew not; but it had the color of silver and was hard as marble, while the column itself was of the clearest crystal." They took in their oars, lowered their sail and mast, and ran into an opening "under the canopy." Inside, the "sea looked like transparent glass, so that they could plainly see everything beneath them, even the base of the column, and the skirts or fringes of the canopy, lying on the ground, for the sun shone brightly within as without." Obviously, this was a melting iceberg near Labrador.

Later they were carried along by the Gulf Stream to Iceland, which because of its erupting volcanoes and spectacular waterfalls, they took to be the infernal regions. Here, the various biographers of the saint let themselves to with a relish for the grotesque. The Devil shows Brendan the gate of Hell–and the saint watches demons dragging sinners down mountains of eternal fire; there are dragons, scorpions, vultures, beetles, leeches, scratching cats, rending hounds, stinking lakes, and all sorts of horrors. The party sails on into the infernal place, and in a scene that obviously inspired Dante, they spy a figure marooned on a rock, battered eternally by a merciless sea: it is Judas Iscariot.

Finally, at the end of all the voyaging, the party reaches the Land of Promise, which is described as possessing an extremely wide river and being in itself so big that it would take a long time to reach its other side, thus identifying it as part of the North American mainland, the river being thought to be either the Saint Lawrence or the Ohio or possibly the Gulf of Mexico.

Some (non-Irish) experts believe that unknown Irishmen had been traveling to America since prehistoric times. They unquestionably knew of the Northern Route and reached Iceland and probably Greenland even before the Vikings in historic times. These writers believe that Brendan's Voyages are possibly a compilation based on earlier Irish discoveries. Despite the absence of definite proof such as another Vineland map or the discovery of an Irish Ogham stone signed "Brendan" or a Gaelic manuscript, few Irishmen have any doubts that the real name of America should be Brendansland. Of course, few of the Irish peregrini wandered as far as Saint Brendan. The one we shall consider next, for example, stayed close to home most of the time, yet he is no less important for that.

In the library of the Royal Irish Academy in Dublin lies a fragmentary copy of the psalms, called *The Cathach*—the oldest Irish manuscript in existence and the book which probably began a whole movement in Irish manuscript illumination. According to the paleographer Lowe, it "represents the pure milk of Irish calligraphy." It is believed to have been written by Columba himself. Generally known as Columcille, Columba (not to be confused with his kinsman Columban or Columbanus who labored on the Continent) was perhaps the most remarkable and most interesting personality of sixth-century Ireland.

Columcille was born in December 521, in county Donegal, a member of the Irish royal family. Generous and artistic, he was a man of great enthusiasms who surrendered his own claims to the High Kingship in order to become a cleric. His cousin, afterward the High King of Ireland, gave him his first site for a monastery. This was a two-hundred-acre area in a grove of oak trees, which became known as *Doire Columcille*—that is, Derry Columcille (the "wood of Columcille")—a place which since the seventeenth century has been known as Londonderry but is still stubbornly called Derry by all Irish Catholics. Later he founded a number of other monasteries and schools, among them Durrow and Kells. Had he done nothing more in life he would have already accomplished much; but at the then advanced age of forty-two he embarked upon his true mission.

In the year 560 Columcille went to visit his friend Finnen, abbot of Moville. While there, Columcille, a skillful scribe, secretly copied out a portion of a Bible belonging to Moville. The result was *The Cathach,* part of a copy of Saint Jerome's Vulgate. On discovering the "theft," Finnen claimed Columcille's copy for his own. The latter, however, refused to hand it over, and Finnen appealed to the High King, who handed down a famous decision: "To every cow her calf, to every book its copy." Angrily, Columcille still refused to hand over the manuscript, and the king's attempt to enforce his decision resulted in a battle at Culdremna in the county Sligo that caused the death of three thousand men and ended in the defeat of the High King. In consequence, Columcille was censured "by all the saints [abbots and holy men] of Ireland." In remorse, he decided to exile himself as penance. With a number of associates, he set sail for the island of Hy (Iona), which had been granted him by his kinsman, King Conaill of Dalriada. The exile, which began in 563, was a bitter experience.

> Too swiftly my coracle flies on her way;
> From Derry I mournfully turned her prow;
> I grieve at the errand which drives me today
> To the land of the Ravens, to Alba, now.
>
> How swiftly we glide! there is a grey eye
> Looks back upon Erin, but it no more
> Shall see while the stars shall endure in the sky
> Her women, her men, or her stainless shore.

For thirty-four years, until his death, Columcille worked to convert Caledonia. If only a portion of what has been written about him is true, then he is one of the greatest Irishmen who ever lived. Such is his mystique that even today in his ancient Donegal homeland, stories are told of him as though he were yet alive. In early medieval times historians described him as sage, prophet, poet, "dove of the cell," "lovable lamp, pure and clear," "silvery moon," a diadem, a harp without a base chord, a noble child, venerable, man of grace, and "physician of the heart of every age." He was of great height and physique, with a comely face, large and luminous gray eyes, and a loud and resonant voice that could be heard "at fifteen hundred paces." The inevitable Irish "magic" element duly enters his story with the claim that he healed diseases, raised the dead to life, subdued the fury of wild beasts with a word, expelled demons, calmed the waves, changed the winds, and was even able to foresee the future.

His energy and enthusiasm must be counted phenomenal by any standards. Apart from tramping over half of Scotland on foot, he is said to have written three hundred books and to have founded a like number of churches. Adamnan, his biographer, tells us that he was skillful with his hands and clever at making "crosses and writing tablets and book satchels and other church gear." He was a prolific poet, although few of the poems that are attributed to him are thought to be authentic. Adamnan says of him, "He could not spend the space of even one hour without study or prayer, writing or some other holy occupation."

Columcille did not live to see the real triumph of his mission. From his monastery at Iona, Irish missionaries nurtured Christianity and civilization in Scotland and spread their influence to the greater part of England. His artistic work was carried on and encouraged by his successors in the abbacy of Iona and produced astonishing results—*The Book of Kells* (largely written at Iona) and *The Book of Durrow*, plus the whole school of Northumbrian and other English manuscript illumination, which as an English historian has put it, "has only been surpassed by the products of the sister isle itself."

Seven years after Columcille founded the monastery at Iona, another great Irish saint, Columban (or Columbanus), began his missionary career. Columban left Ireland in 570, accompanied by twelve companions. They first went to Britain, where they stayed for four years; then they continued to Gaul. Here they established Luxeuil, which soon enjoyed notable fame for its holiness and iron rule. In the end, the stiff-necked behavior of Columban—typical of many of the peregrini—led to his expulsion from Luxeuil, although his influence continued to be felt there.

Brunehaut, mother of King Thierry, had asked the saint to bless certain bastard sons of the ruler, but the Irishman, insisting they were "the offspring of adultery," refused. The irate grandmother retaliated by ordering a boycott of Columban and his monks. Columban thereupon decided to see Thierry himself. Admitted to the palace, he was not shown in to the king at once but was offered dishes of food and drink, which were put before him with great ceremony. With the marked lack of tact which is perhaps forgivable in saints, Columban pushed them away, declaring: "The Most High looks with displeasure on the gifts of the impious." Then he overturned the table, scattering the food and drink, and stalked out.

In the end, Columban and his Irish monks were simply turned out of the kingdom. They decided to go home and were about to depart from Nantes when Columban suddenly changed his mind and led his party back into the heart of the Continent. They crossed through Neustria and Austrasia, went down the Moselle and then up the Rhine. At Basle, a monk named Ursan set out by himself to explore the Bernese Jura, where eventually he built a monastery at the foot of Mont Terrible. Columban led the rest into Italy. On the way, however, Saint Gall pleaded that he was too ill to continue and elected to stay and become a hermit near the river Steinach, where he died in 646. Seventy years after his death, an abbey was erected on the site, and around it grew up the town of Saint Gall.

The aged Sigisbert also dropped out along the way and elected to take the easier path along the Rhine, where he founded the monastery of Disentis. Columban himself crossed the Alps into Milan and was eventually given land by the King of Lombardy on which to erect his great foundation of Bobbio. Here he settled down and began composing a body of writings, many of which have come down to us. Most are admonishments and instructions to monks on ways to lead a better life—how to develop a contempt for the world, for instance. Fortunately, his observations on women are among those of his works that have been preserved:

> Let every man preserve his soul from the deadly venom
> Which is concealed, unfortunately for him, in the
> tongue of a self-seeking woman.
> It was a woman brought ruin to the blessings of a
> better life;
> But it was a woman who obtained for us the blessings
> of eternal life.

Before he was through, this great Irish saint was responsible for the founding of more than one hundred monasteries and seats of learning on the Continent. Jonas, the Italian biographer of Columbanus, estimated that no fewer than 620 missionaries (not all of them Irish) had left the Irish saint's great foundation at Luxeuil "to concentrate on Bavaria alone."*

Of all the accomplishments of the peregrini, however, the work they did in England perhaps holds a special importance. Indeed, looked at in the light of the history of subsequent Anglo-Irish relations, there is a profound irony in the fact that the Christianity of Britain was largely a gift of her sister island—a gift for which Ireland has never been properly thanked.

In the sixth century, a wide cultural gap existed between Ireland and Anglo-Saxon England. The surviving old British had refused to have anything to do with the Anglo-Saxons, who were said to practice all sorts of barbarities, including cannibalism. This savagery was, perhaps, exaggerated; the device of extolling one's own virtues and decrying those of one's enemies had been already developed to a fine art. Yet the fact that Anglo-Saxon England lay under boycott by the civilized British for almost

* Columbanus and his followers, of course, were just the tip of the iceberg, for the accomplishments of the wandering Irish monks are too numerous to be told. France, Germany, the Low Countries, Switzerland, North Italy, as well as Scotland and England, all benefited from their zeal and energy: The little island gave 25 missionaries to Scotland, 44 to England, 81 to Gaul, 115 to Germany, and 13 to Italy.

two centuries still remains an otherwise incomprehensible mystery. Indeed, the Venerable Bede was to deplore the fact that British antipathy was so great "that they never preached the faith to the Saxons or English who dwelt amongst them." Both Columbanus and Dicuil, great Irish continental missionaries, did make early efforts to Christianize East Anglia, but "found the hearts of the people in darkness." When Gregory the Great dispatched Augustine and his assistants to reestablish Christianity in England, the little band became so fearful at rumors of the horrors that awaited them that Augustine returned to Rome and pleaded with the Pope for permission to abandon the mission. The Pope fortified him with the thought that "the greater the suffering, the greater the reward," and sent him back. In the spring of 597 Augustine arrived in the Isle of Thanet, from where he moved on to establish the See of Canterbury and to Christianize Kent. Roman missionaries, indeed, penetrated as far as Northumbria; but in the end their mission proved a failure. Augustine himself died in 604, and within thirty years his work lay in ruins, all his associates–save Lawrence–fleeing back to the Continent.

It was at this moment that the Irishmen began their great work, invited into England by the Christian king of Northumbria. The French expert Montalembert maintained that the Irish bear the chief glory for the conversion of England: "From the cloisters of Lindisfarne . . . Northumbrian Christianity spread over the southern kingdoms . . . its slow but certain course reached in succession all the people of the Heptarchy. . . . Of the eight kingdoms of the Anglo-Saxon confederation, that of Kent alone was exclusively won and retained by the Roman monks. . . . In Wessex and East Anglia, the Saxons . . . were converted by the combined action of continental missionaries and Celtic monks. As to the two Northumbrian kingdoms and those of Essex and Mercia, which comprehended in themselves more than two-thirds of the territory occupied by the Saxon conquerors, these four countries owed their final conversion exclusively to the peaceful invasion of the Celtic monks." Howorth, in his *Golden Days of the English Church,* says, "The men who really ploughed and harrowed the soil of . . . northern and central England, of Northumbria and Mercia, were not Augustine's monks, but . . . the never-tired, resourceful, and sympathetic spiritual children of Saint Columba, Saint Aidan, and their disciples."

Although Colman, successor to Aidan as Abbot of Lindisfarne, resigned his postion and returned to Ireland in 664 after the Irish church had surrendered to Rome in a controversy over the dating of Easter, Irish influence continued in England for centuries. Not only did Irish monks labor on in England, but Saxon-English continued to be educated in Ireland itself. Colman, for example, established a monastery and school in

Mayo exclusively for the accommodation of English students. Indeed, when a great plague struck England in the very year of Colman's resignation, Bede noted that "many of the nobility and of the lower ranks of the English nation were there [in Ireland] at that time. . . . The Irish willingly received them all and took care to supply them with food and also to furnish them with books to read and their teaching gratis."

Although the work of the Irish was eventually superseded by Canterbury, and English education came to be carried on from the classical school founded there, almost all the great English scholars up to the Norman Conquest, including Aldhelm, Bede, Wilfrid, Cuthbert, Alcuin, and Dunstan, were the products either of Irish teachers or of Irish foundations. Indeed, a plaintive note is often heard issuing from Canterbury, protesting that large numbers of English persisted in going to Ireland for their education instead of being taught at Canterbury. Until the Conquest, too, all Anglo-Saxon manuscripts continued to be written in the Irish script, and Irishmen can, with some justification, claim that a great deal of the art, culture, and learning existing in Anglo-Saxon England was, in general, an Irish transplant.

For centuries, Irishmen were not only reverenced and respected as holy saints and benefactors, but were without doubt the intellectual and moral leaders of western Europe. Even in the ninth and tenth centuries we hear of Irishmen going forth as "conscious teachers and preachers and traders in wisdom." Then they appeared on the Continent "like bees from a hive," arriving in "troops of philosophers." With them they took some of the earliest known Irish manuscripts—which is why so many are found in the Vatican, Vienna, Turin, Naples, or Milan, rather than in Ireland. Some of the earliest known examples of ancient Irish writing are now in Switzerland or Italy. Called *glosses,* they are marginal notes in the Irish language on Latin manuscripts and have been a source of delight to scholars for centuries: small human asides echoing down the ages. One copyist sighs, "Oh, my hand is weary with writing!" Another finds it difficult to concentrate on his task because of the beauty of the world outside his cell: "Pleasant is the glimpse of the sun today upon these margins." On an Irish manuscript kept in the Swiss monastery of Saint Gall, one of the great continental seats of learning founded by Irishmen, we find this still-fresh poem, written before the ninth century:

A hedge of trees surrounds me: a blackbird's lay sings
to me, praise which I will not hide,
Above my booklet—the lined one, the trilling of the
bird sings to me.

In a grey mantle the cuckoo chants to me from the
tops of the bushes.
May the Lord protect me from doom! I write well
under the greenwood.

Perhaps the most amusing of all these glosses is a little poem to a cat inscribed by a monk in the margin of a ninth-century manuscript now in the monastery of Saint Paul at Unterdrauberg, Carinthia:

I and Pangur Ban my cat
'Tis a like task we are at;
Hunting mice is his delight,
Hunting words I sit all night.

'Tis a merry thing to see
At our tasks how glad are we,
When at home we sit and find
Entertainment to our mind.

'Gainst the wall he sets his eye,
Full and fierce and sharp and sly;
'Gainst the wall of knowledge I
All my little wisdom try.

So in peace our task we ply,
Pangur Ban, my cat and I;
In our arts we find our bliss,
I have mine and he has his.

In any history of medieval Europe there is an extraordinary and almost inexplicable silence with regard to the work of Irishmen in bringing Christianity—then synonymous with civilization and learning—to the barbarians. It sometimes seems as though they had never existed. The probability is that if they had been sent from Rome with the blessing of the Pope, their names would now shine brightly. But although the Irish Church had never disputed the Pope's title as head of the Catholic Church, it had proved a stubborn, independent, and troublesome body for a Papacy then busy filling the vacuum left by the destruction of the Western Roman Empire. The Irish peregrini, unable to fathom the aspirations and ambitions of the early Papacy, foraged and worked their way across Europe, oblivious of a grand design. The Papacy had to extinguish them, and when it finally achieved its goal—when the Irish and Celtic churches had been absorbed into the Universal Church—the great Christian heroes of Ireland were those who had fought for the Roman line. A trick question few Irishmen can answer is: How many Irish saints are there? Even the Cerebelaud-Salagnacs have written: "The saints of Ireland are to be numbered in the thousands." Yet the answer–incredibly–is only two: Saint Malachy and Saint Laurence O'Toole, two men largely responsible for bringing Ireland firmly within the Papal fold. No Irishman would contest the fact that proper Church unity and organization were not essential preludes to the inspiring wave of creativity that took place in late medieval times: the rise of polyphonic music and Gothic architecture, the flowering of Dante and Boccaccio, of Giotto and Fra Angelico. Yet, in many parts of Europe it was the peregrini who laid the real groundwork, doing the rough job of converting and dispelling illiteracy, although they never brought with them that episcopal organization which alone could have guaranteed enduring results. Their memory deserves a better fate, however, than the cause for which they worked has ever allowed it.

VIII

THE FALL OF THE GAEL

Fierce and wild is the wind to-night,
It tosses the tresses of the sea to white;
On such a night as this I take my ease;
Fierce Northmen only course the quiet seas.

From a ninth-century Irish gloss
in ST. GALL PRISCIAN

The Vikings came off their great warships clad in heavy mail armor and sturdy helmets, with great battleaxes and long, heavy swords. None of the races in the British Isles stood a chance against them, and initially, Irishmen fared no better than the rest. A land of rivers and lakes, Ireland proved an ideal place for attack from the sea. After small strikes against monasteries around the coast, the Vikings sailed their great-prowed ships up the rivers and deep into the heart of the country. The fabric of Gaeldom shook. Throughout the country Irishmen watched as their monasteries and schools were robbed of sacred jewelry and rich ornaments. Students fled from their desks, leaving their slates, other writing materials, and books to go up in a general holocaust.

In retrospect it may seem surprising that while Irishmen had been making themselves illustrious in the arts of peace, they had made little headway toward developing a really strong central monarchy. The High Kingship had become little more than an honorary presidency, and Ireland was hardly better than the English Heptarchy when the Vikings arrived. The lack of a strong monarchy meant that there was no standing army. Indeed, instead of uniting together, certain Gaels considered how best they might profit from the new anarchy. The Kings of Cashel thought they saw their opportunity to wrest the High Kingship from the O'Neills, who had held it for six centuries. Indeed, in his efforts, the King-Bishop of Cashel destroyed more churches even than the Norse. Soon Ireland became a battleground of Norse and Irish against Irish. The Norsemen gradually became more and more involved in complex Irish rivalries.

If the failure of medieval Ireland to develop a central government is viewed in historical perspective, it indicates no especial backwardness in the Irish people. After all, central authority was unknown to early medieval man; his world was local, sequestered, circumscribed. Men looked only to their own lords or chieftains, had difficulty understanding accents beyond their region, and rarely traveled or communicated with anybody farther away than a day's walk. Anglo-Saxon England lay in a similar state, as did all of western Europe—Charlemagne's empire had crumbled soon after his death.

The Norse invasions rapidly revealed the vulnerability of the island, although eventually the Norse were to contribute a great deal to Ireland. They minted her first coins, introduced modern methods of trade and commerce, increased the prosperity of the country, and built the first seaports, at Dublin, Wexford, Waterford, Cork, and Limerick. Ironically, one of the results of their invasion was the development of a strong central monarchy such as Ireland had never quite seen before—precisely the sort of monarchy that, had it existed earlier, might have led to the rebuff of the invaders. Two of the central heroes of Irish history emerged from the ordeal: King Brian Boru and King Malachy II.

Brian Boru was Ireland's Alfred the Great. The greatest of Ireland's kings, at the height of his power he gloried in the title, Emperor of Scots. Malachy was an O'Neill who became High King of Tara in 980 and won the famed Collar of Gold; he is the king immortalized by Thomas Moore in his melody "Let Erin Remember." In the year of his accession he attacked the main Norse forces at Dublin and captured the city. An intelligent and cultivated man, he perceived the importance of the city to the Irish economy and did not burn it. Instead, he banished the Norse leader, Olaf, and when the latter died the following year, married his widow, Gormflath, and installed his new son-in-law, Sitric, as King of Dublin and his vassal.

Gormflath, however, proved to be one of the most fateful women in Irish history. She has been described by the Norse sagas as "fairest and best-gifted in everything that was not in her own power, but it was the talk of men that she did all things ill over which she had any power." In turn she married Olaf, Malachy, and Brian, and had concluded a deal to marry a Viking leader, Earl Sigurd, who would also have become King of Ireland if he had won the decisive battle of Clontarf. Her matrimonial stratagems prompted the Irish annalists to comment sardonically: "She took three leaps no woman should take—a leap at Dublin, a leap at Tara, and a leap at Cashel." In the end she "lepped" too far.

It was Gormflath and her machinations that led to a great drama. Malachy apparently found her an unbearable consort and soon divorced her. Whether prompted by vindictiveness or by local Leinster patriotism, she hit upon a scheme to undo both her ex-husband Malachy and Brian Boru, who was then merely King of Cashel although one of the most powerful rulers on the scene. In the complex tangle of interwoven sovereignties, Leinster was more or less unique. Originally formed by a separate wave of Celtic invaders, Leinster had always resisted the pretensions of the kings of Tara and Cashel, but found itself at this juncture forced to pay heavy tribute to Brian. At the same time, Malachy, High King of Tara and Gormflath's ex-husband, was exacting tribute from Dublin, the richest and most powerful of all Viking cities in Europe. As a native of Leinster with powerful connections there, and as the mother of Sitric, Malachy's puppet king of Dublin, Gormflath was in an excellent position to do something about the situation.

So she wove her plots: First her brother Maelmora would simply seize the kingdom of Leinster; then she and Maelmora, in alliance with Sitric, would overthrow Malachy, destroy the protective alliance that existed between Malachy and Brian, and thus free Leinster from Brian's grip. For all its simplicity, however, the plan never got beyond the first stage. Malachy and Brian joined forces to smash Maelmora, and Brian ended up celebrating the turn of the millennium by spending Christmas in Dublin.

It proved a fateful holiday, for Gormflath's beauty cast its spell on Brian, who married her and had her son Sitric reinstated as King of Dublin. Whether at her whispered suggestion or from the stirrings of his own ambitions, Brian, realizing that his marriage to Gormflath provided him with powerful allies in Leinster and Dublin, now cast his eyes on the greatest of prizes—the High Kingship itself. Although the results of his decision were not to become manifest for more than a century, Brian in that moment sowed the seeds of Gaeldom's destruction.

He marched to the Hill of Tara, still the symbolic seat of Gaelic majesty, and there demanded Malachy's abdication. The latter protested at the usurpation, but unable to secure sufficient allies, surrendered with dignity. In 1004 Brian Boru made the circuit of Ireland as High King with a pomp never equaled before or since. His rule during the next decade proved a blessing for Ireland. Brian erected churches, bridges, causeways, fortifications—everything necessary to restore an ancient if uncomplex civilization. Wisdom and learning were restored to their pride of place, professors and masters were appointed to positions long vacant, and scholars were sent to the Continent to bring back books for which Brian himself donated the money. Ireland became so peaceful and so orderly and Irishmen so well behaved and law-abiding that a lone woman was able to ride round the entire country without once being molested.

Rich and rare were the gems she wore,
And a bright gold ring on her wand she bore;
But oh! her beauty was far beyond
Her sparkling gems, or snow-white wand.

Lady! dost thou not fear to stray,
So lone and lovely through this bleak way!
Are Erin's sons so good or so cold,
As not to be tempted by woman or gold?

On she went and her maiden smile
In safety lighted her round the green isle;
And blest for ever is she who relied
On Erin's honour and Erin's pride.

Myth or not, modern Irishmen take pride in this episode as evidence of their essential virtue and dignity.

All might have remained well had it not been for Gormflath's fiery ambitions, her zest for intrigue, and her inability to hold a husband. On one occasion her brother Maelmora, King of Leinster, journeyed from Dublin to Brian's castle at Kincora, in Munster, bearing his required tribute of three masts of pine. On the way, while helping his men in a boggy place,

Maelmora burst a silver button from the gold-bordered tunic Brian had given him as a symbol of his vassalage. When they reached Kincora, Maelmora asked his sister to sew on the button again. Gormflath flung the tunic into the fire and launched into a tirade, upbraiding Maelmora for being content to remain her husband's vassal.

When Brian divorced Gormflath, she rejoined her brother and son, and full of revenge and ambition, urged them on to yet another trial of strength. This time she would have the Vikings on her side. To this end she dispatched Sitric to rally Vikings from their settlements in the Orkneys, the Hebrides, Scotland, and the Isle of Man. Earl Sigurd, Lord of the Orkneys, agreed to help provided he received the hand of Gormflath and the High Kingship of Ireland. Knowing his mother's penchant for giving herself to kings, Sitric readily consented, then sailed south to Man to bargain with another two Viking leaders, Broder and Ospak. He made the same promises to Broder as to Sigurd, on the assumption, presumably, that one or the other would fall in battle. Ospak refused to join him, however, because of his admiration for Brian. Indeed, on the fateful day, he battled at Brian's side.

The impressive carnage that took place at Clontarf, just north of Dublin city, on Good Friday, April 23, 1014, was little more than a pyrrhic triumph. Unfortunately, Irish accounts of the battle are so bombastic and bardic in tone that historians have had to turn to the Norse sagas to find out what really happened. It is from these, paradoxically, that we see that the battle had considerable significance for the Scandinavians, for the defeat of Sitric and his allies put an end to any ambitions they still had of totally conquering the British Isles. It was a defeat, certainly, attended by great superstition so far as they were concerned. All over the Norse world these formidable pagans were beset by apparitions, omens, dreams, and other auguries, both before and after the battle. According to the *Saga of Burnt Njal,* they even tried to divine the best day to fight. It seems they were told that if the battle took place on Good Friday, Brian would fall, but his forces would win the day; if the battle occurred on any other day, all who opposed him would fall. Their hearts must have been heavy as they chose Good Friday, the lesser of two evils.

The battle commenced about 5:30 A.M. and lasted until late afternoon. The Norse and Leinstermen numbered about twenty thousand, and Brian's forces little more. A substantial part of Brian's army was composed of Norse and Danish auxiliaries. Malachy did not take part in the battle itself but joined in the rout. Nobody at all turned up from Ulster. The clash was watched from the city walls by the citizens of Dublin, among them Sitric and his wife, Brian's daughter. When the battle opened well for the Norse, Sitric remarked with some satisfaction, "Well do the foreigners reap the field." "At the end of the day they will be judged," his wife answered boldly. Hours later, when it had become clear they were defeated, she piped up, "They're going into the sea, their natural inheritance"—a comment that earned her "a blow that broke her tooth out."

Strangely enough, it was at this precise moment that her aged father, now in his seventy-fourth year, and her young nephew, fifteen-year-old Turlough, both lost their lives. The boy plunged into the sea in pursuit of two Norsemen and drowned. When his body was found, he was still gripping a Viking head in each hand. The death of the great King was full of irony. Brian had stayed in his tent just north of the battlefield all day, praying and watching the course of the contest. When it became clear that the Norse were routed, he gave leave to his bodyguard to join the rout, and they left him alone with but a single attendant. By chance, the fleeing Broder and his men sought escape that way. According to the Irish account, Broder had already passed Brian, thinking him "a noble priest," when one of his men identified him as "the great king." Broder at once turned aside and attacked Brian with a battle axe. Although the aged king sliced off his assailant's legs, he had his own skull cleft simultaneously.

Clontarf was won. The Norse themselves were happy enough in the outcome, gradually assimilating into the population so that today Viking names—Kennedy, Doyle, Kettle, and others—are now considered native Irish. Twenty-four years after Clontarf, the Christianized Norse began building Dublin's oldest church, Christ Church Cathedral; and the first bishop of Dublin was a Viking.

The real significance of Clontarf was that the three great pillars of the O'Brien dynasty—King Brian himself, his son Murrough, and his grandson Turlough—all perished. The history of the next two centuries, as a consequence, emerges as a period of paradox and ambiguity. Irishmen continued to flood on to the Continent; to found the famous *Schottenkloster* (schools) at Ratisbon, Würzburg, Mainz, and other places in Germany; to produce men of the caliber of Marianus Scotus and Marianus of Ratisbon. There was a Renaissance in Irish art. And yet in church and secular life, it has been alleged, there was only growing anarchy.

Ireland in fact was really no more anarchic than medieval Christendom itself. On the continent corruption was widespread—churchmen selling church offices; noblemen, in their turn, selling clerics, bishoprics, or abbeys. Bishops and priests married or took concubines, and there was a general permissiveness about sex. Even the Papacy itself was bought and sold among a group of Roman families, and on one occasion no fewer than three men claimed the office as a family right. There were infamous Popes, such as John XII, who set houses on fire, openly indulged in love affairs, and once drank the health of the devil. But with the introduction of the Cluniac and Hildebrandine reforms, abuses were removed, and the Church, which for a time had become the plaything of secular princes, regained her independence.

The two great catalysts of disorder in Ireland were the efforts of a Church-Reform party and the ambitions of individual Irish kings, fired by the "illegal usurpations" of Brian Boru.

In Ireland, as on the Continent before reform, bishops and clergy had become subordinate to the secular power. Abbots were usually laymen—relatives of a local prince and appointed by him. In the circumstances, the "warfare" that sometimes broke out between Irish monasteries was as inevitable as between the city-states of medieval Italy. As Frank O'Connor has written: "The Church had become absorbed into the elaborate social system to such a degree that it was no longer distinguishable. When we read of the burning of churches we must remember that the Irish did not think of them any longer as places set apart for worship, but as fortresses whose abbots were members of a branch of the ruling family."

Tales of violence to priests and nuns, of the burning and destruction of church property, of a general spiritual and moral laxity, were carried to Rome—to a Rome where, until reforms had been made, Popes were being assassinated by poisoning to such an extent that the average period of incumbency had been reduced to three years.

It probably was not easy for Irishmen to detect danger in the comings and goings of churchmen and in an increasing disposition on the part of the Archbishops of Canterbury, as representatives of the Pope in the British Isles, to claim jurisdiction over the Irish church and to order reforms in Ireland. In a strange irony, the reform movement began with the newly-Christianized Norse of Dublin. In 1074 they sent their bishop, Patrick, to Canterbury, where he was consecrated by Lanfranc, the Pavian-born Archbishop of Canterbury, after he had successfully extracted an oath of obedience to the Holy See. Lanfranc took the opportunity to write to Turlough O'Brien, the High King of Ireland, drawing his attention to "abuses" in the Irish church. Rome demanded that the Irish forsake their ancient monastic-based Church; that they conform in all essentials to the practices of the Western Church, and in particular accept the supreme organizational and administrative authority of the Pope. In addition, they were enjoined to observe a mutual ritual, observe canonical marriage, establish an episcopate under Roman Authority, and free the church from all lay interference or domination.

Native reformers were not wanting, and eventually Turlough O'Brien's successor, Murrough, sided with the reformers and in 1101 presented the Rock of Cashel, ancient seat of the Gaelic kings of Munster, as the seat for a new archbishopric. Armagh, traditionally the headquarters of Saint Patrick, joined the movement, and at Cashel in 1106 its abbot was inaugurated Archbishop and Primate of the Irish Church—titles and pretensions Irishmen had never even heard of. Other reforms were quickly pushed through, and Ireland became a fully paid-up member of Western Christendom. Or so it must have seemed to most Irishmen.

Meanwhile, oblivious of all this religious to-ing and fro-ing, the princes of Ireland still jockeyed for the supremacy of Ireland, and as in the days of Gormflath, it was largely petticoat influence that proved decisive. By 1120, Turlough More ("The Great") O'Conor of Connacht had become High King. He was a great king who built forts and bridges and attempted to strengthen the Crown along the lines of the Norman feudal model. Previously, for instance, no Irish prince had taken land from a defeated rival; Turlough, however, behaved differently. He dismembered the ancient kingdom of Munster and raised up the "free" tribe of MacCarthys to be princes there. To settle the problem of the still-rebellious Leinstermen, he made his son Conor king there—a decision fraught with tragedy, for the deposed heir, a certain Dermot MacMurrough, whose name is still execrated in Ireland as the National Traitor, retaliated by ousting Conor O'Conor and becoming the implacable enemy of the whole O'Conor house.

Despite the hatred associated with his name, Dermot was unquestionably a man much to be reckoned with; perhaps, indeed, he has been unfairly treated by history. Tall and handsome, with an imposing figure, he was a patron of culture and religion to whom succeeding Irishmen owe much. It was he who commissioned *The Book of Leinster*. He also founded an abbey at Ferns, his capital, and endowed abbeys at Jerpoint and Baltinglass. And he had a sense of humor. When he attacked the abbey of Kildare, he enjoyed bundling the abbess into bed with one of his men. He was a man most women found difficult to resist, and Devorgilla, the wife of Tiernan O'Rourke, one of Conor's allies, actually connived at being abducted by him. While her husband was away from home, she asked Dermot to seize her—an offer which the fiery Dermot could hardly refuse. When O'Rourke found out, he appealed to the High King, who eventually succeeded in returning her, though not before Devorgilla had borne Dermot a daughter. O'Rourke cuckolded before all Ireland, conceived an undying hatred for Dermot.

Ireland had enough trouble from its own princes at this time, without Pope Adrian IV suddenly deciding to get into the game. What his motives were we shall never know, but we do know that he had reached the conclusion that a document known as *The Donation of Constantine* gave him the right to "dispose" of Ireland—a right that had never before lain in Roman hands.

Now generally considered to be a forgery, *The Donation of Constantine* purported to be a bequest by which the first Christian emperor had given to the Popes of Rome "dominion over the islands of the sea," which in this case meant Ireland. Genuine or not, Pope Adrian IV issued his Bull *Laudabiliter* and then charged his right worthy and trusty son, Henry Plantagenet, Duke of Normandy and King of England, to invade Ireland "and reform its Church and people." A significant condition was that Henry must pay "an annual tribute to the Blessed Peter of one penny from every house" in Ireland. To make certain that Henry understood, the condition was mentioned twice.

The title "King of England" gives little idea of Henry Plantagenet's position in the West. A Frenchman by birth and culture, he was inferior in rank only to the Emperor and was stronger, indeed, in resources. As Duke of Aquitaine, he was master of the richest region in the West, with traditions even older than those surrounding the King of France. He was also Duke of Normandy and Count of Anjou, and for him, as for his successors, France was the place where everything happened. England itself was a mere province of his vast domains. As for Ireland–well, for a time he had tinkered with the idea of giving it to his brother, William of Anjou. In his own person he was an exceptionally able and energetic man. He built palaces and churches throughout his dominions, particularly at Caen, Rouen, Angers, Tours, and Chinon. He loved learning for its own sake and could speak every language "between the Bay of Biscay and the Jordan." It was said of him: "His Majesty's hands are never empty; they always hold either a bow or a book."

Yet even with all his power, a commission such as the Pope's could only occasion raised eyebrows at Henry's royal council meeting. Invade a land so long regarded throughout Europe as holy ground? Reform the saints of Ireland? The Empress Matilda, Henry's aged mother, said no. Perhaps with regret, perhaps with relief, her son Henry dutifully obeyed. The Bull was laid aside, although the dust that fell upon it was not fated to gather for long.

Whether Henry II would ever have landed in Ireland if it had not been for Tiernan O'Rourke's undying hatred of Dermot MacMurrough is a disputable question. But land he did, attended with all the color and panoply of medieval knighthood and waving, if only metaphorically, the Pope's commission to restore Irishmen "to order"–a task, incidentally, that neither he nor any of his successors managed to accomplish in the 749 years, 2 months, and 30 days they managed to stay there. (Oddly enough, one reason why Henry landed in Ireland was to get away from the hullabaloo created by his murder of Archbishop Thomas à Becket. The wonder must remain that the High King of Ireland was not empowered by the Pope to invade England and restore it to Christian civility.)

Acting on his mother's advice, Henry, as we have just seen, had actually put Irish escapades out of his mind and may well have kept them out of it had not been for Dermot MacMurrough. In the continuing warfare between Dermot and O'Rourke, the former had been decisively routed. Deserted by his allies, he had watched his enemies burn his encampments and demolish his castle at Ferns stone by stone. A lesser man might have accepted defeat, but not Dermot. On August 1, 1166, he sailed for Bristol, taking his beautiful daughter Eva with him, determined to recover his kingdom. There he consulted a merchant named Fitzharding, who advised him to see Henry II. The Frenchman, of course, was in France, and Dermot went to Guinne to see him.

The great king received Dermot graciously, but refused to take up his cause. Most historians agree that by then Henry had dropped all ideas of personally invading Ireland. He did not turn down Dermot entirely, however; he gave him letters patent permitting "anyone within the bounds of our dominions" to aid and assist him. Dermot hurried back to Bristol, where he was put in touch with an impoverished Welsh knight named Richard, Earl of Pembroke, known subsequently to Irish history as Strongbow. Securing Strongbow's support, Dermot then enlisted the aid of some other Welsh knights (Fitzhenry, Carew, and Fitzgerald) and of some members of a Flemish colony in Wales (Prendergast, Fleming, Roche, and others).

Meanwhile, the native princes of Ireland were enjoying the last lovely summer of Gaelic Ireland. The great Fair of Tailten, with its feasting, lovemaking, music, and games, was held in the county Meath in beautiful and cheerful weather. There were dancing and athletic contests, and the poets recited the epic tales while musicians made joyful din. Then, on May 1, 1169, in answer to a summons from Dermot, who had returned secretly to Ireland, three long ships sailed into Bannow Bay on the south Wexford coast. The boats were open ones, with a single mast and a square sail, and along the sides hung shields to give protection to the rowers. They were run up on the sandy beach, and there one hundred knights and men-at-arms clad in mail and armor and six hundred archers armed with crossbows disembarked. The landings were unopposed, and the Norman invasion of Ireland had begun.

IX

LAMENT FOR ULSTER

Even if a poem were but make-believe,
it is a lasting make-believe in exchange for a passing one.
All wealth is but make-believe
and even so is he for whom the poem is made.
If poetry were destroyed
so that there were no history or ancient lays
every man would die
without hearing of any ancestor except his father.

from the thirteenth-century
Irish of GIOLLA BRIGHDE MAC CON MIDHE,
hereditary chief-poet to the
O'Gormleys

Few Irishmen could step back and take such a long and lighthearted look at their fellow countrymen as Luigi Barzini has done with Italians:

> Why did Italy always behave so feebly? Why was she at all times so prone to catastrophes? She has been invaded, ravaged, sacked, humiliated in every century. . . .
>
> Travellers did not hide their contempt for us. . . . Yet they never stopped coming to Italy. Many begin to admire us today, listen to us, imitate us, and even envy us. Why? . . . Could it be that foreigners are no longer certain that their virtues are best? Or could it be that our vices have turned out to be desirable advantages in the modern world, qualities essential for survival? Did we or the rest of the world change?

Much of what Barzini says could be applied to Ireland and the Irish. Yet, lack of military success and domination by foreigners have made a far smaller impact on the Italian mind than on the Irish. No other nation in Europe has harbored such a long and sullen resentment against its conqueror. The Irish memory still rankles at defeat, wrestles to understand how and why it was unable to eject the foreigner, sighs over the lost chances, and debates bitterly why certain victory always and inevitably turned to catastrophic defeat. Irish history is a succession of terrible "ifs"—if King Rory O'Conor had not been inept; if Shane O'Neill had not been treacherously slain by his allies; if Hugh O'Neill had not listened to Red Hugh O'Donnell on the eve of Kinsale; if Owen Roe had lived long enough to face Cromwell. . . .

There is something almost Chinese about the Irish tendency to regard their own civilization (in a general and indefinable way) as superior to that of the conqueror; to see the invaders simply as "foreign devils." Men who are seemingly sane in all other respects retain an apparently irrational hostility toward foreign influences—which usually simply means anything British. This particularly applies to members of the Gaelic League, an organization founded in 1893 whose alumni include that triumvirate of immortal heroes—Patrick Pearse, the poet who led the Rebellion of 1916; Michael Collins, the daring Irish Pimpernel; and Eamonn de Valera. The League was founded in a dark hour, and both Ireland and the world owe it a debt, for from it sprang not only the intense political movement that finally gave Ireland independence, but also that Gaelic revival which led directly to the modern Irish literary movement of Yeats, Synge, and O'Casey. The problem for modern Ireland is that the League, lost in the mists of abstract idealism, still largely refuses to deal in reality. Their diehard attempts to turn Ireland into a "Gaelic state" (whatever that would mean today) continue to cause havoc in Irish life—particularly in their insistence that children should be forcibly taught Irish. As Timothy Patrick Coogan, a Dublin journalist, has written: "Much of the ardor which went into fighting for Irish freedom now goes into the fight for the language. People go to court rather than pay their radio licenses if the necessary forms are not made out in Irish. An undue hostility to foreign influences and a concentration on the pastoral aspects of Irish culture have tended to create an uneasy vision in the public mind of what the country would be like if the Gaels ever controlled it. The concept of the Gael as propagated by the extreme wing of the movement is of a man approximately six feet and five inches in height, noble-browed and with the faraway look in his eye which comes through perusing Erin's past glories. His wife is serene, beautiful and the mother of eleven children. In view of the mandatory chastity of the couple, conception, it will be understood, occurs non-sexually . . . . "

Despite the zealots, there is a growing recognition today that Ireland cannot be a wholly Gaelic state if only for the reason that her population is not entirely a Gaelic people. John B. Keane, a popular playwright, insists that Ireland cannot afford to show hostility toward "any nation or culture" and leads a movement to free schools from compulsory Gaelic. A reaction has also set in against the Establishment view of Irish history. Sean O'Faolain, in his book *The Irish,* emphasized "the Norman gift"–Norman keeps, Gothic churches and monasteries, cities and towns, "English" law, the jury system, Parliament, and trade and commerce. Today, too, efforts are being made to soften the teachings of the Irish Christian Brothers, a dedicated body of men who since 1802 have provided Irish youth of all classes with free education up to university standard, but whose ideas of Irish history have always been extreme.

The story of how Ireland came to be subservient to Britain is, therefore, today no longer a tale told starkly in black and white. There is little doubt that the Norman-Frenchman, a soldier of fortune with no roots and little history, could have conquered all Ireland; there were few peoples in Europe capable of standing up to him. Native Irishmen, therefore, have less than they imagine with which to reproach themselves. A Norman view of what it was like to fight the Irish in the fourteenth century is given in the *Chronicles of Sir John Froissart:*

> Ireland is one of the evil countries of the world to make war upon or bring under subjection, for it is closed strongly and widely with high forests and great waters and marishes and places uninhabitable; it is hard to enter to do them of the country any damage . . . for the men draw to the woods and dwell in caves and small cottages under trees and among bushes and hedges like wild savage beasts, and when

> they know that any man maketh war against them and is entered into their countries, then they draw together in the straits and passages and defend it . . . and when they see their time, they will soon take their advantage upon their enemies, for they know the country and are light people . . . they are strong men in the arms and have sharp weapons. . . .

The Irish were so simply armed however that within eighty years of the first Norman landing three quarters of the country had been overrun by the Norman-French and their allies. The Norman, having learned his warfare defeating French kings, knew how to hold his gains he built fortresses—first of wood, later of stones—and defied the Irisn to dislodge him.

Yet in a sense, the Irish were conquering their conquerors even as they went down to defeat. Assimilation was rapid, intermarriage became common, and soon there were Norman barons who could speak nothing but Irish. They allied themselves with Irish chieftains, dressed, lived and ate as Irishmen; ordered their households and cultivated the arts in the same manner as Irishmen. They became, in the classic phrase, *Hiberniores Hibernicis ipsis*—"more Irish than the Irish themselves."

Unfortunately, the Norman monarchs handled Ireland with striking ineptitude. Ireland as much as England could have benefited from the arrival of a vigorous, eloquent people; but the Norman monarchs were too preoccupied elsewhere, and as a result the so-called Conquest never became much more than a half-conquest. Even the "Irish" Parliament that was set up in 1297 existed primarily for the new colonists. The native Irish received few benefits; chieftains were dispossessed without a qualm; and even those who swore allegiance to the new "Lord of Ireland" and did their best to comply with the new order found themselves continually tricked.

Yet paradoxically, Ireland began to flourish as never before, despite the fact that no proper effort was made by the English Crown to create a new nation living harmoniously with the sister domains of the Angevin empire. Peace and order obtained over large tracts of country; systematic agriculture and estate management were introduced; towns were built and regular markets held; mills and workshops sprang up; monasteries and friaries appeared, staffed by continental orders of Dominicans, Franciscans, Carmelites, and Augustinians. Trade flourished; as the Reverend F. X. Martin, Professor of Medieval History at University College, Dublin, has pointed out, in five years the customs duties on wool and hides alone for the town of Ross brought in the equivalent of £100,000 of modern money to the Crown treasury. Local government was introduced, with mayors, town clerks, and councils, and the Irish Parliaments of 1297, 1299, and 1300 (whose proceedings were held in the French language) were attended by representatives of the whole community. Education revived, and a university was founded in Dublin in 1320. Sadly, it failed to survive, mainly because Irish students preferred to attend the University of Paris or its daughter school at Oxford. Large areas of Ireland were pacified, and the endless forays that had marked Gaelic civilization now took place only at the limits of the new settlements; faint echoes only of the clash of arms reached the peaceful burghers and businessmen going about their daily business. Yet, out there, beyond the cleared forests, the pride and arrogance and spirit of the Gael were reviving.

Indeed, they revived so well that by the beginning of the Tudor era little remained of the Norman conquest in Ireland. The Gaelic tide had flown back over those areas of country grabbed in the first dynamic inrush of the French barons. Henry VIII's officials reported that the Irish had "diminished the King's jurisdiction from a large forest to a narrow park." This was no hyperbole, for the Crown's power scarcely extended beyond Dublin and a small border area called The Pale (from which we derive the phrase *outside the Pale* to connote an outsider). To make matters worse, this was hardly the sort of area Henry could have been proud to number among his dominions. It was filled with large numbers of landless natives living in conditions of great squalor–a fact that reminds us that the great Irish slum populations of Britain and America are not entirely the result of industrialization or forced emigration. Indeed, Ireland has possessed her own awful slums since medieval times, for while the Normans were enriching Ireland, they also were creating the Irish slum dweller. The stench, pestilence, and agony of Irish townships, the mountains of stillborn flesh that arose in these cesspools are often only too easily forgotten in the contemplation of a Gothic abbey or church. Ancient Ireland was no paradise; but at least the old Irish had enjoyed a more dignified living.

Yet if by Tudor times Gaelic Ireland had largely rid herself of the yoke of Norman conquest, she also had rid herself simultaneously of the prosperity (if not the slums) that went with it. She seemed unable to rediscover any impetus toward social advancement. For a country that had produced a magnificent art and scholarship in the past, Ireland contributed almost nothing to European culture in her own dark centuries. There was some poetry and music–and the Normans themselves were not without cultivation. Yet while Johnny-come-lately England produced a great literature Ireland languished in a way that seems baffling until one realizes that her cultural attainments could scarcely flourish because she had become a land of great warlords.

There was still no real power in Ireland capable of imposing cohesion and common purpose. The natives remained preoccupied with the recovery of their lost possessions, the Normans with survival. Not until Gaelic resistance was broken forever did English colonists, enjoying privileges denied to the natives, launch themselves on a cultural and artistic spree that was to amaze Europe. The eight centuries between the Norman invasion and modern times were certainly not a cultural or social void; yet regrettably they saw the native culture stifled—even though there still remained enough to inspire that synthesis which emerged in modern times.

No great native prince—fortunately or unfortunately, depending upon how one views the outcome—arose in those centuries of reviving Gaelic power to assert the paramountcy of the old order. The Pale might shrink until even its lords were forced to administer the Brehon law; Irish chieftains might live in wild independence in the Wicklow Hills, gazing down upon Dublin itself and permitting peace and order in lands around the capital only at the price of "black rent." Had the native order then possessed a Brian Boru or Turlough More O'Conor, the pretensions of the British Crown might have been summarily ended. Instead, it was England which threw up the grand figure, in the person of Henry VIII.

Henry VIII is largely remembered as an ogre in Ireland; and yet a study of Irish state papers reveals that this is an unfair assessment of him. His aspirations were hardly tyrannical. On the contrary, he attempted to overcome the problems with which he was faced like a statesman. Ireland lay in an anarchic state just short of chaos; in attempting to bring it to the kind of order achieved in England, Henry faced a hydra's task. Nor could he have simply ignored the place, for Henry sincerely believed he possessed a legal title to Ireland. He also had cause to fear trouble from her. The English colonists there had favored the Yorkist party during the Wars of the Roses, and two pretenders—Lambert Simnel, who was actually crowned King in Dublin in 1487, and Perkin Warbeck, who was received there as a royal personage—were reminders that Ireland was a natural base for those who boded him ill.

At first the King tried to govern through the most powerful of the Anglo-Irish lords, the Earls of Kildare of the house of the Geraldines. Yet even these men of Norman blood were unable to rise above the general chassis; they abused their power and insisted upon ruling to the exclusion of anything but their own interest. When the Earl was summoned to London to answer charges, his son "Silken Thomas" impetuously rebelled and soon had most of Ireland in flames. Eventually, Silken Thomas and five of his uncles were executed in the Tower of London. Both he and his family have been long regarded in Ireland as patriots whose fate adds to Ireland's countless wrongs; but there have been better reasons for Irish indignation.

When the Silken Thomas affair had quietened down, a religious dispute soon arose to bedevil relations afresh. In 1536, following his dispute with the Pope, Henry declared himself Head of the Irish Church. Immediately, a new difficulty presented itself: Henry's title to Ireland derived, in fact, from the Pope, so that once he refused to acknowledge the Pope as his suzerain, the Irish could claim that they no longer owed him allegiance. On June 16, 1541, the Irish Parliament therefore was forced to declare Henry VIII King of Ireland.

Although Henry's religious goings-on were badly received in Ireland, his political moves were impeccable. His policy was "a politic reformation." Irishmen were no longer to be treated as "enemies," but as the "king's subjects" and were to be admitted fully to English law. "If the people were caused to know the ways of justice," Henry noted, they might abandon their "unlawful demeanours. . .no doubt, if there were justice used amongst them they would be found as civil, wise, politic, and as active, as any other nation." A measure of Henry's wisdom in handling Irish affairs is that his policy was blessed with success. In 1545, the Council of Ireland reported that the country was "in such peace, as it was not in any time of our remembrance."

Only three things marred this engaging scene. Neither Henry nor his advisers really understood the Irish social system nor the Irish mind. Henry–perhaps deliberately–misconstrued the position of the Irish princes, or chieftains. He himself, in his feudalized way, assumed that all Irish land was his and that under him an Irish chieftain was the equivalent of an English lord (ignoring the fact that a chieftain held title to his lands only on behalf of the whole clan, and that even the chieftaincy itself was an elective office).

His second mistake was to ignore the power of tradition and ancient custom in Ireland. There was and still is something marvelous about the old Gaelic tradition and culture; but Henry made no provision for this tradition, with the result that today his name is anathema in Ireland. Few of the Irishmen who honor the harp as the symbol of their country, for instance, now remember that it was he who made it so.

His third mistake was to try to extend the Reformation to Ireland. Ironically, it was the very corruption of the Irish Church that proved his undoing. Many churches lay in ruins; priests never preached; there was a shortage of schools. Religion in Ireland existed principally through the work of mendicant friars, who moved freely about, owing loyalty neither to parish priest nor bishop, yet instilling in all Irishmen an ineradicable loyalty to the Holy See. These men were the true heirs of Columba and the ancient Celtic church, and the reforms Henry and his successors imposed upon the organized Irish church passed them by. When the traveling friars spoke out against Henry's church, the Reformation in Ireland was doomed. Nor did Henry send Irish-speaking missionaries among the native people, who remained, therefore, in ignorance of the issues involved—although it is hardly probable that he would have changed their views, anyway. There were riots when the tactless reformers publicly burned the Staff of Jesus—alleged to be Saint Patrick's own crozier, which had been preserved in Christ Church Cathedral—and destroyed an image of the Blessed Virgin at Trim and a crucifix in county Westmeath.

Ironically, it was not until a Catholic queen, Mary Tudor, ascended the throne that the Irish found themselves with real cause for complaint. Not that she claimed to be practicing Catholicism in this instance. Indeed, her actions had little to do with religion and more with the thoroughly secular problems which she faced in England. Among them was the job of controlling the buccaneering propensities of the English, fostered by growing economic difficulties resulting from overpopulation. In a flash of inspiration, her administration saw a quick method of killing several birds with one stone. Gaelic nobles bordering the Pale were still exacting black rents and maintaining a sturdy independence; if the penalty for treason were made confiscation of land, then large areas could be settled with Englishmen. It was such a brilliant idea that no one was capable of resisting it.

The area confiscated by Mary and planted with "new English" was known as Queen's County—after Mary herself—and King's County—after her husband, the Catholic champion, Philip II of Spain. Despite its failure, this "Plantation" provided a pattern for future emulation. Elizabeth I, in her turn, seized another three hundred thousand acres; and James I, son of the Catholic Mary Queen of Scots, grabbed exactly ten times that amount. During his Protectorship, Oliver Cromwell, never a man to be outdone in such matters, helped himself to an enormous eleven million acres. With further confiscations under William of Orange, who assumed the throne of England in 1689, the seventeenth century ended with no fewer than fifteen million of Ireland's twenty million acres having passed into alien hands. It was in Ireland that the Anglo-Saxons perfected their arts of exploitation.

All this sorry history, however, cannot be traced solely to bad intentions. For example, Elizabeth I is execrated in Ireland mainly because of religious prejudice; yet initially, she did her best to treat the country justly. She opened her reign in the same spirit of conciliation which had marked the policy of her father, Henry VIII. Her personal relations with Irishmen and Irishwomen were excellent. If only because she added the word *blarney* to the English language—thus providing modern Ireland with a tourist attraction—she deserves to be remembered more kindly. This occurred when the lord of Blarney, Cormac MacCarthy, continually evaded demands to conform to her authority, making one promise after another and keeping none of them. "With fair words and soft speech" MacCarthy put off fulfilling his obligations until Elizabeth finally declared: "This is all Blarney—what he says he never means."

Despite the good humor with which the Queen received the lord of Blarney's blarney, the inescapable fact remained that in the end either the English or the Gaelic social and political structures had to prevail in Ireland, for there was no room for both.

As her reign advanced Elizabeth saw Ireland grow ever more chaotic and rebellious. It is easy now to view the whole thing as a noble effort by Catholic Ireland to throw off an increasingly oppressive Protestant and alien yoke. The truth is more complicated, however. We find not only Gaelic lords rising in rebellion, but members of the great Anglo-Irish houses, the Geraldines, squabbling with their traditional rivals, the Butlers. We find native and Old English nobility resisting Elizabeth's proselytizing officials and clergy and intriguing to place the Catholic Mary, Queen of Scots, on the throne of Britain. Geraldines were in rebellion, Butlers in rebellion, Burkes in rebellion, O'Neills, MacCarthys, O'Byrnes, Maguires, O'Mores, and O'Connors in rebellion. Sir James Fitzmaurice, cousin of the Earl of Desmond, on promises of aid from Philip II of Spain and the Pope, raised the Catholic banner.

Philip sent a small force of seven hundred Spaniards and Italians to Ireland. They landed in Kerry in 1580 and fortified a place incongruously known to Irish history as *Dun-an-oir*—"the Fort of Gold"; but eventually they surrendered to an army led by the Lord Deputy and the gallant Sir Walter Raleigh in exchange for a promise of fair treatment. The English, of course, slaughtered them all in cold blood.

It was a time of treachery, violence, and cruelty. Shane O'Neill the Proud died at the hands of his erstwhile allies when invited to a feast; Sir Henry Sidney, that paragon of civilization, who indeed had sought to administer Ireland with justice and toleration, showed no compunction in inviting four hundred Irishmen to a conference and then slaughtering every one. The fate of Dermot O'Hurley, Catholic Archbishop of Cashel, even now induces a shudder.

Such cruelties, however, cannot conceal the fact that under Elizabeth's reign, democratic forces first stirred in feudalized Ireland. From the start of the Norman Conquest the poor people of Ireland had known little but oppression. In old Gaelic Ireland most men had lived free and independent lives, and if their chief prospered, they shared in the common spoil; under the half-baked feudalism that Tudor Ireland knew, only the lord prospered. As Sean O'Faolain has pointed out, the first people to show any interest in the common folk "were not native Irish but invading

English who were shocked at their condition." In 1585, under a scheme known as The Composition of Connacht, tenants of the Connacht lords were relieved of many feudal exactions in return for payment of a fixed rent. Most, it seems, welcomed the measure, and historians of every persuasion agree that it was equitable. Yet the Irish nobility—both Norman and Gaelic—saw nothing good in it; it was merely a way of depriving them of power and revenue, of raising "the churl as good as a gentlemen." The gentry, even those prepared to remain loyal to Elizabeth and to tolerate her queer religion, now poured their hatred and scorn on the English middle-class gentlemen who made up Elizabethan officialdom in Ireland. Even the English language became a symbol of loathing.

Of course, the reception accorded these economic policies was always complicated by the fact that Irishmen genuinely detested the religion of the English. In the words of *The Annals of the Four Masters*: "A heresy and a new error [sprang up] in England, through pride, vainglory, avarice and lust, and through many strange sciences, so that the men of England went into opposition to the Pope and to Rome."

When English and Scots were settled on confiscated Ulster lands a few years later, an Irish poet wrote: "In their place [that is, in the place of the native warriors] we have a conceited and impure swarm: of foreigner's blood—an excommunicated rabble—Saxons are there and Scotsmen. We have lived to see . . . dark thickets of the chase turned into streets . . . the mountain all in fenced fields." One can sympathize with the poet; yet most common people were happier for the changes.

The first important result of the resistance to Elizabeth's ideas was the Plantation in Munster, consisting of lands confiscated from rebels of one sort or another. For the first time "carpetbaggers" appeared on the Irish scene—hordes of lawyers and assorted brethren who proceeded to cheat the natives of their property. As a result, men like Sir Walter Raleigh ended up with forty thousand acres of Munster, although no single undertaker was entitled to more than twelve thousand acres.

The tide was flowing inexorably against the Gael, and as Elizabeth's glorious reign drew to its close Gaelic Ireland was brought to its last stand. Whatever the faults of the system, the motives that impelled Elizabeth and her followers were discreditable. Even officials like Sidney were forced to protest.

For over a century English greed and avarice had looked to Ireland for satisfaction. Englishmen had learned that great estates could be gained through provoking rebellion and then buying up the lands confiscated by the Crown after the defeat of the rebels. In an age of licensed piracy, Ireland was El Dorado, and even the Queen was not above dipping her hand in the till. With neither justification nor legal right, she permitted Sir Thomas Smith to attempt the colonization of the Ards peninsula in 1572.

His project failed, as did an even more ambitious attempt by Sir Walter Devereaux, Earl of Essex, to "plant" the northeast the next year. The latter was a particularly shameful transaction, for the Queen herself had put up half the expenses in return for a promise of half the dividends. Sir Henry Sidney criticized the adventure as a mean and shameful bargain, although he had little hand in the opposition which prevented the venture's success. Treachery, deceit, intrigue—even bloody atrocity—marked the preliminary onslaught on the north and soon began to make the name *Englishman* stink in Irish nostrils.

In the midst of all this turmoil stood Hugh O'Neill. Educated at the English court and possessing the manners and graces of a high European gentleman, O'Neill had been trained to play the role of a political puppet; but never had such a misjudgment of character, intellect, and personality been made by a great sovereign. In any other country O'Neill might have made a name to shine throughout Europe. He was a born soldier, a born statesman, a born leader—capable of mixing caution and cunning with an ability to strike like a tiger. He matched himself and the remnants of his devastated society against the brilliance of burgeoning Elizabethan England—and almost won. He reduced the glittering Robert Devereaux, Earl of Essex, who had, in Elizabeth's own words, led "the royallest army that ever marched out of England," to impotence. But in doing so, he caused his own tragic downfall. On August 14, 1598, at the Battle of the Yellow Ford, he imposed on the English the greatest defeat in arms they had ever suffered in Ireland. For nine tortuous years, 1594-1603, O'Neill, captain of a small confederacy of Gaelic chieftains, became the *de facto* ruler of Ireland. Such was his power indeed that he finally declared himself High King of Ireland—as by descent he had every right to do—and made the formal Circuit of Ireland.

O'Neill had never intended to be a rebel. He had taken his seat in the Irish Parliament as Baron of Dungannon and had agreed to rule a third of Ulster in the Queen's name. In 1587 he had returned, as an old Londoner, to the Queen's Court and accepted an English title, Earl of Tyrone. He was a prop and pillar of the rule of justice and law and had a clear concept of the new forces moving not only England but all Europe. He seems to have been neither intractable, intolerant, nor unreasonable. His demands and conditions for peace, even now, seem reasonable:

> That all persons may have free liberty of conscience. That the Earl may have pardon . . . The Earl, O'Donnell and the rest, if these requests be granted, will remain dutiful; and after a while, when the great fear which they conceive is lessened, they will draw themselves to a more nearness of loyalty to Her Highness . . . That the Catholic, Apostolic and Roman religion be openly preached and taught

> throughout all Ireland . . . that the Church of Ireland be wholly governed by the Pope . . . that all cathedrals . . . be presently restored to the Catholic churchmen . . . That there be erected an university upon the Crown rents of Ireland wherein all sciences shall be taught according to the manner of the Catholic Roman Church . . . That the Lord Chancellor, Lord Treasurer, Lord Admiral [etc.] . . . be Irish men . . . That all principal Governments of Ireland . . . be governed by Irish noblemen . . . That all statutes made against the preferment of Irishmen, as well in their own country as abroad, be presently recalled . . . That all Irishmen, of what quality they may be, may freely travel in foreign countries for their better experience, without making any of the Queen's officers acquainted withal . . . That all Irishmen may as freely travel and traffic all merchandises in England as Englishmen, paying the same rights and tributes as the English do . . . That all Irishmen may freely traffic with all merchandises, that shall be thought necessary by the Council of State of Ireland for the profit of their Republic, with foreigners or in foreign countries . . That all Irishmen that will may learn, and use all occupations and arts whatsoever.

In brusque fashion, Elizabeth's chief minister, Sir Robert Cecil, answered these demands with a single word: "Utopia." It was a word that was to cause much blood, agony, and bitterness and was to leave a legacy that is the direct cause of the fighting that has been taking place in Belfast and Derry in our own day.

If Hugh O'Neill represents one facet of the Irish character-learned, skillful, disciplined in emotion and behavior, capable of thoughtful planning and sustained effort—then his great ally in the struggle, Red Hugh O'Donnell, Prince of Tyrconnell (Donegal), embodies those qualities of dash, courage, and impetuosity that are generally associated with Irishmen. Never, from that twelfth-century morning when the Normans arrived until that January forenoon in 1922 when Michael Collins strode into Dublin Castle to accept the handover of government from the King's Lord Lieutenant, did two Irishmen come nearer to physically ejecting the invader. They fought for the Catholic as well as the Irish cause, creating, unfortunately, that association of Irish nationalism with Catholicism that has bedeviled political progress ever since and lies at the root of much of the trouble in Ulster today.

The battle of Kinsale on Christmas Eve, 1601, was the final turning point for Irishmen–an irrevocable end of the old order. Following defeat, Red Hugh hastened to Spain to seek further help, only to die at the hands of a poisoner hired by Cecil. O'Neill retired to his Ulster fastness, holding out until his antagonist, Elizabeth, died. Under James I, the great earl lived for a time at peace on his ancestral lands. By the terms of his submission, however, his powers and privileges were drastically reduced, and he became aware of the constant intrigues and pressures by Englishmen who coveted his domains. On September 16, 1607, he embarked on a ship in Lough Swilly, accompanied by other northern chieftains–in all, ninety-nine of the leading men of Ulster–in an episode still remembered as The Flight of the Earls. Nine years later, blind and in his dotage, the last great Gael died at Rome and was buried there. None of his family has ever returned to claim their patrimony.

X

THE CURSE OF CROMWELL

Ho, brother Teig, dost hear the decree,
Lillibulero bullen a la,
That we shall have a new Debittie,
Lillibulero bullen a la.
Lero, lero, lero, lero, Lillibulero
bullen a la, Lillibulero, lero, lero,
Lillibulero, bullen a la.

There was an old prophecy found in a bog,
Lillibulero bullen a la.
Dat our land would be ruled by an ass and a dog,
Lillibulero bullen a la.

So now dis old prophecy's coming to pass,
Lillibulero bullen a la,
For James is de dog and Tyrconnell's de ass,
Lillibulero bullen a la!

Seventeenth-century song

Cromwell! For three centuries the name of Oliver Williams,. known to history as Oliver Cromwell, an ex-brewer of Huntingdonshire, has been execrated above all others in Ireland. Perhaps only the name of the Devil himself could invoke greater detestation. In his person, beliefs, and behavior, this ugly, wart-faced descendant of Henry VIII's equally detestable Chancellor, Thomas Cromwell, has been the symbol of everything Irishmen have ever loathed about England and what they imagined, rightly or wrongly, to be her aspirations and methods, her greed, unscrupulousness, perfidy, and ruthlessness in the pursuit of wealth. Neither England nor Ireland was ever to be quite the same again for Oliver's living; but whereas England has so mellowed her view of him as to regard him now as the Great Democrat, Ireland still sees him as the Great Rapinist.

The irony is that Oliver only went to Ireland because she had become embroiled in the internal politics of England. His object was not so much to extirpate the Irish people as to crush the Royalists there and to ensure that the Catholic Counter Reformation did not succeed. Even the greatest atrocity against his name—the massacre at Drogheda—probably involved the cold-blooded murder of more Englishmen than Irishmen, for many of the defenders were his own countrymen. Yet historians have not failed to note the rogue's material interest in the country by virtue of his directorship of a body called *Adventurers*, who lent Parliament £250,000 against security of 2.5 million acres of Irish lands which, it was hoped, would be confiscated.

By Cromwell's time, the rape of Ireland—much of it conducted under the banner of religion—had proved a profitable enterprise for the rising new men in England. Following the Flight of the Earls in 1607, the Government declared the departed chieftains traitors and escheated their lands. In 1609, these were offered to English or Lowland Scottish undertakers, who were, of course, Protestant. Over a half million acres were parceled out in what is known as the Plantation of Ulster—the basis of that Scotch-Irish colony which still stubbornly maintains a separate identity from the rest of Ireland. Native Catholics were not entirely excluded. Untainted landlords were permitted to retain their properties, and others were given tenancies. The labor force could be anything it liked. So many Catholics remained on the land. indeed, that the Plantation almost failed, and it was nearly a century before Ulster assumed its present rather awful character. Such extensive seizures did not take place without protest from important Crown officials in Ireland. Sir Arthur Chichester, the Lord Deputy (and ancestor of a former "Ulster" Prime Minister, Terence O'Neill), and Sir George Carew, an old opponent of O'Neill and O'Donnell, insisted that the Irish were being wronged and that the policy was sheer folly. From now on, they argued, England would face even greater difficulties in Ireland, inasmuch as both natives and Old English (that is, Normans) would be driven to unite in a common Catholic cause. It was an accurate prophecy.

Fundamental and far-reaching changes were beginning to take place in the character of Ireland and her people. With the Rebellion of 1641, which was launched with a horrendous massacre of new colonists in Ulster, the harried and persecuted Irish gave vent for the first time in their history to their pent-up fury. In England there was uproar, and even today the echoes still resound in Ulster, where the Reverend Ian Paisley, Ulster's leading demogogue, often resurrects this moment of madness as yet another excuse for his own conduct. In no time at all the Irish, who longed only for peace and to be allowed to follow their fathers' faith, found themselves not only embroiled in the English Civil War but also being used as unwitting pawns in the great European battle of the Counter Reformation. In the loggias of the Vatican; in the gilded halls of Versailles, where Cardinals Richelieu and, later, Mazarin whispered their advice to Louis XIV; in the bare corridors of Whitehall Palace, where Charles I maneuvered for his crown, Irishmen were moved about on the international chessboard. Both the Papacy and the French sent aid to the Catholic Confederacy. Charles dangled promises.

It was a period of much complexity—far too complex to submit in its details to anyone other than Irishmen. In no time at all, no fewer than four armies were counterattacking each other all over Ireland—a Royalist army, a Cromwellian army, an Irish "rebel" (or Catholic Confederate) army, and a Scots Presbyterian army, reinforced by Ulster Presbyterians. The issue at stake for the Irish rebels was religious tolerance. Charles I, leader of the Anglican church, had indicated his readiness to enact legislation tolerating Catholicism and securing Irish Catholics in their properties. His difficulty was that he was unable to do anything about this promise as long as his recalcitrant Westminster Parliament was controlled by zealous Puritans who were as likely to tolerate Catholicism, even in Ireland, as they were to sup with the Devil. Aware that if the Puritans succeeded in their ambitions, all Ireland would be turned into another Ulster, the Catholic rebels sought to forestall such an eventuality. Their object was neither to eject the Crown from Ireland nor to seek separation from England; it was, rather, to secure the repeal of a fifteenth-century Act of Parliament called Poyning's Law, which required that all legislation enacted by the Irish Parliament had to be approved by Westminster. But with their own free and independent Parliament responsible to the Crown rather than to the English Parliament, the Irish would be safe from the molestation of the militantly Protestant English legislature.

Upon the outbreak of civil war in England, however, the Irish suddenly upped their aims. This was a move dictated by the Vatican. The

Pope, in return for his aid, dispatched Cardinal Rinuccini to Ireland charged with securing the public restoration of Catholicism and the Crown's recognition of the Pope's spiritual authority. In 1645, at the height of his difficulties, Charles indeed went so far as to offer a secret treaty to the Catholic Irish if they would provide an army of ten thousand soldiers to fight the Roundheads. Next year, in even more desperate straits, he improved on this offer, and the bulk of the Confederates would have been glad to accept had not Rinuccini declared that he would excommunicate all who did. It was a fateful decision, for the Nuncio's intransigence sealed Charles's fate, thus–no small irony–leaving Cromwell indebted to the Pope for his ultimate triumph.

The martial qualities of Irishmen have never really been in doubt; their fault–if it is their fault–is that they tend to win battles but inevitably to lose wars. Of the armies in the field in 1646, that of the Catholic rebels was by far the most efficient. Led by Owen Roe O'Neill, nephew of the great Earl and a colonel in the Spanish army, they inflicted upon the Scots and Ulster Presbyterian army, led by General Munroe, an ex-officer of Gustavus Adolphus, the bloodiest defeat ever suffered by any British army in Ireland. Along that same river Blackwater where his uncle had crushed the English, Owen Roe scored an even more emphatic triumph. The Scots and Ulster Protestants left more than three thousand of their soldiers dead on the battlefield. So much for the Ulster Protestants' traditional boastful celebration of "their" Boyne victory every Orange Day!

Volte-faces are not uncommon in civil wars, however, and with the defeat of King Charles, the Scots and Ulstermen suddenly became allies of the Catholics. The latter, however, split by Rinuccini's intransigence and the sudden death of Owen Roe O'Neill, had lost much of their unity and purpose. It was into this situation that the triumphant Oliver, flushed with his success over the Crown, finally stepped personally.

Irishmen argue that had Owen Roe lived, the fearsome legend of Cromwell in Ireland would have never existed. As it is, for all the military glory associated with his name, his exploits in Ireland reveal him as something less than a superman.

He landed in Dublin on August 15, 1649, at the head of a highly disciplined, battle-scarred army of twenty thousand men, all fired with a burning zeal to see Papists perish. His declared aims were to recover Ireland for the Republic of England, to enforce the Adventurer's Act of 1642 (a matter in which he had his own small interest), and to punish all Irish Papists for the Ulster massacres. Dissimulator that he was, he lulled the Irish with initial declarations of friendship and goodwill. A Jesuit was even admitted to his camp to play chess, and his soldiers were warned not to "illtreat or spoil the peasantry," who were invited to bring their produce to the army. So far, so good. Then he showed his iron fist. He marched north to Drogheda, a poorly fortified place held not by the Catholic Confederates, but by Royalists. The commander was an English Royalist and his troops were a mixture of English and Irish. After a week's investment, during which Cromwell's unopposed artillery did as it pleased, the walls were breached. Some of the garrison surrendered on promise of quarter; but after the town had fallen, Cromwell himself gave his notorious order: Every soul in the town—some thirty-five hundred fighting men, civilians, women, and children—were slaughtered in cold blood. Cromwell, in what must rank as almost the oddest Christian utterance of all time, reported to Parliament: "This has been a marvelous great mercy."

Two months later he repeated his tactics at Wexford. But this time he found himself in dire danger. To add to his casualties, his army had begun to melt away under the rigors of the Irish climate. In desperation he had to call for further reinforcements from England. Then, at Clonmel, he received his first check, which at least morally was an Irish victory. The town was defended by young Hugh O'Neill, nephew of Owen Roe, and Lord General Cromwell lost two thousand men in several futile attempts to take it, before retiring "as much vexed as ever he was since he first put on a helmet against the King." O'Neill, down to his last cartridge, told the town's mayor to negotiate surrender, and in the darkness slipped away. Cromwell, more than satisfied, granted terms, only to be roused to chagrin when he found the birds had flown. Despite his fury, however—and this has to be said in his favor—he adhered to the terms and made no attempt to make the townspeople suffer. It was his last engagement in Ireland. He sailed away on May 26, 1650, leaving his son-in-law Henry Ireton to carry on the war.

Despite the savagery with which Cromwell had conducted the campaign, despite the fact that he had supposedly cowed the Irish, the war dragged on for another three years and only ended when disunity and conflict of aims among the rebels made it impossible to continue the struggle. One by one their armies surrendered, each making its own terms. These were surprisingly lenient, for already the cold men of business behind the Cromwellian machine had begun totting up the potential gains. First, Irish soldiers were "permitted" to enlist in foreign services—and some thirty thousand potential resisters were thus got out of the way. Then thousands of able-bodied common people, including women and children, were transported to Virginia and the West Indies as slaves. The end of the Cromwellian wars saw the population of Ireland reduced to a mere half-million.

The real barbarity of Sectarian (*i.e.*, Puritan) intentions toward Ireland—the real curse of Cromwell—was not revealed until the Parliament of England passed the Cromwellian Act of Settlement in August 1652. Religious bigotry undoubtedly played a part in the formulation of this act, for it has to be remembered that these narrow-minded men already had fought and triumphed militarily over the Anglicans of England and the Presbyterians of Scotland before vanquishing the Catholics of Ireland—for whom, of course, as adherents of an even more detestable religion, an even worse fate had to be devised. And yet the whole thing, in the end, was settled along sound business lines—as might have been foretold. The mass of the Irish Papist poor, those who owned no more than £10 in goods, were pardoned. (After all, somebody still had to do the actual work in Ireland.) But by virtue of further ordinances and the final Act of Satisfaction of 1653, all Irish gentry and landowners were ordered to remove themselves lock, stock, and barrel to the stony province of Connaught. In Cromwell's own words, they could go either "to Hell or Connaught."

The rest of Ireland—some eleven million acres—was given to Cromwellian officers and men who were in arrears of pay as well as to various English adventurers. Large numbers sold out their shares to speculators and returned to England; others stayed on to form a new and substantial element in the Irish population, molding a new Irish character and in general creating that landlord class which came to be known as the Ascendancy.

As for the common Irish, the settlement left them mere cottiers or tenants-at-will and gave rise to the smoldering discontent which flared into rebellion and then agrarian war, even into Victorian times. The real victims, of course, were the Irish aristocrats, who were almost entirely wiped out. Nevertheless, even today—and among all classes—intense satisfaction is felt at Cromwell's ultimate fate. In 1660 his remains were dug up and hanged at Tyburn. Afterward, the moldering relics were flung into a pit and covered over. Ironically, the place where they still lie is called—and it is, of course, pure coincidence—Connaught Place.

During the next forty years, the inability of the English to settle their own affairs without involving others again proved fatal to an Ireland by this time heartily sick of her turbulent and aggressive neighbor. When this tiresomely energetic people finally restored their monarchy in 1660, Irishmen hoped they might be allowed a period of peace and reconstruction. Under Charles II, indeed, they were not denied this. The population expanded to two million, and Dublin became the second city in the British Isles. A big butter and meat trade developed, and the rough Irish wool (the manufacture of fine Irish wools had been prohibited in Charles I's reign in order to protect the Yorkshire woolen industry) found a market in

England. Yet the country's expansion was quickly stifled under pressure from the new English commercial classes, which now shared power with the Crown. Irishmen were forbidden to export cattle, the main basis of their wealth. All wool had to be exported to England; and even this miserable remnant of what might have been a great trade was killed once and for all when England imposed ruinous import duties in 1699. By far the worst blow, however, was the restrictions imposed on the flourishing Irish shipping industry. Irish ships were forbidden to trade directly with the new colonies in America or elsewhere, and Ireland could thus send and receive goods only through England. Within a century, even the new English settlers in Ireland, inspired by the example of the American colonists, were in rebellion against this sort of treatment.

At the Restoration, the Crown had found itself in a familiar dilemma over Ireland. Throughout medieval times, every effort by the monarch to extend English justice to the Irish countryside had been thwarted by self-interested baronial magnates. Now Charles II found himself caught in the same trap. He tried to do what he could, and some Catholics did indeed have their lands restored. Others were permitted to live again east of the Shannon—as lawyers, doctors, merchants. But the majority had to make do with their stony Connaught acres. By 1672 Protestants owned at least three-quarters of profitable Irish land, dominated the Irish Parliament totally, controlled the government and the civil corporations, and held most of the country's trade in their hands. Despite efforts by Charles himself, by Prince Rupert, by the Lord Lieutenant, and by others, all attempts to right Irish wrongs were repeatedly frustrated. The English Whigs remained stubbornly hostile, and the recurrent religious hysteria in England—especially after the discovery of the so-called Popish Plot of 1678, whose ramifications involved the execution of the Catholic Archbishop of Armagh, Oliver Plunkett—further hindered the spread of justice. Irishmen became a bitter and intractable people—no longer because of abstract principles or ancient traditions, but because of practical, day-to-day grievances. Yet hopes were still placed in the Stuart monarchy.

With the accession of the Catholic convert, James II, the Irish at last saw a ray of hope. Under Colonel Dick Talbot, created Earl of Tyrconnell and appointed to the Lord Lieutenancy, they eventually were admitted to full civil and religious rights, which meant that they could hold government, municipal, and legal offices. Tyrconnell even prepared to call a truly representative Irish Parliament in the hope that such a body would repudiate the authority of the English Parliament while at the same time remaining loyal to the Crown. In England, however, James had run into difficulties. Although his motives were impeccable by twentieth-century standards, even a king could not stand against bigotry and self-interest. The King's aim was to legislate the toleration of all religions and thus heal the divisions that had existed in the British Isles since the Reformation. He sought to cut through the political difficulties by using his royal prerogative. At once the Whig Party hurled the British Isles into yet another revolution, this one destined to deprive a large number of inhabitants of the islands of even their most elementary civic rights. A handful of self-interested magnates invited James's son-in-law, William of Orange, to invade England on the pretext of "protecting the Protestant interest." Five months later, Ireland once again found herself a battleground.

In the ensuing struggle the Irish once more found themselves playing the role not of rebels but of defenders of the lawful British sovereign, who in turn was backed by the most powerful monarch in Europe, Louis XIV. It was also known that large numbers of English Tories were ashamed of having permitted their rightful king to be turned out; and there were also thousands of loyal Highlanders in Scotland ready to fight. With no thought that they were, in fact, opposing the Papal interest (for William of Orange was an ally of Pope Innocent XI in the complex, constantly shifting balance of forces that characterized European politics in the seventeenth century), the Irish welcomed James. Thousands of raw recruits straight from the bogs and hillsides joined his "army."

The Williamite wars have left their indelible mark on Ireland—a mark that extends even beyond her shores. Memories of the campaign are still celebrated annually in the six northeastern counties, in Glasgow and Liverpool, and in far-off Toronto. In Northern Ireland, on the anniversary of the battle of the Boyne, thousands of bowler-hatted Orangemen, wearing sashes and parading gaily colored banners, march through the cities and towns to the din of thunderous Lambeg drums as the bands blare out old songs of triumph:

> The lowland fields may roses yield
> Gay heaths the highlands hilly-o,
> But high or low, no flower can show,
> Like the glorious Orange Lily-0.
>
> Then Heigho the lily-o,
> The royal, loyal lily-o,
> Beneath the sky, what flower can vie
> With Ireland's Orange Lily-o?
> There's not a flower in Erin's bower
> Can match the Orange Lily-o.

The names of the battles and sieges of the Williamite wars ring down sonorously through Irish history: Derry, Aughrim, Enniskillen, and the Boyne! Athlone and the walls of Limerick! For 105 days the citizen-soldiers of Protestant Derry, under their slogan, No Surrender!, defied the army of King James until finally *The Mountjoy*, sent to relieve the starving garrison, crashed through the great boom across the Foyle to end the siege.

The Battle of the Boyne, one of the great turning points of European history, was in itself hardly more than a skirmish. Raw Irish recruits, sent into action with little training, poor officers, and inadequate weapons, were never a match for William's professional veterans, particularly the famed Dutch Blues. James was the first member of his army to reach the temporary haven of Dublin, from whence he immediately fled back to France.

With James himself out of the way, however, the encircled Irish, "blooded" by their experiences at Athlone and Aughrim, showed their real mettle at Limerick. The siege of Limerick lasted almost fifteen months, from July 1690, until October 1691. It was marked not only by the heroic defense of Patrick Sarsfield, a giant of a man and a magnificent cavalry leader, and by a display of fighting fury by Irishwomen, but also by a daring exploit when Sarsfield stole out of the city and intercepted William's siege-guns, then on the way from Dublin. As Sarsfield came up in the dark, the sentries demanded the password. As a jest, his own name had been chosen, and Sarsfield, having learned of this roared: "Sarsfield is the word and Sarsfield is the man!" He then led his small force forward to cut the escort party to pieces. The lasting significance of Limerick to the Irish mind, however, is that it not only wiped out the inglorious memory of the Boyne and the charge of cowardice made by James, but set a new high-water mark in English perfidy.

Sarsfield's exploit delayed William's attack on the city; but fresh guns and mortars were brought up, and bombardment began on August 17. On the twenty-seventh, the British Grenadiers advanced into the city, only to be captured or thrown out. A second massive attack almost succeeded, but this time the women of Limerick joined in, hurling stones and broken bottles; they "boldly stood in the breach and were nearer our men than their own," a Williamite historian has noted with awe. On August 30, after fifty-three days of siege, William gave up the fight and returned to England, but the next year his army returned again, under a Dutch commander named Ginkel. Ginkel's attacks failed, but the indomitable Irish of Limerick, with their provisions exhausted and with no hope of fresh help from France, were forced to accept his terms. On October 3, 1691, the Williamite wars ended in the Treaty of Limerick. Under it, Catholics were "to enjoy such privileges in the exercise of their religion . . . as they did enjoy in the reign of King Charles the Second." On October 12, under the eyes of Sarsfield and Ginkel, the Irish troops, in an episode known as the Flight of the Wild Geese, marched out "with drums beating and colours flying." Twelve thousand of them left to go into exile and join the armies of Louis XIV.

Seven years later—against the personal inclinations and efforts of King William, who, having accepted his throne not from God but from the English Parliament, found himself its prisoner—the Treaty of Limerick was repudiated, and the Penal Laws descended upon Catholic Ireland. Such were the injustices to be visited upon the country as a whole, however, that almost a quarter of a million Scotch-Irish Presbyterians from Ulster fled to North America, where they were to stand in the vanguard of the American Revolution. Eighty-four years after Limerick, the grandsons of the defenders of Derry fought shoulder to shoulder with the grandsons of the defenders of Limerick at the battle of Bunker Hill.

XI

BIRTH OF A NATION

I met with Napper Tandy,
And he took me by the hand,
Saying, How is poor old Ireland,
And what way does she stand?
She's the most distressful country
That ever yet was seen;
They are hanging men and women
For the wearing of the green.

I care not for the Thistle,
And I care not for the Rose;
When bleak winds round us whistle,
Neither down nor crimson shows,
But like hope to him that's friendless,
When no joy around is seen,
O'er our graves with love that's endless
Blooms our own immortal green.

Eighteenth-century song

Jonathan Swift, fretting at the disappointments which had deprived him of a brilliant career in London and forced him to spend his life in the second-rate atmosphere of Dublin, suddenly became less of an English gentleman who happened to be born in Ireland and more an Irish patriot who happened to be born of English parents. In 1729 his Irishness surfaced, and he published his famed *A Modest Proposal,* a savage satire in which he offered to the British people a scheme for killing off year-old Irish children, whose flesh, he promised, would "make a most delicious, nourishing and wholesome food."

Ordinary Irishmen had never been so badly off. There had been famine before in Ireland, but in the eighteenth century it became chronic. In 1720 Archbishop King declared, "The cry of the whole people is loud for bread; . . . many are starved, and I am afraid many more will." In 1740 the worst hunger the country had ever known, not to be surpassed until the Great Famine exactly a century later, carried off more than four hundred thousand people. And if famine were not enough, a system of screw and rack rent flourished, further grinding the faces of the poor. Even in the Big Houses, as Professor Corkery has put it, "The Lord of Misrule governed everywhere." Great Protestant landlords lived as absolute monarchs. Richard ("Humanity Dick") Martin, King of Connemara," was asked if the King's writ ran upon his lands. "Egad, it does," he answered. "As fast as any greyhound if my good fellows are after it."

The physical face of Ireland itself was rapidly changed. The new settlers, eager to squeeze the very last penny from their unexpected bonanzas, hacked down trees at a profit of sixpence a stump to feed England's new industrial machine–leaving Ireland the relatively deforested country she is today. "Undertakers" rented estates to middlemen and then went off to enjoy the pleasures of London and Bath; the middlemen flung themselves into the viceregal swirl of Dublin, leaving their agents to put the squeeze on the peasants; and then between agent and peasant came yet another class who insisted on getting their cut–the bailiffs. Following a period when England's cattle herds were decimated by disease, the new Irish landlords saw an even quicker way of getting rich. They rapidly turned every acre they could over to pasture (on which tithes, anyway, were not payable) and threw family after family out on the roads.

Bereft of natural leaders after the flight of the aristocrats to the Continent, ordinary Irishmen turned for help to the only people available–the Catholic clergy. In an age when priests were outlawed and savagely persecuted, clerical influence waxed stronger than ever. Most clergy undoubtedly deserved well of their flocks. In particular, they advised and educated. At first the Government had tried to suborn them by offering them fixed salaries to join the Established (Protestant) Church; when this failed, the policy switched from honey to vinegar, and priests were declared potential rebels. A gathering for Mass was labeled a conspiracy, and Masses had to be said in deep glens or on remote mountainsides. Priests caught saying Mass in the open were hanged, drawn, and quartered. In 1720 the Irish Parliament proposed that all Popish priests" should be branded with the letter *p.* Priest-hunters, like the bounty hunters of the American West, became legion. Priests had to hide even from their own congregations—by wearing veils or saying Mass from within a closet with holes cut in the door—so that congregations could truthfully swear that they "hadn't seen a priest." Yet despite these conditions—or perhaps because of them—the influence of the clergy grew. By the end of the century, Catholic clergy were the *de facto* rulers of "native" Ireland. During the rebellion of 1798, they even led the people, not as priests but as generals and military men.

Not that the Irish poor were entirely helpless without their priests. Secret societies—the White Boys, the Cork Boys, the Defenders, and so on—sprang up everywhere. Essentially, these were primitive rural trade unions, although their methods were often as desperate as their plight. As the eighteenth century merged into the nineteeenth, they roamed an increasingly anarchic countryside by night, lynching hated landlords or their agents or maiming the cattle belonging to new tenants who had moved into holdings from which previous tenants had been evicted. They burned stables and hayricks and outhouses and tore down fences; they slaughtered or hamstrung cattle and sheep. In extreme instances, they even raped women or seized them and held them for ransom. They invented a new weapon called *boycott,* named after Captain Boycott, a landlord in the west of Ireland against whom the weapon was first employed.

The main causes of peasant misery were not totally attributable to the malice and oppression of English government. Many of the problems could be traced to the rapid expansion of the Irish population, which caused rents to be pushed higher and higher. But even here English policies aggravated a situation that would have been bad enough in its own right, for the trade restrictions imposed on the country by the British Government meant that agriculture was forced to remain the country's sole source of wealth.

Yet, as Maureen Wall, College Lecturer in Modern Irish History at University College, Dublin, has pointed out, "It would be wrong to think of the life of the peasantry as one of unmitigated sadness and despair." When harvests were good, "they led a carefree enough life. The arts of the shanachie, singer, dancer and musician were widely cultivated and appreciated; and these people, though poor in the world's goods, had a rich treasury of folk culture." Indeed, it is startling to find life being lived in such a normal fashion, even in the seventeenth century, that the

Catholic Church had to launch a campaign against excessive drinking and merriment at that supposedly unique Irish institution, the wake. No amount of misery or oppression, it seems, could dull an Irish wake, which, it has been maintained, was a far more uproarious affair even than an Irish wedding. Thus in 1681 a traveler named Thomas Dineley attended a wake at which "young frye . . . appeare as gay as may be, with their holyday apparell, and with pipe, harper or fidler, revell and dance the night throughout, make love and matches." At some wakes, lewd songs were sung, and at others obscene dances performed. (Lewd games were normal at German and Scandinavian wakes, where actual lovemaking often took place.) There was much horseplay, mourners sometimes pelting each other with sods of turf or potatoes. Other ways of passing the time of the long night's vigil were by playing cards, reciting riddles, making up jingles, or trying tongue-twisters. Sean O'Sullivan, archivist of the Irish Folklore Commission, has unearthed no fewer than 202 games that were played either inside the house or in an adjoining field just prior to the funeral next day. These ranged from contests in agility and strength, accuracy of aim and so on, to tauntings, mockery, and even booby traps. Cockfights were popular, with mourners laying bets. Youngsters played all kinds of pranks on mourners, who often had to undergo moments of real trial. Pepper was sometimes mixed in tobacco served to the guests or blown in through a keyhole to set the whole assembly sneezing. Chimneys were blocked with sacks or sods of turf, so that mourners were half suffocated; a refinement here was to tie the door shut on the outside. Tobacco was put in teapots; old boots substituted for meat in the cooking pots. Ancients, dozing off, might awake to find their beards shaven off or their coattails sewn to the corpse's shroud. The corpse itself only too often was involved in the amusement. If the dead person suffered from arthritis or rheumatism, relatives would sometimes attempt to give it more dignity by straightening the twisted limbs with rope; pranksters often cut the rope, causing the corpse to sit up as though it had just come alive again. Some corpses were "invited" to take a hand at cards, and joined the players at the table. Often the merriment reached such a pitch that the corpse was dragged to its feet and made to join in a dance. On one famous occasion in the county Limerick, following two successive nights of fun and music, people from the neighboring parish "borrowed" the corpse for *their* party.

Perhaps the apogee of merriment was reached during the eighteenth and early nineteenth centuries, when nearly every wake broke up in a glorious fist fight. These were the days of "faction fights" in Ireland—when gangs of tinkers or unemployed farm laborers were hired by election agents to stage demonstrations or to start riots. The factions bore fanciful names such as *The Molly Maguires* or the *White Cockades.* Often they sought out rivals at wakes and if no other excuse were available, would invent one to start uproar. A feature of these battles, according to O'Sullivan, was that relatives of the dead man often felt aggrieved if there were *not* a fight at their wake.

One explanation for such seeming irreverence is that primitive peoples believed that the dead possessed awesome powers—that they could in certain circumstances take the living with them; therefore, it became necessary to placate them. O'Sullivan concludes that behind most of the pranks lay an intention of letting the dead man know that he was still a popular chap and that he was in no danger of being forgotten. Much of the merriment, too, actually arose from hospitality customs. (It is rare even today, for instance, to enter an Irish house without being offered wine or spirits or perhaps a cup of tea—which usually means bread and butter, eggs, cold ham, cake, biscuits, and a *pot* of tea.) When death occurred, the first task of the surviving relatives was to lay in ample stocks of food and drink for the callers. Then, too, there may well be a correlation between the burdens a people must bear and the defiant jubilation of their rites for the dead. Just as the poor blacks of New Orleans used to march at funerals to ragtime music, so the Irish waked their dead with reels, jigs, and hornpipes.

Despite the deplorable conditions of the bulk of the population, education in Ireland was not sacrificed. When Thackeray toured Ireland in 1842, he wrote: "I listened to two boys almost in rags; they were lolling over the quay balustrades, and talking about *one of the Ptolemys*! and talking very well, too. . . . Another day, I followed three boys, not half so well dressed as London errand boys; one was telling the other about Captain Ross's voyages, and spoke with as much brightness and intelligence as the best-read gentleman's son in England could do."

It was the poets who provided much of this zest for learning and kept alive the ideals of the ancient culture. At a time when more than 70 percent of the population of England could neither read nor write, the ordinary people of Ireland still read books, learned poetry, and studied Greek, Latin, and the humanities. Even when the entire countryside could clothe itself only in rags, the ancient bardic schools survived, transforming and adapting themselves from schools of poetry into academies for the humanities—what became known as "the hedge schools." While Protestant children, from 1733 on, were superbly educated at government-subsidized Charter schools, so good that Lord Chesterfield declared Irish education to be better than English, poor Catholic Irish had only these hedge schools. The masters, of course, as successors of the *aes dana,* spoke Latin and Greek, but they had to do other work to support themselves:

My craft being withered with the
change of law in Ireland
O grief that I must henceforth
take to brewing.

It was even said that cows were being bought and sold in Kerry in Greek.

The poets, of course, suffered in the collapse of Gaelic Ireland. Many fled to the Continent where they became lawyers, doctors, and professors. Others stayed behind, to sink into the general penury. Neither the new settlers nor the common people were interested in a "type of verse that, cramped with rules and swathed in technicalities as it was, was yet the only kind that had till then been deemed worthy of serious notice." The poet Mahon O'Hernan complained:

Such an art as this is no profit to
me, although it is a misfortune that
it should fall to the ground; it
were more honourable to become a maker of combs–
what use is
it to anyone to profess poetry?

One of the wildest of these Gaelic poets was a drunken, lecherous, desperate man named Owen Roe O'Sullivan, who lives on in the folk memory of Kerry as a kind of priapic figure. Variously a laborer, drunkard, schoolmaster, wanderer, vagabond, seducer, and adventurer (he was once press-ganged into the British navy and later joined the British army), it is reported of Owen of the Sweet Mouth that as he lay dying the woman of the house, unsure whether he had gone or not, ordered her daughter to lift up her skirts, at which the dying poet opened his eyes and stammered out some verses beginning, "Nine and twenty young women have I seduced. . . ." Once, while working on the farm of a Cromwellian as a *spalpín* (common laborer), Owen heard a woman servant declare that she wished to write a letter to the master but did not know how. Probably as much from a desire to show off as to annoy the settler, Owen Roe wrote the letter in four languages–Greek, Latin, Irish, English. The stunned Cromwellian at once hired him as tutor to his children–although shortly afterward was forced to chase him from the house with a shotgun when he found Owen seducing one of his daughters.

The Gaelic poets at first tried to earn a living from the common people, whom they despised almost as much as they did the new bosses. The celebrated Eochaidh O'Heoghusa, once chief *ollave* to the Maguires, princes of Fermanagh, finding himself pauperized, wrote wryly:

I have abandoned the delicate series
of keen and earnest admonitions

for a common sort of
easy art which brings me
more praise.

O'Heoghusa's attitude reflects the true Gaelic mind, which was at variance with the new influences then being introduced from both "vulgar" and English sources. These new influences meant that on the one hand "the Irish poetical spirit burst its bonds and rhythmic, assonantal poetry came into its own . . . true lyric poetry," as one expert has put it, while on the other, it meant a steady descent of the poetic craft into the sentimental and jocular balladry of the nineteenth century:

Oh, did you ne'er hear of the Blarney,
That's found near the banks of Killarney?
Believe it from me,
No girl's heart is free,
Once she hears the sweet sound of the Blarney.

For the Blarney's so great a desaiver,
That a girl thinks you're there–tho you lave her.
And never finds out
All the thricks you're about
Till she's quite gone herself, with your Blarney.

Little was known of the works of the "lost" Gaelic poets until revival of interest in the old culture at the turn of this century–an interest that led to the great flowering of Irish literature in English and to the founding of the Abbey Theatre. Only then did the verses of O'Bruadair, Egan O'Rahilly, Owen Roe O'Sullivan, Sean O'Twoomey, Red Donough MacNamara, Donough O'Mahoney the Blind, Brian Merryman, and others become widely known.

Donough MacNamara the Red was typical of these roistering, turbulent literary men who set a pattern for a type still recognizable in Ireland today. He was a "spoiled priest" and so reckless that once, although still a good Catholic, he applied for–and obtained–the parish clerkship of a Protestant church. His boisterous humor comes out in a "pass" he wrote naming the teachers of his district: Christopher Mac Heavy Bottom; Coxcomb O'Boland; dirty, puffy John O'Mulrooney; Giddyhead O'Hackett; Tatter O'Flanagan; Giggler O'Mulcahy; and Blear-eyed O'Cullenan–a tradition of nicknaming that still lives on in Dublin and on which O'Casey drew for his "Juno and the Paycock." Yet he was also capable of writing the beautiful "Fair Hills of Holy Ireland" (the transcription is by James Clarence Mangan):

Take a blessing from my heart to the land of my birth
And the Fair Hills of Eire, O!
And to all that yet survive of Eber's tribe on earth
On the fair Hills of Eire, O!
In that land so delightful the wild thrush's lay
Seems to pour a lament forth for Eire's decay—
Alas! alas! why pine I a thousand miles away
From the fair Hills of Eire, O!

The most Rabelaisian of them all, in content at least, was a quiet farmer and mathematics teacher called Brian Merryman. He wrote only one work: a bawdy 1206-line masterpiece called *The Midnight Court.* By virtue of its scale and imagination, it is the most considerable work of all these lost poets. The following extract, in which a beautiful girl defends the conduct of an unfaithful woman married to an old man, conveys some suggestion of the general tenor and style of this ribald epic:

Down with marriage! 'Tis out of date,
It exhausts the stock and cripples the state.
The priest has failed with whip and blinker
Now give a chance to Tom the Tinker,
And mix and mash in nature's can
The tinker and the gentleman;
Let lovers in every lane extended,
Follow their whim as God intended,
And in their pleasure bring to birth
The morning glory of the earth.
. . . .
Is there living a girl that could grow fat
Tied to a travelling corpse like that;
Who twice a year wouldn't find a wish
To see what was she, flesh or fish,
But dragged the clothes about his head
Like a wintry wind to a woman in bed?

Was it too much to expect as right
A little attention once a night?
From all I know she was never accounted,
A woman too modest to be mounted.

Merryman, O'Sullivan—and the late Brendan Behan, perhaps—all represent a boisterous earthiness that is as much a part of the Irish character as the humble and docile who accept the dictates of authority in general and of the Church in particular. A probe of Irish character shows that an obsession with religion is no more than an expression of a deep awareness that given half a chance, every Irish man and woman would gleefully go to the devil.

It was from these years—years when Ireland swarmed with spies and informers—that we inherit the beautifully poetic synonyms for the country—*Cathleen Ni Houlihan, Drumin Down Deelish, My Dark Rosaleen.* The poets delighted in circumventing British officials by apostrophizing Ireland, and would toast Rosaleen even as they laughed up their sleeves:

O my Dark Rosaleen,
Do not sigh, do not weep!
The priests are on the ocean green,
They march along the deep,
There's wine from the royal Pope
Upon the ocean green;
And Spanish ale shall give you hope,
My Dark Rosaleen. . . .

If the rigid, aristocratic verse of the bardic schools had to give way to new forms, Ireland, all the same, could have done with less of the maudlin, sentimental rubbish that replaced it. The debasement of the poetic art proceeded rapidly—and as with all revolutions, threw up much that was marvelous alongside more that was meretricious. There was no single responsible factor. The trained poets were capable of adjusting to assonantal poetry; but as English became more and more the prevailing language and the poets, ending up in the Dublin stews, were forced to construct verses in that language, their work lost much of its edge. Worse, no longer protected from untrained and unlearned poetasters who had once held them in awe but who now grew familiar with them in taverns and alehouses, they soon found the unlearned trying their hand at those skills which had been formerly an esoteric "science." Before anyone quite realized it, the Irish pub and street ballad had been born:

They're going to tax the brandy, ale and whiskey
rum and wine,
They'll tax the tea and sugar, the tobacco, snuff
and pipes
They're going to tax the fish that swim and all
the birds that fly,
And they're going to tax the women who go drinking
on the sly.

Any event was good for a ballad—murder, death, a hanging, politics, the triumph of a horse, of a greyhound, of a boxer. Ballads became the newspapers and television of their time. They were sung at fairs, at the firesides on dark winter nights, in the alehouses and taverns. Trite and banal words were often set to authentic and beautiful old Gaelic airs. By 1860 the new synthesis was at full throttle. "Irish" songs were actually being *invented* for the music halls of Britain and America. A circus clown called Johnny Patterson wrote "The Garden Where the Praties Grow," "Goodbye, Johnny Dear," and "Bridgie Donohue." The "jintry," of course, hardly could be expected to keep their hands off, either. Their reckless, spendthrift, irresponsible mode of living had created a new image of Ireland: of a rakish country inhabited almost entirely by hell-raisers—hard-drinking, hard-riding, hard-wenching fire-eaters—and propped up by a poor if witty peasantry. Thomas Moore to some extent had paved the way by taking old Gaelic airs and bending them to fit his own rather sweet verses; now the "jintry" took and bent and borrowed as they pleased, and into the historiography of Erin passed an Anglo-Irish image of hunt-balls, lively parties, and something called *ructions.* A typical product of the new age was "Lannigan's Ball":

The boys were all merry, the girls were all hearty,
Dancing around in couples and groups,
Till the accident happened young Tommy MacCarthy,
He put his right leg through Miss Flaherty's hoops.
The crayture she fainted and roared meelya murder,
Called for her friend and gathered them all,
Ted Carmody swore that he'd go no further,
But he'd have satisfaction at Lannigan's Ball.

In the midst of the row Miss Corrigan fainted,
Her cheeks all the while being as red as a rose,
Some of the ladies declared she was painted,
She took a small drop too much, I suppose,
Her sweetheart, Ted Morgan, so powerful and able,
He tore the left leg from under the table,
And smashed all the chins at Lannigan's Ball.

Oh, boys, it was then there were ructions,
I got a big kick from Willie MacHugh,
But soon I replied to his kind introduction,
And kicked up a helluva hullabaloo,
Ould Casey the piper was near to being strangled,
They squeezed up his pipes, bellows, chanters and all,

The girls in their ribbons they got all entangled,
And that put an end to Lannigan's Ball.

Not that all the "jintry" produced doggerel like this. Percy French wrote many songs that accurately reflect the thoughts and emotions of Irish countrymen—although they would have been scorned by the old Gaelic aristocrats and poets, and indeed, to some extent are still regarded as phony or pseudo-Irish. Perhaps his most famous song is "The Mountains of Mourne," sung to a traditional air already used by Thomas Moore for "Bendermeer Stream":

Oh, Mary, this London's a wonderful sight,
With the people here workin' by day and by night;
They don't sow potatoes, nor barley nor wheat,
But there's gangs of them diggin' for gold in the street—
At least, when I axed them, that's what I was told,
So I just took a hand at this diggin' for gold,
But for all that I found there I might as well be,
Where the mountains of Mourne sweep down to the sea.

However, with the founding in 1893 of the Gaelic League by Dr. Douglas Hyde, Professor Eoin MacNeill, and Father Eugene O'Growney, the genuine Irish note was at last rescued from obscurity:

Put your head, darling, darling, darling,
Your darling black head my heart above;
Oh, mouth of honey, with the thyme for fragrance,
Who with heart in breast could deny you love?

In an earlier day Owen Roe O'Sullivan had written:

'Tis not the poverty I most detest,
Nor being down for ever,
But the insult that follows it,
Which no leeches can cure.

Ireland, and some of her ancient culture, had managed to survive—had survived even the insults.

If a single event can be said to be responsible for creating modern Ireland, that event was the American Revolution.

The British colonists in Ireland at the end of the eighteenth century found themselves in much the same position as their American counterparts, and sympathies ran high for men whose fight seemed also to be Ireland's. With Britain facing war on two fronts—both France and Spain threw their weight into the scales on behalf of the Americans—the threat of an invasion of Ireland gave leading Irish Protestants such as James Caulfield, Earl of Charlemont, their opportunity to form the Irish Volunteers, ostensibly to guard her shores. Soon the slogan England's difficulty is Ireland's opportunity was heard. Agitation for an independent status for the Irish Parliament grew, under the leadership of Henry Grattan. The British government, watching an empire crumble, gave way on all points, and in 1782 Grattan was able to declare: "Ireland is now a nation!"

She was far from being a united nation, however. Although most great figures of the time desired the removal of the legal disabilities then in force against their Catholic fellow-countrymen, there was still a solid bloc who feared that any relaxation could only lead to a loss of privilege for the non-Catholic population. These men were less concerned with justice than with well-lined pockets; they were simply British businessmen operating from an Irish base who wanted exactly the same freedoms as their counterparts in England, and they were fervidly joined in these sentiments by the Scotch-Irish of the North. Indeed, the British Government, fearful of a Catholic fifth column in the British Isles and yet desperate for Catholic recruits for its armies and navies, became far more liberal than many of the men controlling the "Irish" Parliament.

Yet, in the end, it was Protestant Irishmen who gave the mass of Catholic Irish hope and set the country on a path that saw the emergence, 120 years later, of an Ireland able to direct her own affairs. Wolfe Tone, "one of Ireland's few Europeans and real revolutionaries," insisted that Ireland would always be England's lackey while Catholics and Protestant radicals were not represented in the Irish Parliament. With the help of Napper Tandy, leader of the Dublin radicals, he founded the Society of United Irishmen. Other radicals in Ulster, although only a small proportion of the population there, supported him enthusiastically.

Finding itself in a war with Revolutionary France, the British Government finally insisted on the removal of disabilities against Catholics, who were then permitted to vote. Full Catholic Emancipation, however, was still opposed by diehard conservatives, and Wolfe Tone, no longer hopeful that agitation could succeed in moving the British government, left Ireland for Revolutionary France, by way of America. At home, agrarian troubles worsened as the population explosion continued and rents rose ever higher. In Ulster, Protestant smallholders–the "poor whites" of their time–clashed with Catholics hoping to buy their land. The bitterness between Orange and Green, latent from the days of the Plantation and Derry, Aughrim and the Boyne, was revived in the virulent form that still sunders Ireland today and has made Ulster a battleground. It was an hysterical age, of course, with both English and Irish conservatives scared out of their wits by Revolutionary France, and spies and conspiracies were uncovered nightly under every bed.

Not that such men had no reason to feel frightened. In Paris, Wolfe Tone persuaded the French Directory to send an expedition to Ireland, and in December 1796 a fleet carrying fourteen thousand men, under the command of the brilliant General Hoche, put out from Brest. The British fleet proved singularly inept, and a French landing in Ireland would have succeeded had not Hoche's fleet encountered a storm. Some ships reached Bantry bay, where Admiral Grouchy debated whether to land, then lost his nerve and returned to France. In Ireland a frightened government introduced repressive measures primarily designed to force the Irish into rebellion so that they could be crushed before fresh French help became available. When Lord Edward Fitzgerald and other leaders of the United Irishmen were seized, the Rebellion of 1798 was finally ignited. Terrible massacres and cruelties were perpetrated—alike by Protestant and Catholic, English and Irish. Bottled up hatreds, hope, fears, and wrongs led to scenes that the pagan princes of ancient Ireland could never have dreamed of. For all the veneer of civilization, Ireland had never known such savagery. In the end, the rebellion was crushed, a second French invasion stamped out, and Wolfe Tone, captured aboard a French warship in which he was serving as a commissioned French officer, escaped hanging as a common felon by committing suicide. Two years later the Irish Parliament voted itself out of existence, passing an Act of Union with Great Britain.

The great architect of this move was William Pitt, whose laudable aims have been overshadowed by his methods of bribery and corruption. Pitt's ideas were the opposite of spiteful. He believed a solution to Ireland's troubles lay in making the British Isles a single free-trade unit, so that Ireland could share in the blessings of growing empire. With one goverernment speaking for both countries, British capitalists would then feel safe to invest money in Ireland, thus raising her living standards. The fears of the Protestant minority in Ireland would be assuaged because at Westminster they would find themselves members of an unassailable majority. Catholics, therefore, could be safely emancipated and all their grievances remedied.

It was a course deserving of success, for union with what was then the world's richest country could only have been to Ireland's benefit. Yet Ireland by then was too far gone in her misery. Throughout the nineteenth century, agitation followed hard on agitation, usually because of chronic agrarian grievances, but heightened by stark crises such as the Great Famine, and what was worse, the mass evictions that followed. There were constant turmoil and minor rebellions. The century opened with the great O'Connell agitating for Catholic Emancipation and the Repeal of the

Union; leading mass demonstrations, often a million strong, pledged to nonviolent civil-rights-style methods. The patriotic Young Ireland movement had its day; then the Invincibles assassinated the Chief Secretary in Phoenix Park, and the Fenian Brotherhood and the Irish Republican Brotherhood were launched in America and in Ireland. At Westminster the Irish Parliamentary Party, led by "the King of Ireland," Charles Stewart Parnell, argued, filibustered, and disrupted the business of Empire with demands for Home Rule. The British government alternated in policy between just and wise treatment sparked by genuine feelings of sympathy and stark coercion. Land acts were passed, making Irish peasants a more privileged class than their English counterparts. Gladstone even introduced two Home Rule bills, and in the twentieth century, on the eve of World War I, yet another British Liberal Government actually passed such an act, only to see it all blown away by the Ulster Orangemen and the last of all Irish rebellions. Then, after nearly eight centuries of almost unremitting struggle, most of Ireland discovered herself free to decide her own destiny—only to find, with a terrible irony, that the real struggle for survival had just commenced.

XII

THE TWO-EYED IRISHMAN

PHARAO'S DAUGHTER

In Agypt's land contaygious to the Nile,
Old Pharao's daughter went to bathe in style,
She tuk her dip and came unto the land,
And for to dry her royal pelt she ran along the strand.

A bush tripped her, whereupon she saw
A smiling babby in a wad of straw,
She took it up and said in accents mild,
"Tare-an ages, girls, which o' yees own the child?"

Verses attributed to MICHAEL MORAN
("Zozimus")

"No people are more immersed in the marvel and wonder of being Irish than the Irish themselves," the actor Michael MacLiammoir insists. Indeed, an obsession with themselves and their image, amounting almost to narcissism, is responsible for an Irish tendency to be at once intensely self-critical and complacent. The Irishman undoubtedly lingers lovingly over his lineaments in the looking glass, steadily growing more and more enamored of every wart, pimple, and elongated tooth. Yet invariably he wishes he were someone else.

Between the pressures of his religion and his harsh history, the Irishman has been driven to a state of national neurosis, which shows up in the form of a discernible inferiority complex. In Dublin an American nudged me and warned, "See how cautious an Irishman gets when an Englishman walks into the room." Indeed, a deep-rooted fear of insult or contempt persists to the present day, betraying itself in an acute sensitivity to outside criticism.

A Danish designer working at the government-sponsored Kilkenny Design Centre told me how difficult it was for a foreigner to work in Ireland. "The Irish are very friendly to strangers and have a sophisticated sense of humor, and I like a great deal of the way they live. But I've upset them more than once by openly criticizing them. I was invited to come to Ireland to help improve Irish designs—which I took to mean that they weren't satisfied with their own. Yet when I criticized their work they resented it. It's very difficult to be diplomatic when you're working with such a sensitive people. They used to ask me what I thought of Ireland, but they didn't want a *real* answer. All they wanted me to say was 'It's marvelous.' In the beginning, I was stupid enough to say exactly what I thought. I'd say, 'Well, the scenery is beautiful, but the houses could be greatly improved; the interiors lack color and warmth and attention and so on.' Then they either looked bored or simply resented it."

A London journalist who spends his holidays in the county Cork said: "You'd be floored if you imagined you could talk to an Irishman the way you would to an Englishman—that he'd be sensible enough to accept criticism of Ireland in the same way that you'd offer it about English institutions. Instead of admitting that what you're saying might be even partly true, he'll start extolling the virtues of whatever you're attacking beyond all credibility, with the clear inference that if Ireland hadn't been stifled for hundreds of years, heaven alone knows what might not have happened to the world."

These observations seem to be well taken, for the Irish themselves admit to the charge. A Dubliner said helplessly: "We simply can't be objective—I don't know why. If you said 'There's a lot of litter about Dublin,' somebody would immediately bite back at you 'I've seen worse in London' and leave it at that, never dreaming of doing anything about

Dublin's litter." In Ireland one often hears the exasperated groan "You can't tell an Irishman anything!"—an echo, perhaps, of the old Roman cry that the Celts were "unteachable!" Yet too little notice has been taken of the Irishman's humility. He has long been obsessed with the hereafter, intensely aware of his own finitude. Each Sunday he still goes through the solemn exercise of humbling himself anew before God. Real modesty and humility are almost as natural to him as breathing, although he often tries to bury them (even from himself) by braggadocio or self-deception. In his more sober, less dreamy moments, however, he is conscious of his own simple role, and it is merely the pretensions of others that annoy him. Yet he cannot help feeling, at the same time, that he possesses an old wisdom—in particular an ability to perceive and understand cosmic purposes and forces—that gives him a unique advantage.

The Irishman's inability to allow strangers to criticize anything Irish is matched only by his inability to refrain from criticizing everything Irish himself. Indeed, the one aspect of the national neurosis that is not so easy to tolerate is the backbiting that does much to undo the real charity and generosity that distinguish Irish life. A criticism that outsiders have to make of Irishmen is that they usually are not only incapable of saying anything good about each other, they simply cannot be stopped from saying something awful. One Dublin pub-wit puts it like this: "If there were only three Irishmen left in the world, you'd find two of them in a corner talking about the other." "An Irishman would never say to your face what he'd rather say behind your back," admits another. "There's nobody so poor in Ireland that he hasn't got a knife in his back," says a third.

Irishmen, in fact, have invented their own form of Chinese torture—the death of a thousand tongues. The mockery and the backbiting are at their worst in the very place where there is most ambition and where it is obviously most thwarted—the capital. After a few evenings spent in a famous Dublin literary haunt, London critic Cyril Connolly declared, "The atmosphre was as warm and cozy as an alligator tank."

Alistair Cooke, the journalist, found that "in Dublin, you have this impression that when you leave the room, they all turn to each other and say, 'Isn't he a charming man?' and then, after the briefest of intervals, 'but did you notice the way he picked his nose?' "

A Dublin television drama producer insists: "To understand Dublin and the way it thinks, you've got to remember that if you manage to put on a successful play here, people will come up to you, and after warmly congratulating you and telling you 'That was bloody marvelous,' will immediately add 'But d'ye know what's wrong with it?' " Another

Dubliner told me, "If someone's doing a fine job and you mention it, someone else will immediately leap in, 'Ah, isn't he well paid for it?' "

If the acid is not directed at an individual, it is likely to come in the form of a cynical dismissal of Irishmen in general. Two Dubliners were walking past a bank clerk's club in Saint Stephen's Green when they heard a burst of applause. "Something unusual must be going on," said the first. "Sure," agreed his friend bitterly, "one of the members must have stood a drink." Two more were on top of a bus one day when the first noticed a passenger reading a book called *The Rise of the Celts.* "Jaysus," he said, "wud you luk at that? The only time a Celt ever rose was when the fellow sitting on top of him got up." Once I carelessly remarked that I'd read somewhere that Dublin was like the Dead Sea–you couldn't sink in it. "How the hell could you?" exploded someone. "Aren't we squatting on the bloody bottom already?"

Irish writers, on the whole, have done their best to stir the national cauldron of self-doubt and self-hate although by a strange paradox, through their international success, they have helped Irishmen to rise from their knees. James Joyce, like Shaw, "hated" Ireland with that intense hatred which in Ireland is the mark of a true patriot. "Ireland," he declared savagely, "is an old sow who eats her own farrow." Of his fellow Dubliners he once said, "They are the most hopeless, useless and inconsistent charlatans I have ever come across." Yet despite a lifetime's sojourn in Paris, Trieste, and other places, he could never forget Dublin or write about anything but Ireland. When a friend bumped into him and inquired, "Jim, when are you coming back to us?" Joyce replied simply, "I have never left you." Sean O'Casey also excoriated the land of his birth. "It takes courage and patience to live in Ireland," he declared. Yet he could never stop writing and dreaming about her.

The root of it all has variously been ascribed to a fundamental instability in the Irish nature, or to a definite lack of social cohesion. Chesterton once confused the issue by deciding that Irish inability to do anything but run each other down was because "when one is oppressed, it is a mark of chivalry to hurt oneself in order to hurt the oppressor"–as though the Irish had somehow or other anticipated the immolations recently practiced by Vietnamese monks.

The novelist Jack White points to a prime reason for the critical way Irishmen look at themselves. "The real fear of the Irish people is to be jeered at, to be laughed at. As a matter of protection, therefore, they try to be first with the jeer. I remember one year–we're awfully bad here at pageantry or anything like that, as you've probably noticed–we had a festival, and I was one of the radio commentators at the parade in O'Connell Street. Part of the parade was meant to be a historical pageant. I remember a character in a clawhammer coat, top hat, Victorian trousers and beard, shambling down O'Connell Street, supposed to be representing Parnell. Now, if you think of Parnell as anything, you think of him as a fine, upstanding, exceedingly proud man. But there was this fellow ambling along with his hands behind his back and grinning as much as to say, "Jaysus, will ye look at me in the oul' clawhammer!' He was conscious of the laugh that was coming, and he felt he had to get it in first."

Much of the backbiting, calumny, slander, libel, envy, and smoldering resentment is little more than a game, of course—part of the great Dublin sport of gossip and conversation. It is often no more than a counterpart to the gossip and tittle-tattle that have always distinguished aristocratic or privileged societies, exempted as they are from the pressures of industry and commerce. Unlike heavily populated countries, where the pressure of fellow-humans upon each other has become so intense that people have retreated into their shells if only to avoid self-destruction, the Irishman can afford to indulge in his gregariousness (and its attendant talk) to the hilt.

Then, too, many of the vicious remarks whirling about are offered as tentative judgments designed primarily to catch a visitor out. If the unwary stranger agrees with a condemnation, then he may suffer a backlash of resentment. If he opposes it, then he will have done no more than confirm the native in his good opinion of himself, for the Irishman has been simply fishing for compliments to whatever Irish individual or institution he attacked. In this sense, venomous phrases may be used to get the outsider to confirm Irish abilities that the Irishman has come to suspect. Or they may be warnings not to attempt to sneer at anything—that the poverty and mediocrity that are only too observable in Ireland must not lead a stranger into a conceit of himself or a feeling of superiority, nor must they be considered a reflection on an Irishman's mental status.

Too often, however, there is no explanation for a remark other than that it is a plain, unadulterated, old-fashioned piece of backbiting. Thus Brian Inglis explains the venom away as "only the small-mindedness of any provincial society. There's no question, for instance, that every Irishman is intensely pleased and rather proud that both Paddy Campbell and I have done so well in London. [Campbell, now Lord Glenavy, like Inglis became well known by appearing on British television.] When any Irishman does well, everybody is pleased. But that doesn't make anybody *like* Paddy Campbell and myself any the more. They'll admire us, certainly—but at the same time they'll resent the fact that two such clowns as Paddy and I should have succeeded where they haven't."

The derisive comments about other Irishmen—and, indeed, about everything Irish—"What a bloody, God-forsaken hole," Irishmen continually complain to each other—and the unceasing self-mockery are sometimes carried to such excess, however, that they can be seen starkly for what they really are—long-standing expressions of national frustration.

Bernard Shaw once remarked that the Irishman had developed "two eyes"—meaning that with one eye he saw only a dream and with the other saw that it was *only* a dream. Goethe, too, might have had the Irish in mind when he made Faustus declare, *"Zwei Seelen wohnen, ach! in meiner Brust"* (Two souls dwell, alas! in my breast.) The task of anyone setting out to interpret or explain the Irish character is to make it clear that there is a distinction between the dreaming Irishman living a real life and the real Irishman living a dream—but that sometimes both merge.

When Cromwell dumped all Irishmen into the same social bog, they set about escaping from reality through a perfect Darwinian gambit—by developing a dreaming eye. With it, they saw the vision of an eternal reward and also found a means to preserve their present dignity by escaping back into the world of the ancient Gaels, to misty recollections of antique magnificences and past glories. The enchanted eye transmogrified everything; so that even Shaw could describe to English audiences the land on which he had turned his own back thus: "You've no such colours in the sky, no such lure in the distances, no such sadness in the evenings. Oh, the dreaming! the dreaming! the torturing, heart-scalding, never satisfying dreaming!" The dreaming always ended abruptly, however, when an Irishman was shaken from his own tiny universe by the discovery that another bogman was gaining on him. Then his two Irish eyes swiveled madly, and he experienced an unholy mental chassis: *How did that fella manage it, and me—me!—get stuck like this?*

He has rarely bothered to focus his analytical eye on his own ego. In any contemplation of his personal cosmos, it is invariably the eye of the dreamer which he brings to bear. It is only when he switches to a contemplation of his fellows that he focuses his realistic eye, an eye become all the icier because what it sees is usually in such unfavorable contrast to his own transfigured self. The result of such conflict is a thing of incredible wonder. Whatever inadequacies he feels, he simply transfers to the other fellow—and then doubles them. If unable to do something himself, for instance, he has no difficulty convincing himself, through a swift swivel of his eyes, that the other fellow is even less capable than he.

Thus even now, with the Irish economic and social structure changing rapidly, there are Irishmen who still console themselves with the thought that another's success is due only to a mixture of good luck and chicanery: "Ah, hadn't he the luck of the devil!" To which is invariably added a curt dismissal of the man's genuine capacities: "Ah, sure, that fella couldn't skin a cat–and if you gave him a book of instructions at that!" A memory of when they were both bogmen is also certain to intervene. "Don't I remember him when he hadn't the arse in his trousers and was running about, holding out his piece of bread and hoping somebody would put jam on it!" Even in governmental and professional circles there is a penchant to suspect native abilities. Dublin professional men tell alarming tales of instances where American, British, or German experts have been called in to undertake surveys which the natives were perfectly capable of doing themselves. Germans, Japanese, Swiss, Italians, British–anybody can get large government subsidies for wildcat schemes that would get a native certified. This contrast is all the more remarkable, of course, because as a nation, Irishmen remain convinced that they are better than anybody else at *anything*. In no country, as a corollary, is the prophet more without honor than in Ireland. Edward Delaney tells how he got his personal comeuppance when he drove down to College Green, Dublin, for the unveiling of his controversial statue to the patriot Thomas Davis. "There was this old doll, so I leaned out the car window and said, 'Isn't that an absolutely monstrous statue?' 'No!' she snapped back, 'it's just great.' I said, 'I'm glad–because I did that!' So she took one look at me. 'G'way out of that–a dirty idiot like you–you couldn't have done that!' Now, that's a typically Irish attitude–proving we're not even ready for democracy. If I'd been wearing a tall hat and had an English accent or called myself the Marquis Edouard de Laney or worn an American mohair suit and talked with a twang, she'd have probably kissed my foot."

This tendency showed again in Dublin's initial appreciation of Jack B. Yeats, the poet's brother and one of the few modern Irish painters (Louis le Brocquy is another) who has managed to establish an international reputation. According to Bernard Vandeleur in his autobiography, *A Fretful Midge* (edited by Dublin journalist Terence de Vere White), "scoffers there were in plenty" in Dublin when Yeats held his first exhibition in London. Even people who had never held a paintbrush in their hands declared, "Give me a few tubes of paint and I'll squeeze them out on a palette, and you won't be able to tell the difference from a Jack Yeats." Here, both Irish eyes were swiveling madly at once–the analytical eye performing its destructive function of tearing down poor Yeats, the eye of enchantment working overtime to persuade the frustrated Dubliner that he is at least as good as the next fella.

In such a milieu, of course, hardly anybody is safe from some kind of libel, slander, calumny, or jest. Anybody attempting to strike out of the rut for himself is certain to offend somebody. Irishmen realize–but vaguely and usually in the abstract–that Irishmen are capable of greatness.

This may buoy the individual up—even bolster him for a while against a hostile world. Yet he finds the idea that Johnny-next-door could also be a great man a different matter altogether. Johnny, in fact, is too near himself to possess greatness—one reason why the figure who remains remote and Olympian has a better chance of being adulated in Ireland than anywhere else. If an Irishman were made Pope, for instance, the nation's self-esteem would shoot to Himalayan heights; on the other hand, a national memory of the new Pope when "he had the arse out of his trousers" could destroy the Faith totally.

This case is not merely hypothetical. Consider the instance where the Irish did in fact produce, if not a Pope, at least the next best thing—an American president. The golden aura surrounding John Kennedy ought to have shielded him from Irish invective. His visit to Ireland in 1961 as president of the United States gave an almost mystical boost to every Irishman's self-confidence. Although the Kennedys had been away from Ireland for more than a hundred years, they were—and still are—thought of as Irishmen. (Anyone who bears an Irish name is thought of as an Irishman, irrespective of where he was born. As Peter O'Toole, paraphrasing Lord Macaulay, puts it, "Because a dog is born in a biscuit tin, that doesn't make him a biscuit." Dominic Behan even remembers cheering wildly for a black runner at the Olympic Games "simply because he had a name like O'Brien or MacNamara.") As Kennedy rode through the streets of Dublin the bitter centuries rolled away; the Gael at last had come into his own. (The name Kennedy, in fact, is of Norse origin.) Even an Irish peer, whose ancestors had enjoyed centuries of privilege by virtue of English domination, felt compelled to yell, "At long last, we don't feel like second-class citizens of the world." Yet even as the peasants took down pictures of Robert Emmet and Wolfe Tone from walls where they had hung for a century and replaced them with glossy photographs of the smiling American, setting them carefully beside pietistic replicas of the Sacred Heart and the Holy Father (and, it is rumored, lighting little red sanctuary lamps in front of them), a jest was already going the rounds. Weren't the Americans terrible eedjits at that? Didn't the United States Ambassador go down to the ancestral farm ahead of the visit, and didn't he find that there wasn't a bath or a toilet in the place, and didn't he have half the oul' house pulled inside out to make room for them, and then didn't they all find that that meant there was no place in which to hold the reception? And then didn't they decide to set up long tables in the haggard (hayshed and yard) and didn't that mean that everybody had to go out into the haggard to have their bite and their drop? And sure, didn't that mean that an oul' fellow invited along to the do and staggered by the extraordinary technological achievement of it all, turn to an English newspaperman and say, "Well, aren't the Americans the marvelous people, now? Aren't they desperately clever, don't you think? When you remember that we used to have to eat in the oul' house there and come out here into the haggard to pee, and how haven't we to come out here into the haggard to eat and go into the oul' house to pee?"

If Kennedy drew cheers because he was an "Irishman" who had made good, thereby raising every Irishman a little higher in his own estimation, nevertheless some still found it impossible to overlook the fact that one Irishman's rise is always at the expense of the rest. I listened to Dubliners chatting about him and his visit; most of the remakrs expressed pride, pleasure, and gratitude for his memory. And yet the idol had to be rocked: Wasn't he overrated all the same, don't you think? If the Kennedys had stayed in Ireland, sure would we ever even have heard of them? An Irish political figure put it more bluntly: "We've a dozen fellows here who're better men than any of the Kennedys, if you want the truth. I couldn't have seen Jack Kennedy as President of Ireland, could you? Mind you, I'm not trying to run him down. . . ."

It could be argued, of course, that much of this is no more than the skeptical Irish mind hard at work doing what it does best—pricking pomposity; that nearly all Irish digs are only sensible appreciations of the frailties of humanity, and that the Irish are a nation of satirists because there is so much in Ireland worth satirizing. The envy and resentment of another's success, too, might well be no worse than that in any closed society where ambition and frustration jostle each other. The character assassination only seems worse in Dublin, perhaps, because Irishmen often use words with such shattering effect.

Even the most rabid anti-Irish Irishman, however, usually agrees that Irishmen are generally loth to allow another Irishman to stew in his own juice. "The climber in Ireland can always guess what his neighbors are saying about him," Lynn Doyle, the comic novelist, once wrote. "But in the day of misfortune, he will never lack help—'Ah, sure, isn't he the decent craythure after all!' " To me it seems that secure in the knowledge that he himself is compassionate and surrounded by truly compassionate people, the Irishman feels safe in indulging his mockery and his desire to commit slander to his heart's content, partly because he knows that however strong the current, dry land is always within reach; partly because mockery, slander, and backbiting are not only defenses against the pretensions of the world and an attack, therefore, on the Devil, but an opportunity to exercise both his imagination and his tongue.

There is the story of the two Irishmen who, in the bad days of the Land War of the last century, decided to ambush a dastardly landlord by shooting him from behind a hedge. They waited and waited, until finally one said: "I wonder what's keeping him? He's late this evening." "He's late, surely," agreed the other; "I hope nothing's happened to him." This was the instinctive side of the Irish character speaking.

The Irishman's inner eye—his idealism, if you prefer—manifests itself also in what may look to strangers rather like a slapdash approach to life. "We're told life is real and life is earnest; but frankly, I don't think that's the way we want it," a Dubliner has admitted. Most Irishmen are aware that many things in Ireland are inadequate or wrong; but they often prefer them that way. The task of putting them right might entail the loss of something they regard as more precious—the easy and pleasant pace of their lives.

When a party of French fishermen recently put in at a small harbor in the Mizen peninsula, they expressed surprise that the local fishermen did not work harder; there was a small fortune to be made from the enormous crabs and lobsters walking the heavily mineral-impregnated seabed and the great shoals of fish. Why didn't big Sean Flynn work harder? "Sure, don't I get enough," answered Flynn, "and isn't enough enough?"

Recently, an American food-processing firm, considering opening a plant in Ireland, sent over a scout, who reported back, "The fields are small, the gates are narrow, the climate is damp, and the farmers are stupid." Most Irish farmers, though, contrasting their lot with the horrors of the consumer society, would prefer to make the gates even narrower. And anyway, the Irish ethic has never been the Protestant one—that hard work, designed to bring *material* rewards, is the true work of God. It is the Catholic one: that a man must sublimate his animal nature and needs to the spirit; that his existence has another and greater purpose.

In the short term, of course, this kind of thinking raises obstacles to progress in the industrial field. One foreign-owned factory making radio sets could not understand why a consignment of its products refused to work. They traced the fault back to an Irish employee who admitted putting two fiddling transistors in some sets and none in others. "Ah, sure, would you think little things like that would make any difference," he explained.

A professor of economics insists, "We *are* feckless—there is no question of it. We lack application, persistency, and thoroughness. It is the root of much of our troubles. It permeates all our thinking, and may be caused by the fact that we have lacked challenges and have been isolated." Sean O'Faolain once put it a little differently: "What Ireland needs is fewer geniuses and more men of just plain, simple talent."

In Kilkenny, the Scandinavian designer I mentioned earlier thought that Irish attitudes and skills would quickly change once the country's increasing wealth spilled over into higher living standards. "The Irish are unquestionably very intelligent, but they are not *trained* yet; that is, they are not trained in some of the skills considered elementary in my country. The whole tendency of Irish education is toward religion—toward the metaphysical and the abstract. Ireland is rich in argument and disputation and has many really clever people—but she's short of good plumbers and carpenters. The Irish mind, too, is often too optimistic. It thinks it's enough to imagine, say, the design for a beautiful carpet. If, by some miracle, you did get them to see the process through and produce a beautiful carpet, then you'd find there's no floor to lay it on. They are simply a little too relaxed about things. They don't seem to feel the need for *style*; for keeping things in order. Too much is slapdash and careless. They seem to have this feeling that things make themselves, that it's enough just to think of something, to envisage it, and that—hey presto!—it's there! Their minds leap forward in a single jump from an original idea to the completed version, without bothering about the stages in between. They have no interest in the drudgery that must come between—only in the vision. And when they have conceived one vision, then they simply want to think about another."

Of course, it is the persistent Irish vision, the vision of a Christian Utopia, that is the cause of many of the contradictions in the Irish nature. The ideal Ireland as envisaged by generations of Irish patriots and churchmen bears a strange resemblance to Tennyson's Camelot. A fraction of that ideal was revealed by Eamonn de Valera when he declared: "The Ireland which we have dreamed of would be the home of a people who valued material wealth only as a basis of right living . . . who . . . devoted their leisure to things of the spirit; a land whose countryside would be bright with cozy homesteads . . . with the romping of sturdy children, the contests of athletic youths, the laughter of comely maidens; whose firesides would be the forums for the wisdom of old age. It would, in a word, be the home of a people living the life that God desires men should live." "Dev's" Utopia hardly drew a chuckle. As an old 1916 rebel told me, "We all had this vision of a kind of holy, immaculate Ireland, of modest maidens dancing on the silver strands and manly boys playing hurley and white-haired holy men blessing everybody; even Mick Collins, who was as tough as they come, had this same vision."

It would be unfair to suggest that the patriots ignored all economic and material factors, for even that dreaming visionary, Patrick Pearse, who led the 1916 rebellion—and to an even greater extent, James Connolly, who went out with him—were inspired by the idea of improving the material lot of their countrymen. Yet Connolly was well aware that his fellow countrymen often tended to indulge in a brand of patriotism that never let itself be distracted by reality, and he denounced this tendency savagely. "The man who is bubbling over with love and enthusiasm for 'Ireland,' and can yet pass through our streets and witness all the wrong and suffering, the shame and degradation wrought upon the people of Ireland, aye, wrought by Irishmen upon Irishmen and Irishwomen, without burning to end it, is, in my opinion, a fraud and a liar in his heart."

Even Yeats, however, one of Ireland's three winners of the Nobel Prize for Literature (Shaw and Beckett are the others), although himself a Protestant Anglo-Irishman, could not help believing in some innate sublimity of the Celtic character. Indeed, his transcriptions of it played no mean part in the inspiration that finally led to Irish independence. To his eyes, the Irish were men "who believed so much in the soul and so little in anything else that they were never entirely certain that the earth was solid under their footsole."

This element in the Irish character helps in a small way to explain those riots at the Abbey Theatre that seem to foreigners who read of them now as little more than endearing displays of the Irishman's desire to "raise ructions," or like a whole nation of Victor MacLaglens, to get into a good fight. The real explanation is that the secret Ireland lying in the second Irish eye had been dragged in the dirt.

Ironically, it was Yeats himself who was first thumped with the shillelagh of indignation. Ireland, when he first began to write, was accustomed to a diet of "broth-of-a-boy" comedies such as Dion Boucicault's *The Shaughraun* and Victorian romantic operas like *The Lily of Killarney*. Irishmen had fallen head over heels in love with themselves as romantic, laughing vagabonds, outwitting evil with a light jest and rapier intelligence; Irishwomen melted at ill-fated lovers playing out a tragic destiny. Yeats' play, *Countess Cathleen,* first performed in 1899, harshly opened the door on reality. It hit the Irish with the same impact with which Osborne's *Look Back in Anger* struck postwar Britain. In England, however, there was an entrenched Establishment, which merely stiffened its upper lip and sniped back. In Ireland there was only a people sick to death with reality, who had been able to endure what it had endured largely because of its dreams. The last thing the Irish wanted was someone to tell them that their dreams were merely dreams and to rub their faces in reality—and they reacted with understandable hostility to Yeats's attempt to disabuse them of their illusions. "Revolting blasphemies" and "idiotic impieties" were some of the phrases hurled at *Cathleen* by the critics. Cardinal Logue—with an ineptitude that still distinguishes much of the Irish hierarchy—condemned the play without even seeing it or reading it, insisting that "no woman, countess or colleen, could ever sell her soul to the Devil—even to save Ireland." (Frank O'Connor has related a similar kind of story—of a young man who stood up during a play showing the patriot Wolfe Tone about to kill himself and sternly declared, "As a Catholic, I protest against what I consider a defense of suicide.") The visionary Ireland, it became clear, was meant to be not just Celtic Ireland, but Celtic Catholic Ireland.

The first performances of J. M. Synge's *Playboy of the Western World* at the Abbey also were marked by riots. There were fights inside and outside the theatre, and five hundred police were inadequate to keep the peace. Synge, an Anglo-Irishman, was accused by the "Holy Irelanders" of "patronizing inaccuracies"; Irishmen, it was argued, did not use the word *bloody* or make public reference to female undergarments. On the second night, the play was interrupted by boos, hoots, whistles, trumpets, and hisses, and yells of "Kill the author!"

If the native Holy Irelanders were bad, the expatriates proved a good deal worse. When the play first opened in America, unsuccessful attempts were made to boycott it. Nationalist reviewers pleaded "for the true, old ideals of Ireland as the only remedy against this insidious horror: 'Brothers and Sisters, everywhere, place a little history of Ireland in the hands of each little boy and little girl of the ancient race, and all the Lady Gregorys in the world will not be able to destroy an atom of our splendid heritage!' " In New York, one performance was half-wrecked by an audience that left a collection of missiles, "chiefly stink-pots and rosaries." In Philadelphia, a slice of currant cake hit the actor Arthur Sinclair. When the company reached Chicago, a letter awaited Lady Augusta Gregory, one of the founders of the Abbey Theatre, telling her that her doom was sealed and bringing the point home by a drawing showing a gun, coffin, nails, and hammer. Augusta's only comment was: "I don't think from the drawing that the sender has much practical knowledge of firearms."

Yeats described his American tour as the battle of the "true Ireland fighting the false." Today's Irishmen would regard this as ingenuous—after all, which or what is the "true Ireland"? Yeats, perhaps, was thinking of Ireland as she once had been and as she might become. But with patrician nonchalance, he dismissed the legacy of resentment felt by the larger proportion of the Irish. At the nadir of their fortunes, after all, the Irish had been held together by two mystically-based influences. One was the Catholic Church, which—to the regret of many modern Irishmen—became so intermingled with the fortunes of Irish nationalism that an attack upon one largely became an attack on the other. The other was that old vision of a beautiful, suffering Ireland, embodied in poetic images limned from the mists of time and kept magnificently alive in the dark centuries—an Ireland of matchless perfection, personified in the name *Dark Rosaleen,* or *Kathleen,* the haunted daughter of Houlihan:

Think her not a ghastly hag, too hideous to be seen,
Call her not unseemly names, our matchless Kathaleen,
Young she is, and fair she is, and would be crowned
a queen.

By 1926 an unquenchable passion had earned for Ireland the independence of all but six of her thirty-two counties. By then, however, the visions and poems that had lit the fires of rebellion were passé. New circumstances posed new problems or demanded new solutions to old problems. It was a time, in fact, for a new style of Irish writing and a new direction in political thought. Ireland, however, rejected both.

From the days of Swift, Irish literature in English had been the prerogative of the rich. Now, suddenly, out of the Dublin slums came a new Irish voice. Not that of the old aristocratic Gaelic Ireland; nor of lost, betrayed, and downtrodden rural Ireland; nor of Anglo-Ireland. This time it was the voice of the urbanized poor. O'Casey had no patience with the mystic, idealized rural world of Yeats and Synge and their beautiful verse cadences, nor with the politics of the middle-class Irish who had fought for the revolution and had won independence. His people were the "real" people of the Dublin slums, talking about their "real" sorrows and their "real" problems. Here, and with a vengeance, was yet another "true" Ireland—with every back-street biddy mouthing blank verse and every workingman playing his own Charlie Chaplin. But, like everyone who had ever attempted to show "the true Ireland," O'Casey ran into trouble. *Juno and the Paycock* had to be bowdlerized before Cork could see it. A key speech was cut entirely, to keep the public from being told that an Irish girl had been seduced. Undeterred, O'Casey, with *The Plough and the Stars,* broke all the *geises.* He attacked a trinity of sacred cows—religion, sexual mores, and patriotism. He portrayed the women of the tenements rather than the dead patriots as the real "victims" of "The Troubles"; he showed an Irish girl as a prostitute; he unfurled the national flag in a pub! Was nothing sacred?

In his *Story of the Abbey Theatre,* Peter Kavanagh characterizes those who assailed the company as part of the "world-wide army of philistines . . . . They resemble most closely those who today take part in the St. Patrick's Day parades in American cities—who imagine Ireland to be as green and level as a lawn, where the girls go round with their eyes cast down, green garlands in their hair, and Rosaries at their girdles, while the men, armed only with shillelaghs, beat heavily armed battalions of British soldiers." Nevertheless, this was the impossible dream that had brought the impossible result; and to shatter the looking-glass so violently was to leave Alice bewildered. O'Casey's scorching diabtribes were a bludgeon to a raw wound, and the reception they received has to be seen in that light.

The play opened on February 8, 1926, but it was not until the fourth night that the actual rioting began. Then, from the second act onward, the words of the actors were drowned by shouting, booing, whistling, and singing. During the third act there was total chassis. Chairs, shoes, rotten tomatoes, apples, and eggs were all hurled onto the stage. Stink bombs were set off, and finally a mob clambered onto the stage and began fighting the actors. Barry Fitzgerald, playing Fluther Good, uppercut one man into the orchestra pit before the curtain was run down. After the police had finally restored order, Yeats strode out from the wings and made his famous speech. It was patronizing and authoritarian in the extreme. "You have disgraced yourselves again! Is this to be an ever-recurring celebration of the arrival of Irish genius? Synge first and now O'Casey . . . Dublin has once more rocked the cradle of genius. From such a scene in this theatre went forth the fame of Synge. Equally the fame of O'Casey is born here tonight. This is his apotheosis!" Years later, O'Casey commented, "I'd no idea what 'apotheosis' meant—until I looked it up in the dictionary—but it sounded grand!"

XIII

THE GIFT OF THE GAB

AQUA VITAE

The soile of Ireland is very low and waterish, including diverse little islands, invironed with lakes and marrish. Highest hills have standing pooles in their tops. Inhabitants especially new come, are subject to distillations, rheumes and fleures. For remedie whereof, they use an ordinarie drinke of Aqua Vitae, being so qualified in the making, that it drieth more and also inflameth lesse than other hot confections doo.

One Theoricus wrote a proper treatise of Aqua Vitae wherein he praiseth it unto the ninth degree.

Being moderatlie taken, saith he, it sloweth age, it strengthneth youth, it helpeth digestion, it cutteth flegme, it abandoneth melancholie, it relisheth the heart, it lighteneth the mind, it quickeneth the spirits, it cureth the hydropsie, it healeth the strangurie, it pounceth the stone, it expelleth grauell, it puffeth away all ventositie, it keepeth and preserueth the head from whirling, the eies from dazeling, the toong from lisping, the mouth from maffling, the teeth from chattering, and the throte from ratling; it keepeth the weasan from stifling, the stomach from wambling, and the heart from swelling, the bellie from wirtching, the guts from rumbling, the hands from shivering and the sinewes from shrinking, the veines from crumpling, the bones from aking and the marrow from soaking.

Vistadius also ascribeth thereto a singular praise, and would have it to burne being kindled, which he taketh to be a token to know the goodness thereof. And trulie it is a sovereigne liquor, if it be orderlie taken.

RICHARD STANIHURST, *1586*

The Irish do too much talking. "Everything drains away in talk," declares Lord Longford.

"And the trouble is you can't get a word in edgeways," complains an exasperated American woman now resident in Dublin. "Polite conversation as we know it, simply doesn't exist. Everybody wants to hold the floor."

This view is confirmed by J. P. Donleavy, author of *The Ginger Man.* "People consciously get on a stage and take on starring roles before their curtain is lowered with a bottle to the back of the skull. They turn conversation into a combination of insult and rumour, laced liberally with lies. I often myself say it's famous for producing writers, etc., but the writers are failed talkers and people who can't stand on their own in the pubs and who are hurt and emotionally bruised and sneak away somewhere from the ridicule to write and get their revenge. In Dublin, you get shut up by the wit and the insult. My own good American manners were far too gentle for Dublin; I generally broke somebody's face with a lightning right hook from the hip but said little."

"There are Irishmen who will do anything just to get in an extra word–just to hold the floor for a *second* longer," insists Dominic Behan. "I remember in one of my plays we had an old fellow who was supposed to come on and say 'I'm down!' On he walked. 'Ah, Jaysus, I'm down!' he bawled. 'Cut, cut!' yelled the producer. 'Don't you know you can't say that–that's blasphemous!' 'What'll I say, then?' he demanded. 'Say anything you like, but no blasphemy,' shouted the producer. So on he comes again. 'Lord suffering ducks, I'm down!' he roared. 'Cut, cut!' yelled the producer. 'shorten it, shorten it. Say it any way you like, but just say 'I'm down!' Well, we rehearsed for five weeks and that's all he had to say. But on the first night he came out. Did he stick to the script? What do you think? 'Ah, J, I'm down!' he bellowed–then as he came off, he flung me a defiant 'Well, I bloody well *hardened* the part, didn't I?' "

In V. S. Pritchett's view, the incorrigible Irish talker is "an exhausting professional of whom a little is a pleasure," and Pritchett records how Augustus John, who enjoyed "a little of" the Dublin wit Gogarty, once threw a dish of peanuts in his face to shut him up.

There is no unanimity about Irish talk. "Listening to Dublin talk today can be a disillusioning experience," says Brian Inglis. "The talent is for that kind of contrived improvisation shared by dozens of hack scriptwriters for films and radio–an ability to make intellectual puns not substantially different from those which, when we made them as schoolboys, got groans and pinches." Despite his skepticism, Inglis still maintains that conversation in Dublin "usually is better at every level than it is anywhere else." Less sympathetic was George Bernard Shaw, who dismissed Dublin talk as "silly Dublin persiflage!"

In recent years, Shaw's low estimate of Irish conversation has reappeared in a new form. The shyness of many Irishmen, along with inarticulateness and lack of self-confidence, have begun to worry educators. Today, young Irishmen often prove to be noticeably less talkative than Englishmen or Americans. When Irish television began, there was general astonishment at the large number of stammering, hesitant, introverted people in the population. 'I'll give you two absolutely genuine examples of true Irish conversation," Dominic Behan says. "A man married another man's daughter and they didn't meet again until a year after the wedding on a fair day, when they had a pint together. 'How is Mary?' asked the father. The husband didn't answer for a minute or two. 'Ah, she's hard on shoes,' he said finally. And that's all they said. In the second case, a stranger walked into a man's house, where there was a big skillet of sausages on the fire. The stranger sat down after the usual 'God save all here,' drew up a chair, and stared into the fire. Himself just nodded. Then the stranger helped himself to a sausage and the two men stared into the fire together. Again the stranger got up and helped himself to a sausage and then a glass of whiskey. Finally, after about an hour, he got up to go. Not a word had passed between them. He halted in the doorway for moment, then said, 'Ah, the oul' country's never been the same since de Valera' and walked off."

Edward Delaney, son of a Mayo farmer, declares, "They talk about the peace of mind of rural Ireland. What they're really talking about is the lack of mind."

It is almost impossible to square these strictures with the undoubted fact that there *appears* to be a constant flow of talk in Ireland. Patrick Murphy says of the talk in the Mizen peninsula: "There's imagery, imagination, and vividness in most of it. The other day I was in the grocer's when an old lady came in to buy bacon. The grocer explained he hadn't a whole piece—which is the way they like it around here—but would cut rashers do? 'No!' she exclaimed 'You cut them so thin you can still taste the knife!' Another old fellow, after a glass of poteen, declared, 'Yerrah, after a sup of that, you could have operated on me and I'd have cheered you on!' "

Few people, indeed, visit Ireland without being impressed, if not with the quality of the conversation or the memorable character of the wit, at least with the quickness of the Irish tongue and its "odd twist." The wit, in fact, even if it does not always live up to the definition of real Irish wit as "essentially spontaneous with a touch of malice in it," lurks everywhere. A lady trying to cross a Dublin street against busy traffic got as far as the policeman directing it. "I'll be safer here in the middle with you, officer, I think," she gasped. "Ah, ma'am, that's so, but remember that with me you'll only be middlin' safe." A motorist inquired if the road ahead was rough, to which the local replied, "Well, it's not the sort of road I'd like to have to praise." Another tourist, trying to find out which was the better of two hotels in a town, was advised, "Well, it's like this—whichever one you stay at, you'll wish it had been the other."

Recorded Irish wit mainly dates from the eighteenth century because the wits then began speaking or writing in English instead of Gaelic, although long before MacCarthy More's beguiling words had inspired Queen Elizabeth to coin the word *blarney,* we hear of the great Irish-Norman, Gerald, Earl of Kildare, apologizing to Henry VII for burning down Cashel Cathedral by mistake: "I thought the Archbishop was inside," he explained. An English official wrote Henry VIII from Dublin warning him: "Sire, the Irish hath most pregnant, subtle wits."

It was the Irish legal profession of the late eighteenth and early nineteenth centuries, however, that was largely responsible for earning the Irish their reputation for wit and eloquence. Irish court records of this period are unique in their humor, passion, and grotesquerie. With the exception of Edmund Burke, all the great talkers of the time were barristers—Grattan, Flood, Curran, O'Connell. They were fortunate, in a sense, in practicing during an age when it was hard to keep Irishmen out of court, either as plaintiffs, defendants, witnesses, judges, barristers, or even mere spectators. The lawyers themselves were histrionic enough; yet they were more than matched by the procession of individuals who took the stand to lie, bluff, and perjure themselves. The very idea of courts of justice at a time when the majority of Irishmen were suffering massive national injustice clearly lay at the root of the disrespect the Irish felt for their courts. There were other reasons, too, among them the disturbed nature of rural Ireland and even the incorrigible need of many Irishmen to indulge their sense of the dramatic. "Irish courts," explains a Dublin barrister, "became arenas for really crucial battles of wits, in which the most usual casualty was justice."

One judge, the Earl of Norbury, has been described as "capering about the records of Irish law as a grotesque whose antics would have been comic had their effects not been so tragic." When passing sentence of death on a prisoner found guilty of stealing a watch, he remarked, "My good fellow, you made a grasp at Time, but egad! you caught Eternity." Once, when the famous lawyer John Philpot Curran was addressing Norbury in court, an ass brayed outside the window. "One at a time, please, Mr. Curran," pleaded Norbury.

A contemporary description of Norbury's courtroom presents an incredible picture. Norbury often dropped all pretense of impartiality and rushed to the aid of a witness wilting under cross-examination. This would at once put both counsel on their mettle, and soon the courtroom would become "a chaos of noisy sophistries, and dogmatic assertions, and contradictions, and points of law and universal wrangling all swelling to a roar." The bellowings of Norbury, "puffing and blowing, and with an apoplectic hue empurpling his distended visage, would then be heard over the whole Babel din." Norbury would finally "throw open his robes, perhaps fling off his wig and stand up, and pour forth an outlandish, unconnected jumble of anecdotes of his early life—jokes, quotations . . . sarcasms against the defendant's counsel; and possibly a few allusions to trial incidents."

Norbury was only one of several characters adorning the Irish bench at this period. There was Judge Boyd, so fond of brandy that he kept his inkstand filled with it. "His Lordship used to lean his arms upon the desk, bob down his head, and steal a hurried sip from time to time through a quill that lay among the pens, which manoeuvre he flattered himself escaped observation." One day, however, he made the mistake of harrying a witness too forcefully: "Come, now, my good man, it is a very important consideration—tell the court truly, were you drunk or were you sober upon that occasion?" "Oh, quite sober, my lord," interrupted the witness's counsel. Then, glancing significantly at the inkstand: "as sober—as a judge!"

Trickery involving the finer points of the verbal art and the innate paradoxicalness of the Irish mind was developed to a fine art in these courts. Daniel O'Connell had an intuitive grasp of the devious workings of the Irish mind. Retained in an inheritance case by clients who insisted that the will had been forged, O'Connell ran up against a string of witnesses who swore that the deceased had signed the will while "life was in him." The constant repetition of this phrase led O'Connell to smell a rat. "On the virtue of your oath, was the man alive?" he demanded of one witness who had parried every question with this phrase. "By virtue of my oath, *the life was in him!*" repeated the witness. "Now!" thundered the advocate, "I call on you in the presence of your Maker who will one day pass sentence on you for this evidence; I solemnly ask—and answer me at your peril—was there not a live fly in the dead man's mouth when his hand was placed on the will?" At once, the witness broke down and confessed.

On another occasion, a lawyer was puzzled when a client insisted upon thanking him profusely for successfully defending him in a case where the client had been sued for nonpayment of a bullock he was alleged to have bought at a fair. The defense was that the money had been paid in notes in a pub, and several witnesses had attested to this fact. "Oh, it was a fairly simple case," protested the lawyer modestly.

"Begob, you're mistaken all right; there wasn't a word of truth spoken in court that day." He then explained that he and the plaintiff had fought some years before over the price of a beast, and knowing that the man was out to get him, had made up the whole story. He was never even at the fair; nor was the plaintiff.

"Am I to understand that there was no beast, no bargain, no sale, no payment, in fact no transaction at all?" demanded the lawyer.

"That's right."

"Then why didn't you say so in court?"

"Because I knew he'd call a flock of blackguards to say I bought the beast from him at the fair and didn't pay for it. And I knew that if I was the only one to say that there wasn't even a beast in the first place that nobody would believe me. So I got a few decent men to say that they'd seen me pay the money."

This particular ploy was only a variant of the famous Tipperary Alibi, a procedure devised in that country whereby witnesses would come forward to swear that the prosecution's star witness was never even at the scene of the crime. The Tipperary Alibi itself was again merely a simplified version of the even more famous Kerry Alibi. Kerrymen had discovered that phony alibis usually failed because at some point or another a good lawyer could trap a witness into contradicting the others. So they worked out a foolproof method. Every witness told the complete truth about the accused's movements–except that they described events that had taken place on an entirely different day.

Irish juries, of course, were notoriously perverse, and many of their judgments were quite unpredictable–according to law. Once, when a Limerick jury discharged a man who was obviously guilty, the judge summed up judicial feelings about Irish juries by declaring: "Prisoner at the bar, you have now been found not guilty by the verdict of twelve of your fellow countrymen of the atrocious offenses upon which you have been tried. Upon that verdict I do not propose to comment other than to observe that it compels me to direct your release from custody. You are, therefore, at liberty to leave the dock and take your place in society with no other stain upon your character than that you have been acquitted by a Limerick jury."

High-flown oratory, of course, was an essential weapon in the armory of counsel, for Irish juries were more easily swayed by rhetoric and histrionics than by facts. The importance of oratory was never better demonstrated than in the case of the widow Wilkins. The widow had been a great beauty in her day; her husband, Surgeon-Major Wilkins, had died in the arms of General Wolfe after the British had stormed the Heights of Abraham to capture Quebec–and Canada–from the French. She was sixty-five when she suddenly found herself the object of passionate admiration by a twenty-three-year-old naval lieutenant named Peter Blake.

The lieutenant was living on half-pay at the time, and marriage was discussed. The widow, however, soon realized what was going on, and her solicitors wrote Blake in strong terms. He replied by suing for breach of promise, claiming £500 damages.

The widow's counsel, "silver-tongued Phillips," decided the best defense was to laugh the case out of court. Defying etiquette, he decided to poke fun at his own client. "How vainglorious is the boast of beauty!" he began. "How misapprehended have been the claims of youth, if years and wrinkles can thus despoil their conquests and depopulate the navy of its prowess and beguile the bar of its eloquence! How mistaken were all the amatory poets, from Anacreon downward, who preferred the bloom of the rose and the trill of the nightingale to the saffron hide and dulcet treble of sixty-five! Oh, gentlemen, fancy what he has lost—if it were but the blessed raptures of the bridal night! Do not suppose I am going to describe it; I shall leave it to the learned counsel he has selected to compose his epithalamium. I shall not exhibit the venerable trembler—at once a relic and a relict, with a grace for every year and a Cupid for every wrinkle—affecting to shrink from the flame of his impatience and fanning it with the ambrosial sighs of sixty-five!"

Phillips finished a long address in this style by declaring: "For the gratification of his avarice, he was content to embrace age, disease, infirmity, and widowhood, to bend his youthful passions to the carcase for which the grave was opening—to feed, by anticipation, on the uncold corpse, and cheat the worm of its reversionary corruption. Born in a country ardent to a fault, he advertised his happiness to the highest bidder, and he now solicits an honourable jury to become the panders to this heartless cupidity. Nothing less than your verdict will satisfy me. By that verdict, you will sustain the dignity of your sex—by that verdict you will uphold the honour of the national character."

The jury found for the widow without even retiring. The denouement, however, was yet to come. As the triumphant Phillips left the courtroom amid the congratulations of his colleagues and spectators he was suddenly faced by his furious client who, armed with a hunting crop, belabored him all the way to his lodgings.

At the close of the eighteenth and the beginning of the nineteenth centuries Ireland was perhaps the most anarchic society ever to have existed in civilized Europe. Secret societies committed one agrarian outrage after another in the impoverished countryside; Orangemen fought Catholics; highwaymen held up travelers on the roads; bucks and pinkindindies strutted and bullied their way round Dublin; lawyers, judges, and members of Parliament "blazed away" at each other upon any or no pretext; spies and informers plied their trade everywhere; and the poor drank themselves into insensibility. One explanation often advanced for the existence of such a riotous society was the total cleavage in the social structure. On one hand were partisans of the Ascendancy who behaved like a lawless garrison; they had come into Ireland by violence and were aware they would be flung out again by violence, and as a result they became "chronically restless and turbulent." On the other were the Catholics of Ireland who had developed a high sensitivity to insult and were ready at the drop of a hat to assert themselves and their ancient pride. Smarting under defeat, they sought "to prove themselves brave by engaging in any and every eccentric and irregular adventure."

Inevitably, even the language spoken in Ireland tended to the grotesque. This was especially true of some scions of the old aristocracy, who tended to shut themselves up in their castles or great houses and to avoid almost all human contact. They were too proud to talk to the ordinary Irish Catholic peasant, too contemptuous to speak to the new Protestant "aristocracy." All had been educated abroad and thus spoke French, Spanish, and German, which they mingled with a smattering of English and their own Gaelic to produce a conglomerate language "unintelligible to the rest of mankind." A similar jargon was spoken by officers of the famed Irish Brigades who served continental monarchs. In his *Reminiscences,* Michael Kelly, the friend of Mozart, gives an example of this Irish forerunner of Esperanto: "Walking on the parade the second morning of my arrival in Cork, Mr. Townsend . . . pointed out a very finelooking elderly gentleman . . . and told me he was one of the most eccentric men in the world. His name was O'Reilly; he had served many years in the Irish Brigade in Germany and Prussia, . . . 'We reckon him here a great epicure, and he piques himself on being a great judge of the culinary art as well of wines,' explained Townsend. 'He speaks French, German, and Italian and constantly, while speaking English with a determined Irish brogue, mixes all those languages in every sentence. It is immaterial to him whether the person he is talking to understands him or not—on he goes, stop him who can?' No sooner was Kelly introduced than O'Reilly began: 'Bon jour, my cher Mick! Je suis bien sise de vous voir, as we say in France. An bhfhuil tu go maith. J'etois faché that I missed seeing you when I was last in Dublin; but I was obliged to go to the county Galway to see a brother-officer who formerly served with me in Germany—as herlick ein Kerl, as we say in Germany, as ever smelt gunpowder. Dair mo laimh—Il est brave comme son épeé. Now tell me how go on your brother Joe and your brother Mark; your brother Pat, poor fellow! Lost his life, I know, in the East Indies—but c'est la fortune de la guerre and he died avec l'honneur. Your sister, Mary, too—how is she? Dair a marreann; by my word, she is as good-hearted, kind creature as ever lived; but entre nous, soit dit, she is rather plain, ma non e bella, quel ch'e bella, e bella quel che piace, as we say in Italian.' "

Words poured forth like a torrent everywhere. In the Parliament House, that persistent perpetrator of Irish bulls, Sir Boyle Roche, mixed his metaphors to rapturous acclaim; he talked of "smelling a rat; yeah, even seeing it float in the air," but he had "successfully nippped it in the bud." In a debate on the dangers arising from the French Revolution, he announced, "Here, perhaps, sir, the murderous Marshall-law [Marseilles] men would break in, cut us to mincemeat, and throw our bleeding heads upon that table to stare us in the face." (Sir Boyle's mixed metaphors were perhaps not equaled again until over a century later when Tommy Henderson, a member of the Belfast Parliament, won renown by declaring: "A light has been lit this day which will shine through the world–a light, I hope, that will lead us towards the day when we shall see the Lion of Progress marching down Royal Avenue, hand in hand with the floodgates of Democracy." On yet another occasion Henderson declared: "If nothing is done to stop the advance of the bureaucracy of the Northern Ireland Transport Board, we shall find ourselves immersed in the testicles of an octopus.")

"The curse of good conversation," laments V. S. Pritchett, following a stay in Ireland, "is that it must evaporate." An American journalist recently described how a Dublin professor kept him entranced for a whole evening with a conversational *tour de force*; then, when he staggered away stunned, he could not remember a single word. It has been said of Brendan Behan that he poured away enough plays and novels to last for years in a single wild evening's talk in a Dublin pub. Unfortunately, nobody has ever recorded more than a fraction of the verbal saturnalia that seems to be continually celebrated in the Irish capital, to wing more than the odd epigram as it flees into the empyrean.

The best Dublin talk, of course, has been always more than the quip, pun, or wisecrack that Groucho Marx, for instance, made familiar to mass audiences. At the turn of the century, conversation was in full spate in Dublin–"the rich Dublin talk that astonished London when it was first heard on the lips of Wilde." The capital of an island where, seemingly, time had been abolished, Dublin had become a town where, as Oliver St. John Gogarty put it, "every man is a potential idler, poet or friend!" The Countess of Fingall told Gogarty's biographer, "I cannot count the wits and storytellers of those days; you used to see men buttonholing one another at street corners in Dublin to tell stories, and roaring with laughter over them." Within the tiny circle of intellectual life swirled such figures as Oscar Wilde, James Joyce, W. B. Yeats, J. M. Synge, George Moore, George

Russell (AE), Gogarty, Tim Healy, Fitzgerald the physicist, Joly the scientist, Salmon the mathematician, the historian J. B. Bury, the Hegelian expert Macran, the classicists Palmer and Tyrell, the critic Dowden, and John Pentland Mahaffy, Provost of Trinity College.

Of these, Mahaffy is said to have been the greatest conversationalist. Sir Shane Leslie, Winston Churchill's cousin, once wrote: "Until you heard Mahaffy talk you hadn't realized how language could be used to charm and hypnotize. With this gift, there were no doors which could not be opened, no society which was proof against its astonishing effect. Kings and queens, famous men and beautiful women, all must come under its powerful and compelling spell." Mahaffy's verbal splendors were such that he became a regular guest of the Kaiser and a close friend of the Queen of Spain. Wilde hailed him "as a really great talker, an artist in vivid words and eloquent phrases" and as "my first and last teacher" (Mahaffy taught Wilde in the seventies). The two toured Greece together, where Wilde is said to have learned the art of conversation from The Master, who later himself wrote a book called *Art of Conversation.* Mahaffy's epigrams and aphorisms have been largely devalued by time, overexposure, and imitation, yet many are still quotable. Once, when an advocate of women's rights demanded fiercely, "Well, what *is* the difference between a man and a woman?" Mahaffy said mildly, "I can't conceive."

But Mahaffy by no means had a monopoly on good talk. The scholar Tyrell once was refused a drink in a temperance hotel, prompting him to announce to the proprietor: "There's no such thing as a temperance hotel. You might as well talk of a celibate brothel." When a rude fellow interrupted him to ask the way to the lavatory, Tyrell said airily, "The first door on the right marked 'gentlemen'—but don't let that deter you."

Or this from Yeats, when he was asked for view of a colleague: "The worst thing about him is that when he is not drunk, he's sober."

Gogarty has left us an imperishable picture of the kind of antics that often accompanied the small, intimate dinner parties of the period. Sir Thornley Stoker, the surgeon, and brother of the author of *Dracula,* once invited Moore, Augustine Birrell, the litterateur who was then Irish Chief Secretary, and Gogarty to dinner.

> In the midst of it all, the mahogany door burst open, and a nude and elderly lady came in with a cry, 'I like a little intelligent conversation!' She ran round the table. We all stood up. She was followed by two female attendants, who seized whatever napery was available, and sheltering her with this and their own bodies, led her forth screaming from the room.
>
> After a long and embarrassed silence, Sir Thornley asked the company to seat themselves. Then he said,

> "Gentlemen, under my mahogany, I hope you will keep this incident, mortifying as it is to me, from any rumour of scandal in this most gossipy of towns. And now, Moore, I conjure you most particularly, as you are the only one who causes me grave misgivings."
>
> "But it was charming, Sir Thornley. I demand an encore," declared Moore, which led to his immediate ejection.

Gogarty himself considered another wit, Jimmy Montgomery, "the greatest Dubliner of them all." One day, as they walked through Dublin Montgomery's wife reminded him that it was their twenty-third wedding anniversary and what did he propose? "Three minutes silence," replied Montgomery. On being appointed Irish film censor, a tricky job in Catholic Ireland, he declared, "I'm between the Devil and the Holy See," adding that his job was to prevent "the Californication of Ireland." On his deathbed, surrounded by a solicitous family, a friend gently asked how he was. "Hovering between wife and death," he replied weakly,

Sadly, there are few notable wits around Dublin nowadays. The closest thing to a witty remark ever attributed to President de Valera was when he once said, "I have no capacity for saying witty things. It is a fatal gift." Nevertheless, the chatter and malice continue. When Sean T. O'Kelly, a diminutive man, was elected President, the joke was "Don't mow the lawn today—the President's out walking." Sadly, too, Dail Eireann (Irish Parliament) has now earned itself a reputation for dullness and a marked lack of sparkling repartee. Memorable remarks are few and far between, and the debates are invariably turgid. Almost the last notable passage was when a TD (member of the Dail) rose and asked the Speaker if it were in order to call a fellow-deputy a sewer rat. "Certainly not!" ruled the Speaker indignantly. "Thank you," said the inquirer blandly. "The sewer rats will be grateful for that ruling."

It is impossible to leave the subject of Irish eloquence, however, without a poignant note; for despite the frivolity and the roistering, a cloud of melancholy has always hung over the Irish. For a century and more, Irish youth found sustenance and hope in the despairing, impassioned speeches from the dock of other young men who had laid down their lives for Ireland. None, perhaps, has the haunting yet hopeful quality that marks the last words of Robert Emmet, the Irish patriot who died on the gallows in 1803:

> My lords, you are impatient for the sacrifice—the blood which you seek is not congealed by the artificial terrors that surround your victim, it circulates warmly and

unruffled through the channels which God created for nobler purposes, but which you are bent to destroy, for purposes so grievous that they cry to heaven. Be ye patient! I have but a few words more to say. I am going to my cold and silent grave—my lamp of life is nearly extinguished—my race is run—the grave opens to receive me, and I sink into its bosom! I have but one request to ask at my departure from this world; it is the charity of its silence! Let no man write my epitaph; for as no man who knows my motives dare now vindicate them, let not prejudice or ignorance asperse them. Let them and me repose in obscurity and peace, and my tomb remain uninscribed, until other times and other men can do justice to my character. When my country takes her place among the nations of the earth, then, and not till then, let my epitaph be written. I have done!

XIV

SODOM AND BEGORRAH

For thee I shall not die,
Woman high of fame and name,
Foolish men thou mayest slay,
I and they are not the same.

Why should I expire
For the fire of any eye
Slender waist or swan-like limb,
Is it for them that I should die?

The round breasts, the fresh skin,
Cheeks crimson, hair like silk to touch,
Indeed, indeed, I shall not die,
Please God, not I, for any such!

The golden locks, the forehead thin,
The quiet mien, the gracious ease,
The rounded heel, the languid tone,
Fools alone find death from these.

Thy sharp wit, thy perfect calm,
Thy thin palm like foam of the sea;
Thy white neck, thy blue eye,
I shall not die for thee.

Woman, graceful as a swan
A wise man did rear me, too,
Little palm, white neck, bright eye,
I shall not die for you.

ANON., *thirteenth-seventeenth centuries,*
Translated from the Gaelic by
DR. DOUGLAS HYDE

Drink and sex, of course, are widely held to be two of Ireland's greatest problems: too much of one, too little of the other. Visitors, often shocked by the proliferation of licensed premises, are not helped by the remarks sometimes made by Dubliners. "This is the only place in the world where a man will climb over ten naked women to get at a bottle of stout"; "A Dublin queer is a man who prefers women to drink"; "Of course, we're interested in sex—outside pub opening hours." Nor by the comments of Irishwomen: "The men are interested in drink, horses, and women—in that order." Nor, indeed, by the remarks of American writers such as Paul Blanshard, who has written: "In terms of total harm to the community, drunkenness is the most serious Irish crime—but few Irishmen think of it as a crime."

Drinking, drunkenness, conviviality, horses, and sex all certainly interact one with the other in Irish society. *The Practitioner,* a medical journal, has reported that alcoholism accounts for one-quarter of all first admissions to psychiatric hospitals in Dublin and therefore constitutes a major health problem. In one year, 139 men and 30 women were admitted to public and private hospitals—a rate of 34 per 100,000, which for men was twice as high as that of Scotland and twelve times higher than that of England or Wales.

Such statistics, however, can hardly be taken at face value where Ireland is concerned, for it is, as I've already said, a pendulum country. Dublin medical men and other investigators confirm that it is mainly a small hard core of "vocational drunkards" who are the problem. And against this statistic must be put another: The Pioneer Total Abstinence Society claims a membership of 400,000, one-seventh of the total population (including women, children, and the aged)—surely one of the highest percentages of voluntary nondrinkers in the world. The annual figures of liquor consumption, too, show that *on average* the Irishman drinks less than the Russian, American, Briton, or Swede.

SPIRITS	
U.S.A.	2.29 gallons
Russia	2 gallons (of vodka alone)
Sweden	2 gallons
Britain	0.33 gallons
Ireland	0.33 gallons

BEER	
U.S.A.	26.27 gallons
Russia	No figures
Sweden	52 gallons (of near beer)
Britain	25.5 gallons
Ireland	12.5 gallons

Obviously, some Irishmen drink while others are relatively abstemious. In the truly desperate conditions of the eighteenth and nineteenth centuries, Irish drunkenness once reached alarming proportions. The response, however, to Father Matthew's Temperance Crusade in the 1840s was admirable (spirits consumption alone was halved), and Irishmen on the whole have been careful about drink ever since. Drunkenness is rarely considered a crime (except by the authorities) because most Irishmen realize it is partly a legacy of the "bad times" and partly a result of the stiff economic problems many Irishmen still face.

Since the 1960s the economic picture overall for Irishmen has brightened, and if Japanese businessmen move in in great numbers, as they threaten to, the whole Irish economy could "take off." As it is, along with the better living standards, Irishmen and women are progressing toward a more social or moderate form of drinking. Once, respectable women were never seen in pubs; now—escorted, of course—almost as many women as men are seen in the lounge bars of Dublin, Cork, Limerick, and other towns, where one finds little to indicate that one is still not in London's West End. It is in the towns, of course, where the consistent drinking is done. The rural community rarely drinks at home, and then usually only at weddings, wakes, or when special visitors arrive. Fair Day is another matter; but a farmer usually attends a fair only when he has business to transact, and there may be intervals of weeks or even months before he gets the chance to almost literally stiffen himself.

American psychologists have described the tendency of some Irishmen to drink too much as a method of drowning their normal pyschic conflicts. The inference is that drink is a substitute for sex. Well, of course, sexual problems are as likely to be the reason for one man's drinking habits as an inability to pay the electricity bill another's. Demonstrably, it is not always sex that is the problem; the late Brendan Behan, "who had a mouth on him" if ever anyone had, was a happily married man. Many of Dublin's steadiest drinkers are observably well supplied with feminine company. Nevertheless, there is something suspicious about a society that combines heavy drinking, late marriages (Ireland still tops the world in this), and a low rate of illegitimacy in a country where contraceptives are not on sale.

To deal with illegitimacy first: On average there are only 1,100 illegitimate births in Ireland every year—a third of the British rate and the lowest in Europe. It has been alleged that these figures are artificial, because unmarried pregnant girls skip to England. Certainly, in one year alone more than 700 illegitimate were born among the 172,493 emigrant, Irish-born population of London; but investigations by journalists and welfare agencies show that most Irish pregnancies there are the result of conduct in London. A Dublin journalist found that "the consequences of St. Patrick's Night dances produce a demonstrable peak in the graph of the year's illegitimacy." In the hard and lonely world of the big city, essentially naïve and unskilled boys and girls grab for solace and consolation where they can.

The "sex problem" in Ireland itself is another kettle of fish. American novelist Sloan Wilson, though happy that his wife "never had her bottom pinched" during their stay in Ireland, nevertheless thought Irishmen had "mentally castrated themselves." A famous Englishwoman once said, "Most Irishmen are content to curse women and leave it at that." The idea, however, that Irishmen are naturally indifferent to sex is laughable. They have been forced to learn to control their appetites more than most people—for two reasons: the first economic, the second religious.

Irishmen and women began to put off marrying at a normal age only under the pressure of the dire conditions immediately preceding and following The Great Famine of the 1840s, which along with the evictions that followed, cut Ireland's population within a few decades by more than half. This terrible nemesis has badly scarred the Irishman's psychological makeup. It was obvious that the small farms of from one to five acres that made up the bulk of the Irish economy could no longer support families of any size—and Irish families were often very large. As the country emptied "consolidation" became the rule. Then, instead of passing a small farm on to his children to be subdivided again, a farmer, if he was able to extend his holding to fifteen acres because others had emigrated, passed it on to only one son. In addition, this small farmer had to raise a dowry for at least one daughter. He simply had not the capital resources to give all his sons and daughters their chance; nor was there land available for them all. All but the favored son or daughter, therefore, faced the choice of permanent bachelorhood or spinsterhood by remaining on the farm, entering the church, or emigrating. Those who elected to remain and to stay unmarried had to learn self-control because church teaching was specific on the point: Sex outside marriage was wrong; even sex within marriage, if it were not intended to procreate children, was wrong. But those who practice celibacy insist that it is not as difficult as it sounds; nor does it necessarily lead to misery. Anyway, a fair amount of "petting" took place.

It is partly this need to steer clear of women, however, that has made Ireland such "a man's society," although some credit also must be given to the fact that Irish society is still tribal and patriarchal. "At any party," a married woman told me, "you'll see all the men congregated together at one end of the room and the women at another. Any man who puts himself out a little to be nice to women in Ireland has it easy."

It is, of course, as difficult to generalize about sex in Ireland as about anything else. More and more young people are certainly marrying earlier as living standards rise. Among the better off, sexual patterns again vary wildly. An Irish journalist has written: "There is little marital infidelity in Dublin—because the men can't be bothered and the chances of being spotted are too high." Yet Benedict Kiely can say: "In one bus ride down

O'Connell Street, I counted ten married people I *knew* were having affairs." Even allowing for the Irish penchant for hyperbole, a Dublin priest more or less confirmed this, adding, "One hears of wild orgies up in the Wicklow Hills." However, a very knowledgeable matron also told me: "Oh, we have a certain class here who think themselves very avant-garde—and they do go in for orgies and sleeping around; but the vast majority of people don't behave like that."

It is easy to blame the church for the overall pervading puritanical attitudes. But asceticism is not foreign to the Irish nature, not difficult for an essentially spiritual people to adopt. And they have adapted well to terrible conditions and yet managed to retain a cheerful good-humored outlook. If the church's teaching on moral law appears to have taken no account of Ireland's special conditions, it has at least produced one of the most demonstrably *good* nations on earth. As John Huston said: "I am not a religious man in the orthodox sense, yet I cannot see how you can overlook the significance of religion in creating the high quality of life in Ireland. There is almost no crime in Ireland—and I've yet to see a fight, or even hear of one, in an Irish pub. From childhood the Irish are taught an ethic, and they retain that moral conscience for the rest of their lives. My own children went to local Catholic schools, and although they haven't become Catholics, the virtue has rubbed off on them, and now they are both, to my delight, completely honest people."

However, there are the inevitable critics of the system. Ninety-five percent of Irish children are taught in Catholic schools run by people vowed to celibacy. Some critics suggest this has produced an unhealthy attitude toward sex, others that the result is not so much a nation of innocents or pure-at-hearts as a nation of sexual ignoramuses. To back up their point they quote instances of cases where girls have written to magazines asking such questions as "Is it possible to have intercourse without being aware of it at the time?"

As a city-bred Irishman, I have never quite understood what the fuss was, or is, about Irish sex. Most men got married when they could afford to. Many I knew had to wait until their positions in their jobs improved, and promotions and pay raises often took years. Wages and salaries were low, often only enough for a man to keep himself—and sometimes he also had an old mother or father to support. It made many men reluctant to engage in anything but short-term dating, and some had grown so old before they were in a position to marry that "the inclination had gone off them." Unquestionably, a lot of Irish people have had to live quiet, desperate lives; but on the whole, they have done so with dignity and accepted their fate stoically. Certainly when I was young, Ireland seemed a marvelous place for a young man. Irish girls are able to make a man feel important; they know how to boost the male ego to an extraordinary degree. Yet even in the west of Ireland, where I used to go for holidays, I cannot say that the girls were simply demure, shy, submissive creatures. They were usually gay, wild, fun-loving wenches who could tumble in a haystack with the best of them. At any gathering, of course, there were always the intensely shy, intensely religious ones who would almost jump if you put a hand on them. But kindness and gentleness could bring their rewards. As for the others, there was a Breughel-like quality about them, a genuinely bucolic earthiness.

Today, I'm told, a harder, more calculating note has crept into relationships between the sexes, particularly among the less well-off and less educated, and even more particularly in the small towns where the big commercial dance halls have encouraged a more impersonal approach. Here girls sit or stand along one side of the hall while the men run an eye over them as though they were a prize herd of cattle. (How different from our own dear London discothèques!) Young fellows mark each other's card in response to the query Does she shift?—meaning does she permit full sexual intercourse. Where cards are not marked, there are plenty who put it bluntly to the girl: Do you car?—meaning is she prepared for athletics in the back seat of a motorcar.

Sex and religion have become the great talking points in the Republic. British television services are easily picked up, and it has been found impossible to censor the wavelengths the way books, films, or newspapers were censored in the past. The result is a more open society, with franker discussion of the topics of the day—sex, contraceptives, permissiveness, abortion, drugs, and so on. Yet Ireland would still appear straitlaced and old-fashioned to most of the inhabitants of larger metropolitan centers such as London or New York. "There's a new vulgarity about," one woman told me; "people necking, even in the Abbey Theatre; that sort of thing." From my own observations, it seems a balance will be arrived at in Ireland. The old obsessive feelings of guilt are likely to disappear in the near future; but both Irishmen and Irishwomen have discovered that life holds plenty of other interesting activities, and will, as ever, tend to put sex in its place. "It's nonsense to say we're not interested in sex here," a Dublin housewife explained. "It's just that we're more sensible about it."

What she means by sensible is, I think, that the Irish will never allow sex to interfere with the delights of conviviality—with good talk and good laughter.

The position of Irishwomen is as ambiguous as everything else in the island. Some Dublin women journalists, in the vanguard of Women's Lib and other fashionable ideas, blame Irishwomen for "letting Irishmen get away with" whatever it is that Irishmen get away with.

In some ways, Irishwomen are the Japanese of the Western world. As a caste, they are gentle, chaste, and feminine. Yet they are naturally flirtatious and approachable, so that every Irishman is made to feel a Romeo or Casanova. The great arrogance of some Irishmen, indeed, may well stem from their womenfolk. Wherever a man travels in Ireland, he is greeted by quick, smiling glances, delivered with a mixture of boldness and modesty.

On the whole, I don't think the Irish are a good-looking race. Centuries of hardship, famine, disease, poverty, and dietary imbalance have played havoc with features and physique. A friend of mine was once commissioned by a London magazine to write an article entitled "In Dublin's Fair City, Where the Girls are So Pretty." His photographer found to his despair however, that he could not find enough Irish girls to meet the required standard and had to hire English models. In general, Irish girls are less pretty than English or German, if more favored than French or Spanish. They are less photogenic than Americans, but have better complexions and are immensely more feminine and attractive. Like everything else about the country, however, even the beauty of the women is a matter of extremes. There is a percentage of bespectacled, befreckled, carroty-haired Irishwomen who are singularly unattractive—yet, by contrast, beautiful Irishwomen are more strikingly beautiful than women anywhere outside Florence.

Relative to their background and education, however, Irishwomen are on the whole a superior breed to Irishmen. They usually make magnificent mothers and dutiful wives. The result, is that Irish children are a joy to have around. They listen instead of talking, and almost as soon as they can walk, they take to washing dishes, doing the laundry, and sweeping the floor. In Ireland, the idea of a child-centered home is considered a perversion. Irish family life, in fact, would have probably seemed normal to an American of Abraham Lincoln's day. For all their backward plight in material needs, the Irish are a sane people who, having lived with desperate and intractable problems for centuries , are often contemptuous of other people's ideas and methods. In the larger matters, however, they seem more often right than wrong, for they know the virtues of simplicity and simple living.

No one would seriously suggest, though, that Ireland was not a much better place for men than for women. Once married, an Irishwoman enjoys less of her husband's company, shares less of his pursuits, enjoys less social life outside the home, and carries more responsibility within it than most other women in western Europe. Some women complain, too, that even when their husbands do take them out, they drink so much that they are unable to perform their marital duties afterward. Females make up a high percentage of psychiatric patients in the Republic. One Dublin woman journalist explained: "Eighty percent of Irish married women have never had an orgasm. Irish husbands are pretty hopeless that way."

Nevertheless, there are more love marriages now than there used to be. In the countryside, in fact, the art of matchmaking is almost dead as traditions change. Once, almost every marriage in rural Ireland was an arranged one. A farmer would meet a prospective bridegroom after a match had been fixed. "You know my place–I've got fifty acres and forty cows. I'm giving £350." Then the "lad" (in Ireland a lad may be as much as fifty years old) would demand: "And you'll give me £50 from yourself?" If this was acceptable, the bargain was struck. The two would then "walk the land," pacing it out to make sure there were fifty acres. After that the couple would meet, have a cup of tea together, and without any further courtship would get married, have a marriage breakfast, and start their married life without any honeymoon. Ireland, alas! was far from being a romantic country for many.

City-bred Irishmen have always regarded these arranged matches as degrading. Dominic Behan says he once heard two men in Kerry arguing over the bargain. "The groom, right there in the pub, suddenly bawled out 'Five hundred pounds in me fist or divil the leg I'll throw over your Nellie!' Now what kind of love and marriage was that!"

There is little unanimity. A Dublin woman journalist writes: "For too long Irishwomen, as mothers, wives, sisters and daughters, have been content to fill the role of self-sacrificing paragons of the virtues, while allowing the men the monopoly of the vices." Another has complained that: "Irishwomen are cabbages and doormats." Yet, Kathleen West, an English girl now working in Cork, says: "It depends on class and education a lot. And whatever is said about Irish husbands, at least they're faithful. They believe in their marriage vows. And on the whole, most Irish middle-class husbands are very good to their wives. And best of all, they're never *dull.* So far as I can see, in fact, Irishmen can be great husbands."

The major problem in Ireland, in fact, is not the imbalance between the fun men and women get out of their lives–after all, men everywhere have it better, and if that is wrong, at least it is not a uniquely Irish wrong. No, the real problem is the one of keeping the girls down on the farm. A Kerry schoolteacher told me: "There are more than one hundred farms around here where the owner is a middle-aged man who would be happy to get married tomorrow if he could find a girl to marry him. The girls don't want the hard life on the farm. They'd rather be up in Dublin or across in England enjoying the bright lights. Everyone of those farms will be sold out." A girl I met on the road to Kilrush, county Clare, on the other hand, said she intended to marry a farmer, come what may. "I know most of my girl friends think I'm mad. We all know that the trouble with Irish farmers is that they're lazy and that they leave most of the work—milking the cows, feeding the hens, and other chores—to the women. Oh, they work out in the fields until it's dark all right, including Saturdays. But there's little work they show for it all at the end of it. Then on Sundays they're in the pubs between one o'clock and three o'clock and in each other's houses for the rest of the day. It doesn't sound like much of a life for a woman, but I'll marry a farmer all the same. Only I won't put up with the way it is now!"

Politically and constitutionally, women have equal rights with men. And today, in fact, women are steadily moving into the better paid and more responsible positions in the Republic. There are women barristers, women surgeons, women executives in business and advertising. One provincial newspaper has a woman news editor, and Dublin television employs a woman as editor of drama and general features. Mrs. Frances Condrell served a term as mayor of Limerick. For the vast majority, of course, the only outlet is marriage, but some do manage to combine a career and marriage.

"The trouble is that women in Ireland feel vastly inferior to men," explains Mrs. Frances Langford, a painter and film maker. "As children, the boys in the family are treated as superior beings, and the girls wait on them and do everything for them, and all most of them hope for when they grow up is they will get married. Even many who are capable of being lively and progressive just don't dare stand up for themselves. They're afraid they'll frighten off the men and won't get married. So they end up getting tied down and living terribly isolated lives, just sunk in lethargy."

I spoke to two Dublin women about this troubling topic. The first was in her early fifties, had been married for twenty-seven years, and has had six children. She lives in a semi-detached house in a good Dublin suburb, and her husband is a pharmacist. She manages to play golf twice a week, bridge twice a week, is a member of the Irish Countrywomen's Association and the Irish Crafts and Design Association, and also paints. But her husband, she complained, was completely happy only "when he gets up to the golf club and has an evening with the boys. I daren't go in either; I have to go to the door and shout Is he ready? But he doesn't come out until the party ends and he feels like it. It sounds awful; but on the other hand, Irish husbands are faithful and they're kind. Education and intelligence make a difference. The better a man is educated, the more he accepts women and treats them as equals."

The other woman, who holds a B.A. and has been married for thirteen years, had five children, and besides running her one-hundred-year-old home as a guesthouse during the summer, found time to tackle five other jobs, including some political activities. Her view: "It's an exceptional Irishman who treats his wife as anything more than a tool. Most Irishmen just don't like their wives to be on the same level. Wives are simply possessions, chattels. And husbands are totally uninterested in the children until they're old enough to be worth talking to. So far as my own husband is concerned, I'm surprised he's as good as he is, for his mother spoiled him completely. That's the trouble with Irishmen—their mothers. They make absolutely no effort to prepare their sons for marriage. All Irishmen have this mystical reverence for motherhood—and they'll even pray to the Virgin Mary. But they expect women to wait on them hand and foot. The mothers of Ireland, I'm afraid, are still at it."

A young television production assistant summed up the matter this way: "The men only want something in bed and something that cooks. Irishmen rarely indulge in the little expressions of affection that Englishmen or Americans do. I think they feel all their friends would laugh at them if they showed they felt deep emotion toward a woman. As for the women—well, they only accept Irishmen because they haven't any alternative."

At which point a male voice broke in: "Ah, the poor wee whoors!"

XV

YOUR EMINENCES GRISES

EPITAPH

If fruits are fed on any beast
Let vine-roots suck this parish priest,
For while he lived, no summer sun
Went up but he'd a bottle done,
And in the starlight beer and stout
Kept his waistcoat bulging out.

Then Death that changes happy things
Damned his soul to water springs.

J. M. SYNGE
("After reading Ronsard's lines from Rabelais")

"In Ireland, it isn't normal for people to argue with the Church," said a priest. "The disaffected," said another, "are like the unemployed—they're mainly for export."

"You hear about Ireland being priest-ridden," declared Father Michael Cleary of Marino, county Dublin, "but too often in Ireland it's the priests who are people-ridden. I got a letter from a woman the other day saying I'd given great scandal to her twelve-year-old son because I'd stood outside the church the other day smoking, and with my hands in my pocket. You see, there's still a great reverence for the priest in Ireland."

Ireland remains one of the last great bastions of the Catholic faith. Religion still permeates Irish life in a way unparalleled even in Italy. Over 95 percent of the Republic gives its spiritual allegiance to that Papacy which has served it so ill over the centuries, and almost 95 percent of that 95 percent are still practicing Catholics. Irish "art" for thousands still means colored prints of the Sacred Heart or plaster replicas of Christ and the saints. Houses still have to be blessed by a priest when a family moves in; missals or prayerbooks too often are the only books in a house besides *Old Moore's Almanac.* The main Dublin churches celebrate seven or eight masses on a Sunday morning (in the pro-Cathedral in the heart of the city three Masses are often celebrated at the same time), and Dublin priests spend an average of six or seven hours in the confessional every Saturday night. In the diocese of Dublin alone, one in every six hundred of the population is a priest, a nun, or a member of a religious order. Ireland still ordains hundreds of priests every year, and in the rural areas it is still the ambition of most parents to see at least one son or daughter enter religion. Patrick Murphy says, "We had an extreme case not far from here a few years ago where all eleven children entered the religious life. And do you know, the parents looked radiant!" There are over 6,100 priests in the country altogether (and another 6,000 have been trained for the foreign missions), giving a ratio of one priest for every 550 Catholics in the country.

This is not excessive by the standards of other Western countries. Malta, for instance, has a priest for every 314 Catholics; Switzerland, 1 for every 454; Holland 1 for every 494; and Britain, 1 for every 507. But what is startling in Ireland is that while the population has fallen by 23 percent since 1870, the number of priests has risen by a staggering 87 percent.

The Catholic Church, in fact, is the great glory of the country—and in the eyes of many, the great national incubus. Cardinals and bishops in their scarlet and purples, their vestments of fine gold and silver, their dazzling chalices and monstrances—all the ornate rituals and formalities of the church—fulfill a need in the hearts of a people whose homes are still abnormally drab by the standards of Britain or America. One sometimes has the feeling that Ireland is a single, great, open-air monastery. The comings and goings of churchmen are faithfully recorded in the press; the visit of a bishop or a cardinal is given the prominence other countries reserve for film or television stars or a few prize athletes. The Primate of All-Ireland occupies a position in his country not unlike that of Queen Elizabeth II in hers—if not officially, at least in hearts and minds. Great weight is given to any utterance by the hierarchy, and even minor clergy get a disproportionate share of publicity. Until recently the Dublin newspapers (with the exception of the *Irish Times*) could easily have been mistaken by a visitor for publications of the religious press rather than the city's main sources of information. In Dublin, priests and nuns are almost as thick on the ground as in the approaches to Saint Peter's in Rome, and the countryside is well supplied with churches, most of them far too ornate and clearly too expensive for such a relatively poor country. Remote wildernesses are dotted with wayside shrines, and the land is still smothered in holy wells (although the clergy draw no direct benefit from these).

The Catholic Church, however, is not a state church. Except for an educational grant toward the running of its schools, it receives no subsidies. But because priests control all Catholic schools, clerical influence is all-pervasive, making it hard to refute the charge often laid against the Irishman that he is priest-ridden. Yet the Celt has always been priest-ridden—by druids and then by the priests of his own Celtic branch of the Universal Church—so that this affliction cannot particularly be blamed on the Roman brand of Christianity.

Nor can the Catholic Church be accused of some form of usurpation of the Irishman's secular institutions. The clergy simply stepped into a power vacuum within the Irish Catholic community during "the bad times." The native aristocrats had gone; the Protestant Anglo-Irish controlled and ran everything; the mass of "old Irish," used throughout a long history to giving their loyalty to their chiefs, had a rudimentary education at best and had not developed powers of leadership and initiative. Only the clergy had the requisite education and opportunity for leadership. In fact, anyone reading the history of the Catholic priesthood (which, after all, was drawn entirely from the people themselves) in the bad times can say only that the ordinary people owe them an immense debt. One can turn this argument on its head, of course: Had the Irish accepted Protestantism as England, Scotland, and Wales did, then their fate might not have been as bad as it was. But to ask the country which had Christianized Scotland and most of England to give up its allegiance to the church of Saint Patrick was to ask the impossible. Yet there is no denying that Irish intransigence on this matter, whether explicable or not, has played an immense role in the refusal of the Irishman to be assimilated into the political and cultural life of his formidable neighbor, England.

The hierarchy consists of four archbishops and twenty-four bishops, presided over by the cardinal, who is also Archbishop of Armagh. This is an impressive apparatus for catering to the spiritual needs of only three-and-a-half million people. (The church operates on both sides of the "Border"—the boundary line with Northern Ireland.) For the most part they have conducted themselves as princes of Ireland. They have been remote figures given to oracular pronunciamentos. Although, up close, many of them turn out to be very human characters—often shy, gentle creatures or jolly extroverts exuding good nature and razor-edged witticisms—they have cultivated an image the result of which is that Irish children grow up with the feeling that to argue with a cardinal, bishop, or even a parish priest is to cross swords with God himself.

Twenty years ago, Catholic clergy were undoubtedly a privileged class in the Irish Republic. They were among the few who could afford to run cars, play golf, drink whiskey, and eat well—so well, indeed, that most Irishmen used to gauge the excellence of a restaurant or hotel by whether or not the clergy patronized it. Priests never queued for anything; they were ushered to the best seats in the best restaurants ahead of people who had been waiting and were shown all the marks of respect accorded an elite. (Since those halcyon days, however, bishops have cracked down on ostentatious display of comfort or privilege, and priests in some dioceses are now allowed cars "strictly for business reasons.") Representative bodies of every type—from local sports committees to the national Arts Council—were automatically chaired by priests, and dictatorial attitudes were the rule rather than the exception. But times are changing. When a parish priest recently rebuked one of his female parishioners for wearing a bikini on a beach, demanding that she wear a one-piece bathing suit, he got the shock of his life when she replied, "Certainly, father. Which bit do you want me to take off?"

For many Irishmen, particularly writers and intellectuals, the clerical atmosphere was often unbearable. Almost anybody who ever let his mind wander outside the standard confines of acceptable thought became violently anticlerical, although not necessarily anti-Catholic. It was easy to see a parallel in which the priesthood was to Ireland what the Communist Party *apparat* was to Soviet Russia. At bottom, both nations were primarily a vast, pliant mass responding to essentially closed ideas. Nor were horror stories wanting. Everyone had his equivalent of the story of the priest who stood at the bedside of a woman who had given birth to an illegitimate child and for three hours denounced her sin so violently that she was driven mad.

The turning point possibly came in 1950 when the Irish hierarchy, combining with the Irish Medical Association, who are as bad in their way as their American counterparts, forced the government of the day to abandon a primitive health scheme known as the Mother and Child scheme. This would have given free maternity care to mothers and welfare assistance to children up to the age of sixteen. The hierarchy has never entirely lived down its part in that affair.

There are signs that as the lay Irishman becomes better educated and begins to regain his self-confidence and to acquire the necessary skills to run an increasingly complex society, the oppressively Catholic atmosphere in the country may begin to dissipate. Declan Costello, a member of the Dail, has warned that although the church still had the active allegiance of most Irish people, "it would be a mistake to depend on an unswerving allegiance in the future." Even more shattering to traditionalists who had come to believe Ireland immune to influences stirring the outside world were the results of a survey taken at University College, Dublin, a school attended mainly by Catholics. A high proportion of young students, the survey revealed, questioned the basis of the Faith, and almost 10 percent admitted they no longer attended Mass. A group of London Irish interviewed on Irish television revealed that only a minority among them attended Mass. (The Dublin archbishop immediately denounced the program as "a travesty of a nation's faith," but that did not change the findings.) At home, even among those who cannot bring themselves entirely to reject the faith their fathers have fought and died for, a new synthesis of ideologies is emerging. Several left-wing Catholic groups have been started, and at a pray-in at a Dublin church, extracts from the thoughts of Chairman Mao were read.

Yet the clergy are far from being down and out. When someone proposed to erect a plaque in honor of Brian Merryman in his home town, the local parish priest roared "We'll have none of that filth here!" and was listened to. When the late Jayne Mansfield brought her sexy act to Ireland, the Bishop and Dean of Kerry combined to have her banned—despite her protests that she was a Catholic herself.

On the rare occasions when they do give interviews, the members of the hierarchy show how conscious they are of a great dilemma. Although writers and intellectuals dismiss them as simple obscurantists and arch-conservatives, the bishops insist that their interest is also "for the church of the poor, the uneducated, and those of simple faith"—echoing the Vatican's own dilemma of how to go about not upsetting the simple faith of, say, the Latin American world and yet somehow restraining the impatience of intellectuals in western Europe and America who demand progressive moves. Timothy Patrick Coogan interviewed three bishops—Browne of Galway, Lucey of Cork, and Birch of Ossory. Browne wondered which was the more important, "a church with a thousand peasants attending Mass, or one professor?" Lucey was convinced that the

Irish church's power was "indirect" and that the people ignored the bishops when it suited them. Birch complained that "people in Dublin who've been to universities think their standards should apply all over the country."

A young American journalist working on a Dublin newspaper, who admitted she was a Marxist, told me: "I thought–and hoped–for another Cuba here. Now that I've lived here for a while, I realize that it's quite out of the question. The Irish are an immature and irresponsible people led into their present predicament by a paternalistic church." On the other hand, Brendan Devlin, a professor at the great Irish seminary of Maynooth, says: "The charge of paternalism is fast becoming a dead issue. The church became paternalistic because it had no option. It was the only power in the country while our people were in such a depressed condition."

I found it difficult to talk to young men like Devlin or Father Tom Stack of Glendalough or Father Cleary without being aware of the supreme goodness and selflessness of their natures. They are walking saints whose opinions, beliefs, and messages cannot help but elicit sympathetic responses from the Irish nature. These are not only good but intelligent and able young men. Some might consider them curious "saints"–Father Stack sitting at his ease in a Dublin pub among hard-drinking, hard-wenching writers, journalists, and actors; Father Cleary making a name for himself as a pop singer and being mobbed by girls in Ireland the way the Beatles used to be and Mick Jagger still is mobbed in Britain and America. I personally found them delightful and stimulating companions and a jolting if refreshing reminder that goodness is still a considerably attractive quality. Against all reason, one begins to believe deeply in Irishmen again–to believe that they still have a role to fulfill that destiny has not yet revealed.

For a last word, I consulted that oracle, the Killarney Boatman, who occupies a place in journalistic tradition rather akin to the New York taxi-driver. This particular one had actually hoped to be a Franciscan monk in his youth, but had dropped out for some reason. "Yes, the Irish character's good today–better in many ways than it has ever been," he said. "The people are more independent. They're less servile and they're less secretive than when I was a boy. They're less ashamed of things, less guilt-ridden about sin. There's more belief in God now and less in superstition. People on the whole are now mainly concerned with what is good for society. *That's* the new Ireland. There was always charity toward and among 'decent' people, but the sinner was too often condemned and the message of forgiveness forgotten by a people who should have known better. Now–and it's not apathy–there is more compassion for the fallen, more charity toward those who need it most."

XVI

NO SURRENDER!

Sure I'm an Ulster Orangeman, from Erin's Isle I came
To see my Glasgow Brethren all of honour and of fame
And to tell them of my fore-fathers who fought in days of yore,
All on the twelfth day of July in the sash me father wore.

It's ould but it is beautiful, it's the best you've ever seen.
Been worn for more nor ninety years in that little Isle of Green.
From my Orange and Purple fore-father it descended with galore;
It's a terror to them papish boys the sash me father wore.

ORANGE SONG

Every man has a skeleton in his closet. Mine is that I was born in Belfast.

I am a Catholic, born in the North when Ireland was an undivided country, of parents born in what is now the Republic. I married a Protestant girl. Both my daughters were educated at a convent school next door to Winston Churchill's old school, Harrow, and when they went home on holiday used to attend The Field, the climactic ceremony of the great Twelfth of July Orange Day parades.

My wife and her family are a kind, liberal, delightful people. Even their country relatives, some with Orange sympathies could not have received me into the bosom of their family more warmly, and my two rather beautiful Papist daughters appear to be the pride and joy of all.

My own immediate family, a sister and brother, both married, still live in Belfast with my father, who has just given up golf now that he has reached ninety-one. All his people live in the west of Ireland, and to me their charm, wit, and innocence are part of that marvelous Irish quality that simply cannot be captured in words. My mother's family were all Dubliners–Campions and Flemings–with not an ounce of indigenous Celtic blood in the lot of them. They were all lunatics who sang with beautiful tenor or soprano voices, and all fourteen could play the piano at birth. All ended up in America, and when I first visited that great country and was asked the purpose of my visit by New York immigration authorities, I answered truthfully: "I'm on a pilgrimage to visit the grave of my grandmother, who is buried in your great city."

Nevertheless, when I started writing this book, I had no intention of including Northern Ireland in it. Geographically and historically, it is part of Eire (the Vikings added *-land* to that, and the first *e* somehow got dropped, which is how you get *Ireland*), but spiritually, psychologically, atmospherically, and pathologically it now belongs somewhere else. Politically speaking, it is part of the United Kingdom, and therefore really lies outside any consideration of the Irish mystique, unless you believe, as many do, that British and Irish are interchangeable. The majority of Ireland's most famous men have been British–Swift, Wellington, Parnell, Yeats, Shaw, Wilde, Synge, Joyce, Field-Marshal Montgomery, and so on; but most of these men cast aside their former origins and were happy to call themselves Irishmen.

Northern Ireland, however, is another matter entirely. She has many people of ability, she has many fair-minded people, she has many people as good, kind, and saintly as any to be found south of the Border. Yet there remains a terrible awfulness about the place that makes everybody else within the British Isles feel highly embarrassed about it. The English are delighted to feel it isn't English (but British, by gad, that's different!); the Welsh, that very great people, wouldn't touch it with a barge pole; and the Scotch–to whom, regrettably, it really belongs, if only spiritually–

affect a genteel Edinburgh accent and pretend it's all the fault of Glasgow. The Irish are torn between wanting to disown the place altogether, as a terrible blot on the national reputation, and a desire to recover it again and go through with the possibly impossible task of civilizing the place.

The difficulty is that although it is the land of Cuchulain and the great Hugh O'Neill, it stands for everything that is *not* Irish. The very existence of this tiny statelet is a monument, at worst, to hatred and bigotry, and at best to greed and imperialism. The energy that keeps the wheels turning has been, in my lifetime, nothing more than *hate.* It has been a weapon used by the large vested interests in Ulster to keep their working classes docile and obedient. Whether the ends justify such means is gravely open to doubt. A Protestant working-class woman, interviewed by a London newspaper, "explained" why she hated Catholics: "I learnt to hate Catholics from my mother. They must have done her some harm." This kind of hate is bred into the bone. Children of five and six, interviewed on British television, have admitted that they "hated Cawthalicks." No regime, however much it feels itself threatened, can justify this kind of behavior, yet the hate is kept going by such institutionalized processes as the Orange Order, whose openly and avowedly anti-Catholic aims are forwarded by the constant staging of parades throughout the summer months to celebrate such past Protestant victories as the battle of the Boyne and the siege of Derry.

Yet I do not find it beyond the bounds of credibility to imagine that in some strange way Northern Ireland itself could not give rise to a mystique. In the same way that the London poet, John Betjeman, professes to find beauty in Victorian gasometers, that the ink-black brush strokes of L. S. Lowry's belching factory chimneys stir a response in those who were born in industrial wastelands, it is possible to feel a sense of *une jolie laide* about this dreadful place. There are Belfastmen who have seen the Parthenon and the Taj Mahal and still stoutly insist that the most beautiful sight in the world is Donegall Place at five o'clock on a wet winter's evening with the lights glistening on the pavements. In fact, I used to be proud of certain things about Belfast myself. It had the world's largest shipbuilding yard; it was the world center of the linen industry. It even had the world's biggest gasometer. It also had the world's biggest cigarette factory and the world's largest ropeworks. Nor could one forget that during Haig's great offensive on the Somme in 1916, the Ulster Division was the only unit to break the German lines; not only did they break through, but they careered on for three miles, in a war in which gains were measured in inches and feet, and were well on their way to Berlin when they discovered that the rest of the British army had been unable to keep up with them.

The local newspapers continually feed local pride. Some ten American presidents, including Andrew Jackson, Ulysses S. Grant, and Woodrow Wilson, had Ulster forebears. Stephen Foster's people were from Derry. The Mellon ancestral homestead still exists in Ulster, and of course, the richest American, J. Paul Getty, is descended from a certain John O'Getty of the county Derry, whose descendent James gave the family name to a well-known piece of American real estate called Gettysburg.

Then, too, there was—and is—the indisputable fact that the countryside of Ulster is hardly less beautiful than other parts of Ireland. The Mountains of Mourne do sweep down to the sea in Ulster; the Glens of Antrim scythe round in a series of magnificent bays and wild headlands, past ruined Dunluce Castle perched on jagged rocks, to the Giant's Causeway with its ranks of octagonal columns squeezed out in basalt from the earth's interior like tubes of black toothpaste. It all complements the scenic gem that is Ireland:

Oh! 'tis pretty to be in Ballinderry,
'Tis pretty to be in Aghalee;
But prettier far in little Ram's Island
Sitting in under the ivy tree:
Och anee! Och anee!

And it has, too, its marvelous songs, one of which has a tune so fine that Beethoven borrowed it to to complete his Seventh Symphony:

As beautiful Kitty one morning was tripping
With a pitcher of milk from the fair of Coleraine,
She saw me and stumbled, and the pitcher it tumbled,
And all the fine buttermilk watered the plain.
Oh, what shall I do now? 'Twas looking at you now;
Sure, sure, such a pitcher I'll ne'er meet again,
'Twas the pride of my dairy, oh, Barney MacCleary,
You're sent as a plague to the girls of Coleraine.

Another virtue of the place is the Northern sense of humor. The Stage Ulsterman has no sense of humor; he is a dour puritan who takes his eye off the Bible only to study his bank account. In fact, however, Belfastmen are often as quick-witted as southerners, if in a drier, less malicious way. Southerners criticize themselves at the drop of a hat, but less often tell or laugh at jokes against themselves; the northerner never criticizes himself, but rarely tells a joke that isn't against himself. There is the characteristic story of the Presbyterian minister denouncing sin from the pulpit. "Will any mon hold his hond in a candle for five minutes? No! Will any mon hold his hond in a candle for two minutes? No! Will any mon hold his hond in a candle for thirty seconds? No! But ye'll live in sin and die in sin, and when the Lord tells you, 'Depart from me into everlasting fire,' ye'll cry out: 'Oh, Lord, Lord! We didn't know. We didn't know!' And what will the Lord say to you?—Well, I'll tell you! He'll tell you, 'Well, you damn well know now!' "

The Ulsterman, in fact, has a keen sense of his own ridiculousness. Belfast roared with laughter once when, following a fuss over the loss of a fine Victorian building, the Ulster branch of the National Trust (which preserves fine houses, buildings, and landscapes) suddenly bestirred itself and took over a Victorian wrought-iron "public convenience" in the center of the city. Normal people read with glee local press reports describing how the unspeakable Ian Paisley and his even dottier wife fought to have the film *Ulysses* banned in Belfast. Mrs. Paisley did not want "dirt from Dublin"—the implication being that dirt from Derry or Coleraine would have been all right. Paisley himself, accused of being in favor of censorship policies that would have put him in the same camp as the Pope, hastily declared that he was against censorship—"Roman censorship." Belfast, it will thus be seen, is in some respects the pottiest part of Ireland.

Unfortunately, it does not stop at being potty. To its sheer lunacy it adds a broad streak of violence. Belfast has always been one of the most violent towns in the British Isles. It is a city whose unofficial motto is a belligerent "What are you looking at?" If you stop on one side of the street to stare into a shop window on the other, someone will come stomping across, looking for a fight, under the impression that you have been staring at him. It is a brutal and brutalized society. It has much in common with Glasgow—although to be fair, it has not had a great deal of crime, and certainly it practiced none of that razor-slashing and bicycle-chain whipping that characterize the denizens of the Scottish slums. In Belfast, violence is straightforward, and you can see it coming. It does not hide and it does not disguise itself. The man who wants to fight you comes up to you in the street with his fists at the ready. The mob that wants to burn you out or shoot you down does so with their Union Jacks flying, bellowing their Orange songs into your ears.

Belfast sits at the head of a glorious *Lough,* (or sea-inlet) surrounded by beautiful hills. Except for Naples, I can think of few large cities so well favored by natural environment. Although it is an ugly town, it is a clean one, possibly because it is continually swept by rain and wind. Nowhere are windows kept so diamond-bright. Even in the poorest slums the little terraced back-to-back houses have their brass door knockers and knobs polished and their doorsteps scoured and whitened.

Having said all this, I have about exhausted most of the good things it is possible to say about Ulster. The human spirit there is continually crushed by the intolerable burden of the sixteenth-century Scottish Kirk mentality, which seems to imagine that all natural joys and freedoms are sin. The place, when I lived there, was religion-ridden in a way the South has never been priest-ridden. Biblical tags stared at you from every hoarding. Little bands of sharp-nosed Bible thumpers constantly gathered at street corners to relate how they had been "saved." Cinemas, theaters, pubs were all sternly closed on Sundays; a wet Sunday in Belfast was a glimpse of hell. Even the local museum and art gallery locked its doors on the Sabbath. It was all good Old Testament stuff, and if you were waiting for fire and brimstone to descend upon you the next moment, then I suppose there was nothing terribly wrong with it. But, as we all used to tell ourselves, the only good thing to be said about Belfast was that it was easy to get out of. And certainly, within five or ten minutes of the city center, you can be in an enchanting world.

Despite his sense of cleanliness and his admirable sense of industry, the Belfastman has developed even less sense of beauty than the southerner. In the better-off suburbs, few citizens plant trees or bother to bedeck their gardens with flowers. The impression given is that such folderol—such concern for beautiful things—smacks of vanity and pleasure and is the Devil's work. But what goes on in the Presbyterian and Orange mind is really beyond my comprehension, and I find it all so totally tiresome and unrewarding that I will not linger on it further.

The fact is that the ancestors of these people knew full well what they were up to when at the time of the Plantation of Ulster in 1609, they settled themselves, at the invitation of the British Government, on lands that had been stolen from the native Irish. If they did not know then, as with the people in the minister's warning, they damn well soon found out. In 1641, some ten thousand of them were either massacred or driven out at the start of the great rebellion. For a while, the future of the colony lay in doubt; then, after the Cromwellian Settlement, there was a further influx of immigrants, mainly from Scotland. The majority were Presbyterians and therefore Dissenters who suffered from the same legal disabilities as the Catholics; many either toyed with republicanism or quit Ireland and made for the New World. More than 250,000 of them flooded into Canada and the United States in the eighteenth century, and because of their bitter feelings they unquestionably played a major part in the establishment of American independence. Their leaders, however, belonged mainly to the established Church of Ireland and stayed on in Ireland, with their nonconformist tenants, to enjoy their good fortune in possessing broad acres that, so far as the Irish people were concerned, did not belong to them. The excesses of the southern Catholics during the 1798 rebellion, when many better-off Protestant families were massacred, more or less permanently alienated even liberal-minded Ulstermen.

By this time almost all memory of King William III and his victory at the Boyne had disappeared from the Ulster consciousness. But among the rough and uneducated tenant farmers, a specter had arisen. As good Protestant families uprooted themselves and sailed for America the poor, dispossessed native Irish bid for the tenancies. More and more of the original owners became repossessed of what had belonged to their ancestors. A Protestant mob called *the Peep-O-Day Boys* was formed to resist such "incursions" and to combat Catholic factions such as the Molly Maguires and the Ribbon Men:

July the Twelfth, at Dolly's Brae, there was a grand
procession
Of Orangemen, in proud array, all haters of oppression;
But Ribbon-knaves soon played their pranks and poured
their murderous volleys;
Which caused our men to thin their ranks and rout the
blood-stained mollies.

Of old their rebel sires had thought to make our fathers
fear them,
But dearly was their wisdom bought when Orangemen drew
near them;
For having formed one mighty band, brave, fearless, and
united,
Full soon they quenched the Popish brand which death-
fires would have lighted.

But with the ancient serpent's love of perjury and lying,
The conquered rebels seek to move men's pity by their
crying;
They swear the Ribbonmen are Saints, whilst Orangemen
are Sinners,
But we but laugh at their complaints–which is but right
with winners.

The Peep-O-Day Boys formed the nucleus of that Orange Order which for almost two centuries now, has ruled Ulster as a kind of Protestant Mafia. At the start of the nineteenth century, therefore, Ulster, hitherto a patchwork quilt of republicanism and right-wing Toryism, was all set to swing to the right. Materially speaking, it was indisputably in much better shape than the rest of Ireland. A tightly knit community, it was driven by the dynamic that distinguishes most societies in a pioneering situation. It was a community, moreover, that did not carry the legacy of bitterness and deep sense of injury and degradation that burdened Catholic Ireland. If it had no aristocratic class, it had a leader class with which it could identify racially and religiously, whereas Catholic Ireland had lost hers and drifted rudderless. In addition, the Ulstermen enjoyed much more favorable conditions of land tenure and—what was even more important—did not have the incubus of absentee landlords to support.

Ulstermen argued, as they do today, that the prosperity of the North, as contrasted with the poverty of the South, was attributable to religious factors; but this is a simplistic or factional view. The majority of landowners in the South, as well as most of the merchant and traders of substance, were Protestant; if the South lagged, it could be said it was because it was led by Protestants.

To an extent, indeed, the Ulster Protestant owed his prosperity to sheer luck. The one Irish industry never to suffer disability at the hands of the British government was the linen industry. On the contrary, every encouragement was given to the infant linen industry because it competed with no English interests. Actually, the industry had come to be centered in Ulster largely because of the skills and energies of French Huguenots who had fled there from France, and not because of Ulstermen themselves. Be that as it may, they found themselves sitting on a good thing and made the most of it. They brought over steam looms from Britain, and Belfast grew rapidly. Inspired with that same sense of industry and opportunity which had by then set England alight, Ulstermen prospered. Often, however, they showed poor judgment. For example, they attempted to set up a cotton industry but found themselves incapable of coping with English competition. What they did do successfully, however, was to start a small port and a shipbuilding industry in Belfast, which later bore fruit. But it was not until the American Civil War, which cut off supplies of raw cotton to Britain, that the linen industry became a gold mine, and Ulster the commercial center of Ireland. With the establishment of Harland and Wolff, the great shipbuilding firm which built the *Titanic* (Harland was a Yorkshireman and Wolff a German), Ulster became a hive of industry and commerce and was enabled to enjoy a prosperity that unfortunately proved to be short-lived.

Today, the place languishes. The linen industry is dead; Harland and Wolff's has had to be bailed out by the government time and again. And Ulstermen, it turns out, show no greater capacity for coping with the intractable difficulties provided by Ireland's meager resources and her peripheral geographical situation than other Irishmen. The province enjoys the highest rate of unemployment in the United Kingdom, and if it were not for a subsidy of £200 million ($500 million) annually from the British government and other forms of help in the shape of navy and aircraft orders, she would not enjoy a standard of living much above subsistence level.

Until 1886, when the British government, spurred by Gladstone's decision to atone for past wrongs, began a campaign of assistance to Ireland almost without parallel, Catholic Ireland simply talked, agitated, and suffered without doing very much. After the change in government policy, however, Catholic southern Ireland flourished as never before, and by 1910 Ireland's trade was £28 per head, as against £20 per head in Great Britain. Exports had doubled within seven years; bank deposits had trebled.

Despite this improvement, Catholic Irishmen, for emotional as well as for what they considered sound, practical reasons, still wanted the Union with Britain repealed, and eventually a British government agreed to give them home rule. When such an act was proposed just prior to the 1914 Great War, however, Ulster Protestants refused to accept it, insisting that "Home Rule meant Rome Rule." In defiance of the democratic decision of the entire electorate of the British Isles, Ulster Protestants announced that if Westminster passed the Home Rule Bill, they would set up their own Provisional Government in Ulster. And to show they meant what they said, they formed a military organization called the Ulster Volunteer Force and ran in arms from Germany. In their determination to resist Home Rule, they even invited the German Kaiser to become ruler of Ulster. In the end, as a result of right-wing machinations in England, the British government caved in and agreed to "exclude" Ulster, temporarily, from Irish Home Rule. By the Government of Ireland Act of 1920, six northeast counties (or two-thirds of the whole Province of Ulster) were turned into the statelet called Northern Ireland, with its own parliament operating under the overall authority of Westminster.

The rest of Ireland got the self-government it had campaigned for, but was appalled at the exclusion of part of Ulster. Under any democratic system the Ulster Protestants ought to have been included in an all-Ireland government. Numbering just over nine hundred thousand, they were—and still are—a minority of the population of Ireland. What is more, by excluding Ulster, the British government condemned almost five hundred thousand Catholics to live under the dominance of a bigoted parliament largely run by the Orange Order. The whole purpose of the Orange Order, its sole raison d'être, was and is "to keep Micks down." Such is its power that almost every Ulster Protestant who has a decent job is a member of the Order, and all members of the recently suspended government belonged to it. In short, between them, the Ulster Parliament and the Orange Order had made it their mission in life to maintain Ulster as a Protestant stronghold and to deny a fair share—in some cases even elementary civil rights—to Papists.

Protestant Ulstermen often defend themselves by pointing out that the condition of Catholics in Northern Ireland is no different from the conditions of Protestants in Republican Ireland. This is true as far as it goes, but it does not go very far. Certainly, Protestants in the South suffer all the disadvantages that attend living in a country dominated by a religion not their own. The censorship of books, films, theaters, and newspapers is dictated by Catholic, not Protestant, moral teaching. Protestants cannot get a divorce, nor can they openly buy contraceptives. In this sense their suffering is comparable to that of Catholics in the North who are forbidden, by the Presbyterian conscience, from attending cinemas or theaters or pubs on a Sunday.

Where the supreme difference between the two areas of Ireland is more blatantly shown, however, is in the economic difference in status between a Republican Protestant and an Ulster Catholic. In the south, Protestants flourish—so much so, indeed, that in the Dublin area they still hold a large majority of the best executive jobs available. Nothing in practice or in the constitution debars them from serving in the government; indeed, the first President of Ireland was a Protestant, the respected Gaelic scholar, Dr. Douglas Hyde, and the deputy premier in the last Government is also one. In the north the reverse has been the case. Catholics have been discriminated against in public and private employment and in housing; electoral constituencies have been gerrymandered so that Catholics have not had fair representation; and they have been constantly subjected to a barrage of display, demonstration, and even intimidation designed to make them continually aware of Orange triumph. In the poorer districts of Belfast, the more polite wall slogans announce "To Hell with the Pope!" and the less polite ones are unprintable. Gable ends are often garishly decorated with Orange "art"—colorful portraits of "King Billy" on a white horse crossing the Boyne. Until World War II, members of the Northern Ireland government, including several ex-prime ministers, constantly made anti-Catholic speeches.

Of course, Catholics in Ulster have not been entirely blameless. The place was created violently, and in violence it has survived. In its infancy it had to cope with armed attack from one of the parties that had launched civil war in the south; this party refused to accept the treaty with Britain in 1921 and waged war against both the new Free State government in the south and the new Ulster government in the north. As the tale is told by the Ulster government and the Orangemen today, however, the impression is given that *all* Catholic Ireland fought to subvert Ulster by force. They also tend to overlook the fact that Protestants certainly contributed at least their fair share to the violence. Catholic families who had no connection with the fighting in any form were murdered. In particular, the "B" Specials attacked publicans, the wealthiest members of the Catholic community. As a child, my blood ran cold when I heard how the entire MacMahon family were wiped out in a massacre hardly less brutal than that which did in the Tsar and his family. Again in 1935, at a period of high unemployment, poorer Catholics were subjected to such a pogrom that the British army had to be drafted into Belfast to patrol the streets.

After World War II, conditions appeared to be changing dramatically in Ulster. The old difficulties remained, but were less in evidence and seemed to engender less heat. The "Twalth" continued to be celebrated, but with less enthusiasm. People were still referred to as "digging with the wrong foot," which meant–depending upon the speaker and his affiliations–that one was Catholic or Protestant. Boys and girls being interviewed for jobs were no longer openly asked their religion, but they were asked what school they had gone to, which came to the same thing.

With some justice, the government and the Orangemen could claim that Catholics were not playing their full part in fostering good relations. Catholics adamantly refused to accept the border between north and south as a permanent settlement, making it clear that when the day dawned when they had attained majority status in the North, they would vote Northern Ireland into an all-Ireland republic. They made little or no attempt to initiate or invest in industry and commercial enterprises and were largely content to remain employees. The Catholic Falls Road area sheltered the outlawed Irish Republican Army, which from time to time attacked targets in Northern Ireland or shot policemen (often Catholics). Nor did Catholic members of Parliament play a constructive role in Ulster politics: They spent their time either making propaganda against the Belfast Parliament or boycotting it.

There was just enough truth in all this to give excellent propaganda to the ruling Unionist Party, backed by the Orange Mafia. In fact, the leaders of the ruling party were simply playing the same game that had been so successful in the nineteenth century. At every election, at every sign of a lessening of the old factional feelings, the Orange leaders whipped up "the danger" to the Border and "the danger" of Papal domination. Although the activities of the IRA were condemned and outlawed by the government of the Republic and by the Catholic hierarchy, Ulster spokesmen, either openly or by implication, manipulated their uneducated masses with the constantly reiterated theme that Catholics were just waiting their chance to rise and take over the province. This totally ignored the fact that the Catholic community in Northern Ireland (save for a few hundred or so in the IRA) did not have the means to do anything of the sort. Indeed, if they had been granted proper treatment from the inception of the Ulster state, the existence of the Border would have probably become irrelevant. The Orangemen's vociferous defense of their own rights and their denial of the same to Catholics have in the end backfired and endangered everything.

Two things sparked off the troubles that began in 1968. The first was a much earlier decision by the then Ulster Prime Minister, Mr. Terence O'Neill, to "build bridges" with the republican south. Ireland, as a whole country, can just about afford one parliament, and the idea of *two* is so preposterous it is small wonder neither of the statelets has been able to make itself viable. O'Neill, an old Etonian with a contempt for the rugged sensibilities of his followers, saw advantage in coming to some arrangement with the south over matters of mutual interest—tourism, transport, trade, and so on. On his own initiative he invited Sean Lemass, then Prime Minister of the Republic, to Belfast. A series of meetings followed, alternately in Belfast and Dublin. It all seemed part of a new spirit of concord, spurred by the election of the first Catholic president of the United States and the extraordinary personality and initiatives of Pope John. But in a place like Ulster the very spirit of concord arouses discord. The tough, intransigent religious fanatic named Ian Paisley, with a doctorate from a fundamentalist correspondence "university" in the American deep South, decided that the ecumenical spirit was a threat to his brand of Protestantism—as it undoubtedly is. Although he insists that he has nothing against Catholics personally, he launched a virulent campaign against ecumenism and against O'Neill for having truck with the Republic. In any normal society, Paisley would have been laughed to scorn as a harmless lunatic; in Ulster he became a major political force.

I ought to make plain that not all Ulster Catholics and Protestants are simplistic fools or knaves. Mob violence is restricted in general to the poorer and less educated, some of whom could hardly be said to be educated at all. Even among the lower middle class, Catholics and Protestants often live side by side and form abiding friendships. Many people stemming from Protestant backgrounds, having discarded formal religious worship of any kind, have been working with rare courage and fortitude to bring about a just society in Ulster. Many Protestants who take their religious precepts seriously have also been working hard at helping to make and keep friends among Catholics. For their part, most Catholics simply wish to live in peace and harmony with their neighbors and are content to let the political thing work itself out without violence.

With the rise of Paisleyism, however, the old antagonisms began stirring again. More and more middle-class Protestants, reasonably well-educated and enjoying a reasonable standard of living, whom one might have expected to rise above such prejudices, began saying: "I don't agree with Paisley's methods, but there's an awful lot in what he says." The parallel with Nazi Germany is fairly obvious.

Into this situation suddenly came the Civil Rights movement. Avowedly nonviolent in its methods, it was met with brute force from the Paisleyites and from the Ulster police, who on government instructions, barred the marchers from demonstrating in certain districts. Behind the Civil Rights movement lay several shades of radical opinion, ranging from student activists, Maoists and old-line Russian-style communists to ordinary Catholics. In some cases, as with Miss Bernadette Devlin, radicalism and Catholicism combined in one person. Their justifiable demand was for the end of all religious discrimination in Northern Ireland and a fair share in housing, employment, and other benefits. Behind it, too, lay the unquestionable fact that the Ulster government had tended to starve the western areas—areas in which Catholics were in a substantial majority—of new enterprises. The inescapable conclusion was that the government's undeclared policy was not to provide jobs for Catholic workers, in the hope that Protestant supremacy would last forever in Ulster.

In the long run, the Ulster problem is never likely to be solved except through a change of heart and mind on the part of all who live there. The simple fact is that Northern Ireland is not in any real danger of being incorporated, against its will, into an all-Ireland Republic dominated by the Catholic Church. Successive British governments have made it clear they would never countenance it; nor does the republican south wish to have within its citizenship almost a million malcontents who would be more trouble than they are worth. As long as any sizable body of Ulster Protestants holds out against a republic, it is hard to see many, other than a handful of fanatics who would wish to force their hand. What is asked of them, only, is that they should grow up and live in the twentieth century with all *its* problems, instead of stubbornly languishing in the seventeenth. If they do not, it is quite likely that they will lose all.

EPILOGUE

The Irishman, I think, deserves the description once given him as "the salt and pepper of our lives." He is a great fellow, and Ireland, with all her mirths and tragedies, a great place.

The noblest share of earth is the far western world
Whose name is written Scottia in the ancient books
Rich in gold, in silver, jewels, cloth and gold,
Benign to the body in air and mellow soil.
With honey and with milk flow Ireland's lovely plains,
With silk and arms, abundant fruit, with art and men.

Worthy are the Irish to dwell in this their land,
A race of men renowned in war, in peace, in faith

—as Donatus of Fiesole, an Irish bishop living in Italy in the ninth century, once wrote.

It is easy to exaggerate the problems and dilemmas of Ireland, even to the point of despair. It is easy to underrate the capacity of Irishmen to use the national reservoirs of common sense. Many, pleased with their new Mercedes and their glossy suits and the prospects of greater "prosperity," see a dynamic future for Ireland; others lament the loss of idealism and that "magic society" that always, somehow, appear to have belonged to yesterday. As ever, a *via media* will probably be found.

A solution to the Ulster problem will be found also. If the English were a less illogical people, the problem might be simpler. The Irishman cannot really fathom the workings of the Englishman's devious mind, but in the end Britain probably will "neutralize" Northern Ireland, with possibly both the flag of the Republic and the Union Jack flying side by side over Stormont, and citizens of both all-Ireland and Great Britain enjoying a dual citizenship.

Most Irishmen are tired of the ancient squabble and want it ended once and for all so that they can get on with the job of building peace and prosperity. Irishmen hope once again to be able to make some contribution to the world, just as Ireland once contributed to the reestablishment of civilization in Europe—a role that many nations that once benefited from her activities either know nothing of or have conveniently managed to forget.

The Irish national character still embraces the widest of spectra. The place is still full of amusing and enlightened people—and their opposites; still full of hundreds of thousands of humble, unpretentious people. It is a land, perhaps, of too many ideals and too much religion. Yet there is a touch of something elusive and ungraspable in the very air, which at moments adds up to pure magic. It is, on the whole, a country of generous spirit, a flickering candlelight in a darkening world.

INDEX